GOING PUBLIC

GOING PUBLIC

MIPS COMPUTER AND THE ENTREPRENEURIAL DREAM

Michael S. Malone

Edward Burlingame Books
An Imprint of HarperCollinsPublishers

FIRST EDITION

Designed by Irving Perkins Associates

Library of Congress Cataloging-in-Publication Data

Malone, Michael, 1954–
  Going public : MIPS computer and the entrepreneurial dream /
Michael Malone. — 1st ed.
    p.   cm.
  Includes index.
  ISBN 0-06-016519-7
  1. Going public (Securities)—Case studies. 2. Entrepreneurship—
Case studies. 3. Computer industry—Case studies. I. Title.
HG4028.S7M19 1991
658.15′224—dc20   90-55933

---

91 92 93 94 95 AC/HC 10 9 8 7 6 5 4 3 2 1

For My Father

Acknowledgments

A book with a tight-focus subject like this one requires a sensibility I had not experienced since my investigative reporting days. It meant dashes at dawn to cover some breaking story and sleepy midnight interviews with sources. And, like investigative work, the people who suffer most are one's family. In my case that meant my wife, Carol Marschner, who, as always, covered for my absences, limited my interruptions, and kept me going during the rough patches. She is my secret weapon.

Equally, a book of this type is built upon a mountain of interview transcripts; whispery words picked out of the hisses, echoes, and clatter of noisy offices and my own lousy recording skills. For that I thank Kathy Chambers.

Much has been written over the years about my agent, Don Congdon. He deserves every superlative. And in my editor, Ed Burlingame, and his assistant, Christa Weil, I've found a professionalism, integrity, and flexibility I've encountered only rarely in the management of the best technology companies, much less in publishing.

Finally, and perhaps most of all, I wish to recognize the courage of the management and employees of MIPS Computer Systems, Inc. Few companies would risk setting a reporter loose within their halls, talking freely to anyone and everyone about very personal matters . . . and to let that process go on for three months, through good days and bad, and during those weeks when the story teetered on the edge of tragedy. For that bravery, I hope this book is worthy of its subject.

Contents

THE MOMENT

THE DAY

Live as though the day had come.
—NIETZSCHE

BEFORE

Silicon Valley, California, 2:00 A.M. PST

BOB MILLER DIDN'T DREAM.

And when his eyes opened at two o'clock on Thursday morning, he was instantly awake—and knew why he was.

He padded down the hall to the kitchen on the thick legs of an old college lineman and made himself a cup of coffee. On the intercom he could hear the rhythmic breathing of his baby daughter. This would be the most important day of her life and she wouldn't even know it. Pondering this, Miller decided to write a letter about this day she could read years hence.

That is, if this really was the day . . .

Sipping his coffee, there at the center island in the big kitchen of his French provincial estate in the foothill town of Woodside, California, Miller went over and over the sequence of events that had led up to this early morning awakening. There were still so many things that could go wrong. He began to write down all the possible disasters that could yet occur and what could be done about them. What if the SEC didn't accept the revisions? What if Latta got delayed getting to Washington, or if they kept him cooling his heels in the lobby? What if the *Wall Street Journal* or *New York Times* picked up the Dow wire pricing announcement and ran it in their first edition? How late could the company wait to go out?

If not today, then surely tomorrow was the last chance. And a Friday Initial Public Offering was almost impossible. Next week was Christmas. You couldn't go public during Christmas week or the week after—the market would be dead. And that would mean the first of the year. And who knew what the state of the market would be in the new year of 1990?

Could they even go public in January? After all, that would be after the end of the fiscal year. The year would have to be reported. That would take several weeks. And the new numbers would demand another killing road trip around the world to bring investors up to date. Just the thought made Miller's stomach tighten. He wasn't up to another such marathon. The last one had literally almost killed him.

If they didn't make it out today, then it might not be until February. February! The economy could be a disaster by then. The market could go through one of its regular slumps. There was a lot of talk of recession. Hell, the market was already falling. The Marines had invaded Panama the night before and were still fighting.

Or, the company could have a bad quarter. Anything could happen by February. Miller tried not to think about the last set of Silicon Valley firms that had tried to make their first public sale of stock. October 1987. One firm had been giving its road show presentation to New York analysts when the word came that the market had fallen five hundred points. That firm had not attempted an IPO since. And the market had never again been strong for high-tech stocks.

Bob Miller sipped his coffee. There were so many things that could go wrong. As chief executive officer he faced enough challenges just trying to run a high-tech start-up company—especially one such as MIPS Computer Systems, Inc. that had tripled in size each of the last three years. Adding the hysteria of an Initial Public Offering made the job too much for anyone to handle well.

Miller had thought he'd known what was coming, but there was no way to really know until you'd been through it. Looking back, he was proud of the way he'd anticipated the chaos and had divided the top management of the firm; he, chief financial officer Dave Ludvigson, and vice-president and general counsel Joe Sweeney managed the IPO and depended on the rest of the executive staff—Boesenberg, Jobe, Vigil, DiNucci, Hime, and the others—to run the firm.

But MIPS was a new kind of company. Not only did it operate in a realm of innovative technology (its name is based on a term that means millions of instructions per second), but its organization was unlike anything seen before in American business. And experience had taught that if the MIPS business model had one weakness, it was an overdependence in the early stages upon the CEO. And for the last two months this CEO had been pulled almost in two. Thank God, Miller had said many times to himself, that this company has a veteran management. What was the line one industry watcher had used? ''The $100 million company with the $1 billion management.'' The analysts had loved that one. And a good thing it was true, or MIPS might not have survived the last few weeks, what with all the publicity and an angry Securities and Exchange Commission. How did young firms with inexperienced management teams ever make it alive through a Going Public Day?

He finished his coffee in the glare of the kitchen lights. Outside, it was still night, the trees black silhouettes. During the process of taking the company public Miller had often said the experience was like being the pilot of a jet airliner and trying to land it on Wall Street. You try to finesse it down through the canyons of office buildings on either side of the street . . . and at any second, it all can go terribly wrong. You catch a wing tip on a cornice or a light pole or snag the landing gear on a pothole or high manhole cover—and suddenly you are out of control, breaking apart, the wings shearing off and exploding.

As the debris-spitting ball of flame goes tumbling past, one stockbroker on the street turns to another and asks, ''Say, wasn't that MIPS Computer?''

''Yeah, poor bastards.''

Bob Miller finished his coffee and dressed in the suit he would wear for the next twelve eventful hours. At five o'clock he kissed his wife, Barbara, goodbye. She remembers saying jokingly, ''Don't come back until this is good.'' Then she added, ''I know you're going to nail it; I'll keep my fingers crossed.''

''I may need more than that,'' Miller told her.

The predawn air was cold and misty as Miller drove his Mercedes to the freeway. The lights at the on-ramp were harsh. Just ahead, on the far side of the overpass, lay the darkened campus of 3000 Sand Hill Road, home of Silicon Valley's venture capital community. Board member Bill Davidow's office was there. And just over the hill, at Mayfield Fund, were the offices of Gib Myers and Grant Heidrich, also board members and the two men who had helped recruit him out of Data General. If all worked out, this would be a big day for them, too.

Miller pulled onto the 280 freeway and headed north in the darkness. On his car phone he called Carol Muratore, a Morgan Stanley principal for Equity Research, at her home in New York City. Do you, he asked, get the *Times* and the *Journal?* No, she said, but I can run across the street and get them. Call me back in ten minutes. When Miller got her on the line again she reported happily that there was nothing in either paper. That was a relief. One possible disaster had been averted.

But, as Bob Miller drove up the Peninsula through the fault-riddled hills toward the Morgan Stanley office in San Francisco, on what could be the pivotal day of his business career, he was haunted by the memory of an event that had occurred a week before. The company's manufacturing employees, a group employed at a building two miles from headquarters, had gathered for a Christmas luncheon.

Most of these employees were assembly line workers, and a large number of them were Southeast Asian, mostly Vietnamese. Miller knew that many of them had experienced terrible ordeals getting to this point in their lives, but beyond that he knew few details. The Vietnamese were hard working, dignified, and taciturn, and it had always seemed rude to pry.

But at this luncheon, Miller sat next to a small, soft-spoken woman who was called by the American name Connie. Miller did know something about her life. He had just learned that she had a husband, a former South Vietnamese army officer, still in Vietnam after fifteen years in a Vietnamese political prison. He knew she was planning to use the money she made from selling her stock to buy her husband out of Vietnam.

Not surprisingly, the talk at the luncheon quickly got around to the public offering. After all, many of the manufacturing people, especially the Vietnamese, were among the company's most tenured employees (many had been at the firm twice as long as Miller and the executive team) and thus were fully vested in their stock options. For them Going Public Day would mean an instant leap in personal wealth of $50,000, $100,000, or more.

With the promise of that sort of payday, the manufacturing employees had become very sophisticated in the workings of the stock market. They asked about the underwriters, the opening price, the stock price in the days and weeks after the IPO, even the likelihood of a split. They knew the exact value of their shares at different opening prices and the date, whether it was a week or three years from now, when their options would be fully vested.

Though he tried to be honest, it gnawed at Miller that he was putting too much of a positive spin on the events leading to the IPO. Sure he could provide evidence for everything he said. But was it the truth? Could he be fooling himself? After all, the most recent set of questions back from the SEC had addressed entirely new topics from the previous set. That wasn't supposed to happen; the new questions were supposed to refine the company's answers to the previous set of questions, not start over on new ground. This endless shifting suggested the terrible possibility that the SEC's questions might leap from topic to topic in a process that might take not days but months.

Should he tell the employees his fears? Were the fears realistic or just a product of his own paranoia and exhaustion? He decided to keep up the brave front. Why frighten them with speculation?

But each time he looked into Connie's eyes, Bob Miller was reminded that for some MIPS employees Going Public Day would mean far more than reputation or money. At least one life might depend on it.

The sky to the east was turning pink as he drove into San Francisco.

At about the moment Bob Miller awakened, Bob Latta's plane was just touching down at Dulles Airport in Washington, D.C.

Latta, who prided himself on his ability to sleep aboard an airplane, to nod off as the wheels left the runway and to awaken as they touched down again, had been awake all night. He was running on adrenaline. Of the fifty stock offerings with which he had been involved in his ten years at the Wilson, Sonsini, Goodrich & Rosati law firm, twenty-five of them initial public offerings, this MIPS deal was not only one of the biggest, but easily the worst. Every time the turbulence calmed some new catastrophe would send the team reeling.

Young associates usually carried the papers and amendments to offering documents back to the SEC. But now here he was, the 35-year-old general partner in the most famous Silicon Valley law firm, on a red-eye flight, two boxes of paperwork on the seat beside him and *Dead Poets Society* showing on the movie screen. What a deal.

Given the history of the case, he had come to expect confusion. On the day before the papers had to be delivered, when John Sandler left Bowne printers to drive back to Palo Alto to be Santa Claus at the firm's Christmas party and then called to see if he should pick up anything on his return, Latta had replied, "Yeah, John, stop at my house and get my wife to give you some clothes for me. Get my London Fog and put the liner in it. And put the gloves in the pocket because I may have to take this if things aren't settled."

And things sure as hell weren't settled. Not after a series of calls back to D.C. during the evening.

Latta had sworn never to make a courier run again, especially in the dead of winter. He could have given the job to Sandler; Sandler always wanted to make the deliveries because he had a babe in D.C. and could get a nice weekend out of the deal. Now Sandler was annoyed, but Latta knew he was right to go.

He had made the decision at ten o'clock, a half-hour before the last flight out of San Francisco that would reach D.C. before the business day.

Latta turned to Sweeney and Ludvigson and said, "You know, I hate to volunteer for this because I haven't slept in several days and it's really not my idea of a fun time, but maybe I should go instead of John in case something happens tomorrow."

Ludvigson said, "Yeah, I'd really appreciate it if you'd go." But the documents—the amendment with all the pricing data that had to be cleared by the SEC examiner and the box of exhibits in support— weren't ready. The deadline to leave for the airport came and went and still the packages weren't ready. Finally, Latta gave instructions to have the papers meet him at the airport, ran out the door, jumped into his car, and raced to the airport.

As he blasted down Bayshore freeway, Latta reviewed his options if the plane started to leave and the papers weren't in his hands. The most extreme scenario was to find another plane. He remembered the high-rolling days of the early 1980s when legendary venture capitalist Art Rock spent $30,000 to rent a Learjet for Latta's paralegal to get packages on the Diasonics IPO back to the SEC after the regular flights had been missed.

That was an option Latta didn't want to use. How about holding the plane? Trotting through the quiet United Airlines terminal, Latta remembered the time eight years before when, as a young attorney, he'd been assigned to deliver some SEC documents: "We were running to catch the plane and I get there with the package and one of the other guys is buying my ticket. I pop the package up on the counter and announce, 'This is a $60 million package'—it was—and you've got to hold the plane for ten more seconds.'

"But they wouldn't do it."

They'd made that flight anyway. But the way things were shaping up, this time might be even closer. And this was a $70 million package.

Reaching the gate, Latta discovered to his dismay that the plane was on time. "I couldn't believe it. It really pissed me off. The first United flight I'd taken in three years that's on time and it has to be this one." He called Bowne: "Have they left yet? Have they left yet? The goddamn plane's on time!"

Now Latta decided his only chance of holding the plane was a guerrilla approach. Searching the crowd, he spotted a kid wearing the sweatshirt of U.C. Berkeley's law school, Boalt Hall. Perfect. No law student would mind a little embarrassment to make some folding money. Latta walked up and asked the kid if he would be willing to make twenty bucks by faking an epileptic seizure and blocking the ramp doorway.

"The kid wanted more money! So I'm negotiating a price with him when I hear this commotion in the distance. I look over and see Dave Segre running his ass off down the concourse carrying this big fucking box.

"Now I know I'm safe. I've got the exhibits. If worse comes to worse I can have the rest telecommunicated to me.

"So here comes Segre just hauling balls down the people mover. And this is like Gate 90 or something, so he's run like three quarters of a mile or something. Fortunately, he's a biker, rides in the mountains and so forth on weekends.

"So he gets to me and he's panting so hard he can't even talk. He's hanging on the railing. They're loading the plane now and I'm asking him, 'What do I have to know about what's in the package? What has to change when I get to Bowne in D.C.?' And he can't talk. So I start shaking him, yelling 'Talk to me!' and meanwhile the last eight people are getting on the plane.

"Finally, I just say, 'Look, leave me a voice mail and walk me through it. I'll pick it up when I get in.' 'Fine,' Segre manages to say.

"About now Patterson, the rep for Bowne—one of the best in the business—finally shows up. And, since he's not a jock, he's panting even harder than Segre. But at least he manages to tell me Bowne's street address in D.C. and some other stuff, and next thing I know I'm on the plane."

But the confrontation with United wasn't over yet. "I've got a bulkhead seat in the coach class right by the galley and I'm just standing there, with the box on the seat behind me, sort of hiding it. And I was going to stand there right until take-off. Well, this stewardess comes up and asks me to sit down. So I start schmoozing her, telling her that the reason I don't want to sit is because I've been sitting for about eight days and I've got a veg butt. Well, she buys it and walks away.

"Soon as she's gone I start stuffing this big box into the overhead compartment. Next thing I know another stewardess shows up and starts giving me shit about the box being too big and heavy, and how it should be checked in. And I said, 'No, you don't understand. This is a $70 million package and I'll hold it on my lap if I have to.'

"Right about then the first stewardess appears and says, 'Aw, lay off him. The guy hasn't slept in three days. Be nice to him.' So I got to keep the papers with me."

After all that, the rest of the flight was comparatively uneventful. Sleepless, Latta first used the on-board telephone ("the first time I'd ever had one work") and called Segre and Sandler to find out what was missing from the documents. "I got a pretty good bill for that call later."

Next, back in his seat, Latta set about doing a "washtub" edit of the materials—lawyer's jargon for clearing your mind to proofread, as if for the first time, documents you've already read and edited a dozen times before. After that, amazed to find himself still wide-eyed, Latta watched the movie, even though he had seen it before.

Landing at Dulles, Latta took a cab into the city to the D.C. offices of Bowne, located in the National Press Building, half a dozen blocks from the SEC. He arrived at about seven in the morning, eastern time, read all the faxes from San Francisco, and, following their instructions, set about packaging and organizing all the documents and exhibits according to the right number of copies of each.

At 7:30 Latta finished the task and used the Bowne bathroom to shower and change out of the suit he'd been wearing for the previous thirty hours. Outside, a Bowne car with a phone was waiting to take him to the SEC.

As he rode in the car, going over what he had to do, Latta thought that finally everything was beginning to go right.

He was wrong.

"My big mistake was that when I got to the SEC I let the driver go. I never should have done that—because it had been eight years since I'd been there and I'd forgotten that there are no pay phones in the lobby of the building. I think it's intentional by the SEC.

"So, I go in. I get to the file desk at five minutes to eight. I wait the five minutes until it opens and I formally file the first set of documents.

Now, of course, that doesn't do me any good because no one will see that shit for days. That's why you also carry courtesy copies for the examiners. I've got four of them, but the courtesy desk, which is down in the basement, doesn't open until 9:00.

"There's a reception area on the first floor, with a phone, that I thought opened at 8:30, so I go wait there. I'm watching all sorts of other guys coming in and making their filings at the main desk and then going down to the basement with their courtesy copies. But I know that's a chump move because you'll end up opening too late on the market if there's any problem with the examiner. So I think I'm pretty smart.

"Then 8:30 comes and goes and still nothing's happening in the reception area. So I go and ask a file clerk, 'Hey, what time does the place open?' '9:00.' And I say, 'Oh shit.' I put my jacket back on and I put the coat back on and go out into the cold looking for a pay phone.

"So here I am. It's now 8:35 A.M. It's also like ten degrees outside, and I'm huddled in my overcoat walking ever-larger concentric circles around the SEC looking for a pay phone and freezing my ass off.

"Finally, I find one a couple blocks away in one of those little bombed-out ten-car parking lots between buildings.''

Latta dialed the number of the assistant director of the SEC, Howard Morin, the man whose questions were delaying making the public offering "effective" [formally cleared to go public]. Instead of Morin, Latta got a recording: "It was like 'Sally and Suzie aren't home right now. Please leave a message.'

"So I'm thinking, what the hell? So then I call [SEC branch chief] Barthelmes . . . and I get a disconnected number. Then I call the examiner and I get a ring with no answer. What the fuck is happening here?

"So I call Segre in San Francisco and wake him up and get him to check the numbers. He gets up out of bed, looks in the directory and, yep, they're all right.

"So I hang up and try Morin again—'Sally and Suzie aren't home right now.' Then Barthelmes—the line is disconnected. Then, David Thelander, the examiner—no answer.

"It's now twenty to nine and I'm starting to panic. At 9:30 the market opens. I know if I have to wait until the courtesy desk opens at 9:00, the copies won't get to the examiner until 9:30. Then he's got to read it, bless it, pow-wow with Morin—and it'll be 10:30 before we're effective. And that's not what Morgan Stanley wants. They want to go at 9:30.

"I don't know what to do. I can't keep leaving strange messages for Howard Morin with Sally and Suzie. Maybe it's the phone, I decide. So I trot back to the SEC to see if maybe there's a phone there I missed. But there isn't. Just a dozen lawyers standing around waiting for the desk to open.

"So, with no other choice, I run once more out into the cold and start making concentric circles again around the SEC looking for another phone."

CHAPTER 1

Breaking the News

ON NOVEMBER 3, 1989, six weeks before the long night, MIPS treasurer Stephen Bennion, 46, armed with only a handful of overhead slides and limited to an hour, set out to explain to one hundred MIPS employees and a video camera one of the most complicated maneuvers in all of business.

The location was the MIPS lunchroom, a classroom-sized space with a handful of tables usually covered with scattered sections of that day's *San Francisco Chronicle* and *San Jose Mercury-News,* a coffee dispenser, three automats selling soda pop, juice, and sandwiches, a display case offering T-shirts, pens, and notebooks bearing the MIPS logo, and, on a far wall, a fading rendering of the new corporate headquarters building.

Bennion, a tall, stocky man with a thick head of hair and metal-rimmed glasses, wore his usual uniform of a patterned tie, button-down oxford cloth shirt, and suit trousers held up by dark braces. As he paced in front of the overhead projector, the shadow of his gesturing hand was intermittently silhouetted on the screen behind him. A hired video team captured his every move and word, packaging it for mailing to MIPS offices around the world.

The audience formed a semicircle around Bennion, some sitting in the few available chairs, but most standing. They watched him intently in a concentrated challenge. About a third of the listeners were from the corporate staff. They wore business clothes. Most of the rest were engineers, wearing open-collar dress shirts and jeans. The few remaining had come over from the manufacturing building. They were Hispanic or Southeast Asian and dressed in flannel shirts or T-shirts and worn jeans.

Bennion knew that fairness demanded that all the employees be given an understanding of the pivotal event in the company's history that would soon occur and be made aware that everything about the company would, to one degree or another, soon change forever. After all, each had helped build this company, and each had a stake in Going Public Day. But how could he reach across such a range of educational backgrounds, cultures, and personality types, especially with a subject as complicated as an initial public offering of stock?

Bennion was born in Ogden, Utah. His father was a bookkeeper and managed a Culligan soft water franchise; his mother was a government employee. Both were staunch Mormons, but in Stephen's case the religion "just didn't take; so I was a sort of heretic."

Beginning at 13, without a driver's license, young Bennion drove the franchise's delivery trucks around town. He attended Weber State College in Ogden, married in his senior year, and went on to graduate school at the University of Utah. His first job was at Big Eight accounting firm Ernst & Ernst (now Ernst & Young) in Los Angeles.

"I thought L.A. was the end of the world and wanted to get back to Utah. So I finally got a job as an IRS agent for three and a half years, and that was the beginning of my government career. Learned a lot about taxes, but chasing after the movers and shakers wasn't what I wanted to do. I wanted to be a mover and a shaker.

"So, I joined a company called Envirotech in 1970. Worked in Salt Lake City, starting as the director of taxes. Stayed eleven years. About halfway through that time I was made vice-president and treasurer. Also did investor relations.

"It was a real interesting company. Fortune 500. Operated in twenty-eight countries, which gave me a lot of foreign travel.

"We moved to [company headquarters in the Peninsula city of] Menlo Park and I've been in the valley ever since."

Bennion next spent four and a half years at Rolm and then "made a bad career move by going to one of those shooting star, flame-out companies, called Xebex. I went there as VP finance. I was there five months, had a major confrontation with the guy running it, then resigned.

"Then I went to another exciting company, Coopervision. It was exciting, always doing big deals, a roller coaster. But I wanted to get back into treasury, and joined Xidex—and that was another strange two years. I tell you, I'm through with 'x' companies forever.

"It was at the time we were selling off Xidex that I was introduced to Dave Ludvigson by a mutual friend. And that led to MIPS.

"When I started here I was all by myself. Didn't have a staff. Didn't have a Macintosh. Didn't even know how to run the electronic mail. But it's been wonderful."

Remarried in 1986 (his second wife runs the tax department at Raychem), Bennion had four children, three from the first marriage (the eldest 23) plus a newborn baby. One of the oldest senior executives, he also looked the youngest, a situation he credited to "loving this kind of work. I thrive on it."

"Good morning!" Bennion shouted in his tenor voice, attempting to make a friendly start. "Quite a turn-out!" This was a new experience for him. Corporate treasurers normally talk more to bankers than to their fellow employees. And acting the expert felt like a pose: after all, Bennion had never been through an IPO himself. Secretly, he was just as excited as the people facing him, whose excitement he would spend the next hour trying to temper.

Bennion knew that in the audience were some mathematical geniuses who'd no doubt already scrutinized the company's prospectus and come to their own conclusions about pricing strategy. He also suspected that there were several employees who'd been through IPOs at other firms and had more experience in the subject than he.

Finally, Bennion appreciated that many in the audience were still bitter about the announcement, a few weeks before, that all company stock was being reverse split by two and a half to one, meaning that one hundred shares of stock were now only forty shares. This inevitable change did not change the real total value of the shares, but Bennion knew that many people had prematurely multiplied their options by the $12 or $15 of a typical IPO pricing, imagined those riches to be already theirs, then watched as they fell by 60 percent. He expected that disappointment to come out in the question session and hoped to forestall it in his presentation.

Given all this, it wasn't surprising that Bennion began his talk by mentioning his back-up: "What we want to do is talk about the process of the IPO and how we value the company, issues relating to your stock options, and then maybe some tax considerations. I have here," pointing to a small, impeccably dressed man in his early forties, "Mr. Sweeney, our general counsel, to bail me out of sticky situations."

He took a deep breath. "Okay, why don't I go through the process of the IPO? It really began five years ago when the company founders, Skip Stritter, John Hennessy, and John Massouris, put together the business plan of the company and had this idea for commercializing this incredible RISC [reduced instruction set computing] technology. In doing that, they went to venture capitalists, who are people who receive money from investors like pension funds, companies, and individuals. These investors want to realize what they hope will be an excellent return by investing in a seedling company and then seeing it do what in fact MIPS is doing.

"And for those of us who have been around Silicon Valley for a while, we know that there are more companies that fail than really make it. Certainly those that do what MIPS has done are extremely rare."

Bennion paced, trying to keep the opening short but still sufficiently complete for newcomers and business neophytes.

"So, the process really started five years ago when we went through our first round of venture.

"As the company grew and developed, we went through additional rounds of venture capital, raising more money for the company's growth and development, purchasing equipment, and so forth. Many of you know that about three and a half years ago, just before Bob Miller came in, the company was not in terrific shape." That was the polite way of saying it. Bennion knew several employees in the audience had, unlike himself, been through that terrible time, when the company was all but dead on its feet and bleeding laid-off employees. "We'd run out of money and hadn't really done what we needed to do.

"Then Bob came in and did it. On the strength of his being here and the new management people and with his new business plans, we brought in our first corporate venture partner, Kubota, Ltd., which purchased about 20 percent of the company—adding significant additional capital to the company, in equity investment in the technology and a manufacturing agreement.

"And the rest is history. We've had a lot of articles written about the company and the growth that occurred." That took care of past events. The audience was still focused, expectant. Now Bennion could start on the slides.

"Okay, we're now at the point that all start-up companies and founders and venture capitalists dream of being. And that is, we're ready to take the company public."

He paused for the notion to sink in. "Now, what does that mean and what is the process? Well, what it means is that we will register our common stock with the Securities and Exchange Commission. And in doing that, we put together with our investment bankers—who are Morgan Stanley & Co. and Cowen & Company, two of the most prestigious investment banking houses on Wall Street—we put together a document that is done with those people, with their outside lawyers, with our outside lawyers, and Joe Sweeney and Dave Ludvigson. A lot of you were involved in writing this—and this is an incredible document which sets forth everything about MIPS and talks about the company's history, talks about the company's products, technology, and our customers.

"It also talks about the risk factors, too, because the SEC's job is to protect the investing public from companies that may want to raise a lot of money and use the exchanges to sell their stock. So this is an extremely important document. We filed this document on November 7 and that is the beginning of the official steps.

"From that, we printed what is known as a 'red herring' prospectus." He held up a copy, though few in the room could read its title. "That's this document, which is an abbreviated version of the information in the S–1. [The S–1, he neglected to say, was the SEC filing document.] And the reason this is called a 'red herring' is that it's a preliminary prospectus and this red wording on the side of it essentially says that this offering is subject to SEC review and approval and therefore this document is not the final document."

Bennion put on the first overhead slide. From then on he didn't stray far from the projector.

"What happens next is that the filing is sent in to the high-tech group in the SEC review section and they go through it with a fine-tooth comb to see if they think we have set forth all of the applicable risk factors, and if we discuss the company and business in enough detail. They'll come back to us no doubt with questions and comments, probably three weeks from the date we filed. Then we'll have to go through all of those, answer their questions, and on and on and on.

"Meanwhile, the investing public is aware that the offering has been filed. I'm sure you've probably seen at least some of the press in newspapers that the MIPS offering is happening; that is one of the most widely anticipated offerings on Wall Street. There has not been an offering of a computer systems company of this magnitude in the past two or three years. We are really breaking through some of the barriers that were set up after the stock market crash that happened a couple of years ago. Certainly in the process of doing this we've also run into a mini stock market crash and run into a major earthquake, but nevertheless, everything is proceeding.

"The investment bankers have formed what they call an 'underwriting syndicate,' which is a group of other investment banking houses, all of whom want to sell the stock to their customers. Most of these customers are institutional investors; in fact, probably 90 to 95 percent of the investors in MIPS will be institutional investors such as pension funds, insurance companies, money managers, mutual funds—they control virtually all of the stock market. . . ."

Bennion inserted a few more words about how proud the employees should be of their company and then returned to the IPO process.

"The timing will be that as the comments and questions come back [from the SEC], we will go ahead and plan what we call a road show, which is a series of meetings scheduled to begin December 4th. It's like a traveling road show where, in a very short period of time, we tell the company story and really sell the company. Our corporate communications people have, in the past, put together a terrific show and Bev Jerman and her people I'm sure have got a great show lined up that will really tell the MIPS story.

"So, the team, which will probably be Bob Miller, Dave Ludvigson, and I think Chuck Boesenberg and the investment bankers, will first go international—to London and Edinburgh one day and then on to Zurich, Geneva, and Paris—to talk to foreign investors. Although we will not be initially listed on any foreign exchange, probably 25 percent of the offering will be sold in the international marketplace.

"At present, our plan is to be only on the NASDAQ exchange, and we have requested the symbol of—guess what—'MIPS.' You've got to have four letters, and it was very clever of the founders to do that."

The audience laughed. Laughter came easy when you were about to get rich.

"So, after the foreign part, they'll go on the U.S. road show, to New York and Boston, then work the West. This will be an intensive series of group meetings with analysts and one-on-one meetings with major investors.''

Time for some more cheerleading: ''We're told that the offering is being extremely well received on Wall Street, that a lot of people want to invest in MIPS, that this offering will kick open the door for some other high-tech offerings. I know that when we were negotiating with printers—the initial printing of this red herring is forty thousand copies— all of the financial printers wanted to be able to carry this prospectus around in their kit bag as they sold printing services to other companies. So, we're really being afforded some very special treatment.''

Back to business: ''You've seen the size of the deal. We anticipate seeing between a $70 million and $90 million offering; with new equity to the company of between $60 million and $75 million. The difference is the proceeds for selling shareholders. These are some of our original investors, like venture capital funds, who have decided that they want to use this opportunity to reap some of the profit of their investment now and get the cash out.

''It's interesting to note that many of our investors did not want to go out with this offering. Very often, you'll have venture capitalists clamoring to be part of the underwriting to get their stock sold. A lot of our investors seem very happy instead to continue holding their stock, perhaps distributing it up to their individual investors. That again is a strong vote of confidence.''

Now it was time to get into the nitty-gritty of pricing, the subject of most interest to the assembled employees. Tonight, when they sat at the kitchen table with their spouses, these would be the numbers they'd multiply against their MIPS shares. The estimated price per share would become the multiplicand of their dreams of riches.

''Okay,'' said Stephen Bennion, armed with a dozen slides comparing MIPS to comparable tech offerings in the past. If he had to, if there was a serious challenge from the audience, he was ready to support his position with considerable case and precedent.

First, there was the touchy matter of the reverse stock split: ''The expected offering price as set forth in the prospectus is between $14 and $17 per share—after a two and a half to one stock split, which will be approved at a special stockholders' meeting.'' He chose not to mention that none in the room would be at that meeting, as the management and venture capitalists constituted majority ownership.

"Once the SEC comments are cleared the deal is priced. That will probably happen in the wee hours of the morning at the financial printers, where we negotiate between the company, all the lawyers, the investment bankers, and management as to what the offering price will be.

"Whether it's at the low end of the range or the higher end of the range depends upon the receptivity to the transaction and what's going on in the market. We are very much governed by what's happening in the overall stock market. The market is good for IPOs right now, but it's not necessarily good for tech companies. Still, it does reward the best high-tech companies with reasonable what is called 'price-earnings multiples.' We'll get into that in a minute.

"In any event, after we finish all this, the offering of the stock is made. We've had stock certificates printed up. The transfer agent is the Bank of Boston. The certificates all get delivered to New York and the underwriter pays us our money. We in [corporate] treasury hopefully have a wonderful plan for investing the money. So when we get it, we'll shoot it off into all sorts of high-quality investments.

"At the same time, we begin trading the stock in the marketplace. Maintaining this 'after-market' is important. It is important that the after-market in our stock remains orderly. What we'd like to see is a gradual trading up from the offering price. You don't want to see wild spikes up and wild spikes down and that kind of thing. [But keeping price growth smooth] requires a lot of experience. And again, we have the best underwriters in the business, we think, so we anticipate that all will go well."

Next, to make the case for the price-earnings ratio, Bennion showed slides bearing tables of P/Es for other tech stock.

"Given the fact that we are not in a particularly strong market for tech stock, nevertheless we've managed to position MIPS as the best of the best. . . ."

"[The price-earnings ratio] is a really important statistic in stock market work and it's what investors look at. What the P/E is is the price of the stock per share divided by the earnings per share. In other words, if a company earns a dollar per share and is selling at 20, the P/E is 20. The higher the P/E, the higher your company is valued."

A table showed the average price-earnings ratio for Standard & Poor's 400 to be 14.4. Another listed current P/Es for selected well-known stocks:

Apple	13	Compaq	10
HP	12	Intel	17
DEC	11	Sun	8.5

[Bennion commented on Intel's high P/E, "It must be all the Intel people who are now at MIPS that did that for them."]

MIPS was anticipated to go public at a stock price reflecting a price-earnings ratio between 17 and 21.

Bennion displayed another slide, listing recent tech stock offerings: "Looking at Sequence, Silicon Graphics, Autodesk, Microsoft, and Oracle, which is a recent IPO, as you might expect, software companies typically are seeing a higher multiple."

Next was a table of offerings with high price-earnings ratios that included, among others, Network General: "These are all companies that we put into our comparable group. And we said to ourselves, hey, we're at least as good if not better than these guys. So our P/E range should be between 17 and 21. Again, based on what the market is doing at the time.

"But 17 or 21 of what? That's times 1990 earnings. So, we're going to have to look at our business plans and see what our profits are predicted for 1990 and that's where we'll get our valuation."

That was a good start, Bennion decided, but it needed more detail to meet any questions about the reverse stock split.

"Looking at the valuation, we think that we will earn a 1990 net income after tax of between $18 million and $20 million. Accordingly, our valuation range, and that's the value of all of MIPS at that point—" He hesitated; like a true treasurer, he wanted to put such a gross number in proper perspective. "Let me emphasize that the only thing that investors look at, the major thing they look at, is earnings and potential future earnings. The market is really short-term oriented. For those of you who follow the market, you know that company stocks will drop on positive news."

Okay, now perhaps people wouldn't panic every time the stock fell a couple of points.

"So, looking at that kind of multiple, we come up with a value for MIPS of $330 to $420 million. If you recall, the value of Sun when it went out I think was about $450 million. And Sun went out in a much stronger market for tech stocks, before crashes and that sort of thing."

Now for the reverse split: "If we look at all the stock options that could be exercised, we'd have about 60 million shares outstanding. That would yield an offering price of $5.50 to $7. We could have gone out at the price, but we didn't do that and there was a very good reason why not.

"After the two and a half to one reverse split, we reduce the number of shares down to about 20 million or so and the range then becomes $14 to $17. That value of MIPS is still $330 to $420 million. So why the reverse split? Simply because we and our investment bankers are convinced that we'll enhance the value of MIPS stock both short term and long term.

"Why is that? Well, Wall Street institutional investors and the like, who buy 90 to 95 percent of all stock, simply don't like single-digit stocks and avoid purchasing them. Many, in fact, actually have prohibitions against buying single-digit stocks.

"One of the reasons is that if you're close to $5 a share—say you're a $6 stock and there's a general market decline and your stock hits $5—at that level investors can no longer do what they call 'margining.' That is where they buy stock at, say, 50 percent of the cost. But when a stock hits $5, the margin gets called. So, if you have an unusual trading situation where your stock hits $5, all your margins get triggered and that causes more to sell off—and that drives the stock down to $4 or $3. We just don't want to see that happen.

"There's a lot of psychology in this as well. If we had not done the reverse split, our quarterly earnings would have started at about 9 cents a share. Investors see that and say, 'huh, a penny stock,' and aren't interested. Whereas, 22 cents a quarter or 25 cents a quarter—that's what they expect to see in net earnings from a quality company."

Was that enough to convince the audience of the value of the reverse split? He scanned the faces. It couldn't hurt to say a little more: "In order to *really* be in the big leagues, you've got to have a dollar per share in earnings. And you just can't do that with so many shares. The point is that your interest in MIPS after the reverse stock split is totally unchanged. In fact, we believe seriously that it enhances short term and long term.

"The other thing is that the reverse split affects all of the employees and all of the officers equally. There's no preferential treatment. Again, it was done to enhance the value of the stock in the offering."

Now to close with some good news: "One of the things that we also want to point out is that we are going to have, shortly after the first of the year, probably February, an employee stock purchase plan which will allow us all to participate even more in terms of MIPS stock. The way that will work is that we'll have an offering period, which is generally a six-month period of time, and we'll take a look at the stock price on the market the first day of the offering period and the last day of the period and employees can buy the stock at 85 percent of the lower of those two prices. So, it's an immediate 15 percent discount from the market and assuming the stock is going like that, obviously buying in at the lower of those two periods is going to be an excellent benefit for all of us.''

Now to find out the reaction. Bennion took a couple steps toward the audience: "Maybe I ought to stop at this point and see if we have any questions on the offering, on the process, on valuation.''

Hands raised.

The questions, as expected, ranged from the innocent to the sophisticated. One asked for more information about the price-earnings ratios of other companies used as comparables to MIPS.

Another asked if the employees would be notified of the IPO in advance. Bennion replied, with more prescience than even he knew: "We probably won't be informed. What happens is that you come right down, in a very frenetic process, to where you've got some questions the SEC wants you to answer. They may want some changes in the final prospectus. So you go back and forth with them. At the same time you're negotiating with the underwriters over the valuation one night at the printers in San Francisco, or maybe in New York. In fact, there'll probably be phone calls to the road show team wherever they're traveling. Once you clear all these questions, get the SEC approval, then you go for it. You get your pricing done, you get your final prospectus, the deal goes through the underwriting syndicate, and it just happens.

"When it does happen, we'll put out an e[lectronic]-mail to let you know. But we know you don't read your e-mail [general laughter], so you'll probably end up reading it in the newspaper.''

Two questions were asked about the underwriters. The first was how many total underwriters would be making the market in MIPS stock. Bennion replied that the syndicate was not yet finalized, but would probably include about a dozen domestic firms and perhaps an equal number of international firms. "We would expect all those companies to make a market in MIPS stock—and even those companies which do not participate in the syndicate can choose to be a market maker. . . . I think we're going to have a lot of market makers in MIPS stock.''

The second question was both more general and more pointed. What was the role of underwriters, and how much money do they make?

Bennion began as if he knew he would soon raise a gasp: "The underwriter is also known as an investment banker and in this country investment bankers are distinguished from commercial bankers by the fact they don't have checking accounts for people or do the normal real estate loans or things like that. They are firms that assist companies in major transactions. They will advise companies on acquisitions and divestitures. They will assist companies in various types of corporate development matters. They also are members of the various stock exchanges, New York, wherever. They have a lot of international networks and linkages.

"One of the pieces of their business in addition to being stockbrokers is to do what they call 'underwriting.' What underwriting is is that they present themselves to Wall Street with their reputation and their credentials behind the company [about to sell stock]. They do this after examining carefully the business of the company and the prospects for that company. They also work closely with that company's management to value the company for the offering.

"At the same time they work with their colleagues—other underwriters or investment bankers—and put together what they call the 'underwriting syndicate.' And this is the group of companies that will sell the stock at the offering.

"The reason they're called underwriters is they actually pay the company for the stock. In other words, they're saying: 'We'll underwrite [the offering], we'll guarantee the deal is going to happen.' It's almost as if they're buying the stock from us because they guarantee the market's interest. That's why they're very much involved in the setting of the price; why there are negotiations between the company and the lead underwriter and the co-underwriters.

"They then distribute, allocate the stock to the underwriters in the syndicate. The company management has a lot of input in what underwriters it wants in the syndicate. And on a deal like the MIPS deal the underwriters are very anxious to get a piece of it because they want to gain favor with their customers who want to buy it."

Now for the punchline: "Also, they make money on the sale. The underwriters' fee will be about 6 percent of the total offering, so they'll make somewhere between $5 and $6 million altogether on the deal."

The crowd stirred. Six million bucks for shuffling paper? Six million bucks that could have been ours?

"In addition to that," Bennion continued, trying to keep things moving, "we have significant legal fees. For our attorneys. It is not a cheap thing, obviously, to go public."

Nor is it an easy thing. To get to the moment when Stephen Bennion could make this presentation, MIPS had not only to help develop a brand new computer technology, but to revise the very nature of business organization.

CHAPTER 2

"The First Company of the 1990s"

CONTRARY TO THE VIEW of many outsiders, few business decisions are made entirely rationally on theoretical or empirical grounds. Rather, most corporate strategies and tactics carry a strong irrational component. Enthusiasms, prejudices, habits, hunches, unrestrained competitiveness, personal vendettas, greed, conservatism, wishful thinking, suicidal tendencies, fear, anarchism, aesthetics, and natural human perversity all struggle to play a role.

So it was that while MIPS had originally intended to go public in March or April 1990, the appeal of timing the event with the turning of a decade slowly began to assert itself.

More than one observer of the company had noted that MIPS's innovative organizational strategy represented a potential model for high-tech businesses in the 1990s, especially for U.S. electronics companies trying to regain lost ground from the Japanese. MIPS suggested a way, through strategic business partnerships and licensing, that the United States could operate from its strength—dynamic, small, young companies—yet still compete on the international scene against Japanese megacorporations. The recognition that MIPS had discovered, or at least refined, a new model of business organization led these observers in late 1988 to begin calling MIPS "the first company of the 1990s."

Like many such phrases, its origin is obscure. Certainly some people inside the company had long used the phrase. Board member Bill Davidow liked to describe MIPS as such to his colleagues in the venture

26

capital industry. The phrase first appeared in print in the influential industry newsletter *Technologic Computer Letter,* edited by former *Wall Street Journal* columnist Dick Shaffer.

By mid-1989 "The First Company of the 1990s" had been adopted by MIPS as its catch-phrase, and the company carted it out regularly (though always prefaced with "We've been called . . .") for visiting customers, suppliers, and members of the press.

Morgan Stanley, anxious to be the underwriter for the IPO, jumped on the bandwagon. In the hundred-page presentation package it left behind after its May 2, 1989, pitch to MIPS executives, the phrase appeared several times in different permutations: "MIPS: The Strategy for Computing in the 1990s," "The First Deal of the 1990s," and on the last page, in a mock-up of a Morgan Stanley tombstone ad for the IPO, "MIPS: The IPO of the 1990s . . . We want your business!"

By the autumn of 1989 the phrase had evolved from a description to a motto to a corporate asset. Suddenly what had seemed a nice poetic symmetry—that the first company of the 1990s should also become the first new public corporation of the 1990s—became a vital part of the company strategy. After all, that was what would be expected from what Morgan Stanley hyperbolically, if not entirely inaccurately, had called in its proposal the "Most Anticipated IPO Since Apple Computer."

Needless to say, that new asset would be at risk with a March or April 1990 IPO. What if some other hot tech firm out there sneaked through the yawning window and declared itself first? No, better to go with a timetable proposed by Morgan Stanley: File the S–1 red herring prospectus November 20, run the road show January 8 through 15, price on January 22, and go public January 29, 1990.

Recalls Ludvigson, "We got ready to go with a plan that we would try to take the company out at the end of January. And then we were in a meeting with [Larry] Sonsini [corporate counsel] in his office—me, Miller, and Sweeney—and Larry, who's done like 75, 80 percent of all the IPOs ever done in Silicon Valley, suggests that maybe we should try to accelerate the process into 1989 on the basis that if we then have any kind of hiccup we can still make it happen in January. Whereas, if we wait until January, then if we have a hiccup we would have to report the year-end numbers and maybe lose a couple months in the process."

When Sonsini, the closest thing Silicon Valley has to a legal god, made a suggestion even Morgan Stanley genuflected. "We liked the idea. It was very typical MIPS: Select the course of action that gives the most flexibility. We now had also chosen to try and ram the thing home on the world's fastest schedule. That was very much MIPS, too.''

The company had now committed itself to making its catch-phrase literally true. But did its technology and corporate organization really fulfill that phrase? And if they did, as many industry experts seemed to agree, what were the lessons that could be gleaned from MIPS's operations that could be applicable to other high-tech firms trying to survive to century's end?

Fundamental to MIPS's competitive strategy in technology is staying in the lead in advances in computer processing speeds, speeds typically measured in mips, millions of instructions per second.

The race to faster processing speeds involves more than just bragging rights. ''There's a relentless drive for price-performance improvement,'' said William J. Filip, IBM's assistant general manager for advanced workstation marketing. For example, the current generation of desktop computers is as powerful as the room-size mainframe computers of two decades ago. There is intense competition not only within each market from supercomputers to personal computers, but among those markets.

Competitors that cannot keep up the pace of change are often left crippled or dead. Such was the fate of Wang Computer. Sometimes, whole industries are left obsolete. The emergence of the workstation and the phenomenal success of Sun Microsystems, Inc. obliterated the once-mighty minicomputer industry and left minicomputer giants like Hewlett-Packard and Data General wounded and scrambling for safety.

Performance improvements are also self-perpetuating. Each increase in processing power opens the door to new applications (or user interfaces or operating systems) until then available only in more expensive computer markets. Such an advance is the means by which one competitor differentiates itself from all others. Not to be left behind, the others make the same improvements, and what was a breakthrough just a few months before becomes an industry standard, the ante for each computer maker to stay in the game. And, as the different computer industries continually migrate upward, brand new industries (hand-held computers, laptop computers, cheap ''clones,'' home computers, and smart video games) fill the vacuum created below. So precise have the steps in this dance become that new performance advances seem to be adopted almost simultaneously across one of these industries, whether the manufacturer is in Taipei, San Jose, or Wiesbaden.

This kind of rapid-fire competition has several interesting effects. One is that it requires extraordinary vigilance by computer manufacturers. They must be able to spot emerging breakthroughs, quickly judge from little evidence their likelihood of success, and then rapidly implement them. This is, of course, a high-risk proposition. The cost of a delay in a breakthrough—as IBM experienced with Windows, Microsoft's answer to the popular Apple Macintosh software—can be a loss of hundreds of millions of dollars in potential sales and a double-digit collapse in market share. For smaller companies the wrong throw of the dice at this table can mean overnight oblivion.

A second feature of this frenetic competition is that, by constantly decreasing the time any competitor can distinguish itself from any other, it places an enormous squeeze on profits. This is less true in the Mac world, where ever-litigious Apple has been able to maintain high margins for a decade by legally crushing any competitive upstarts. But in the IBM world achieving the maximum performance for the price has become an obsession linked to survival.

So, combine these factors: a continual need for new applications, a willingness by computer makers to take chances on radical new technologies, and a rage for ever-improved price-performance, and the result is an industry ripe for revolution. Add to this the arrival of new generations of user interfaces (the "face" the computer presents to the user, such as Macintosh's cartoon figures), increasingly complex operating systems (the language of the computer, such as the PC's MS-DOS), and powerful new applications (such as three-dimensional graphics and relational data bases)—uses that press the capacities of the computers' microchips—and the rifles and cannons are primed and loaded.

The explosion came with UNIX, a universal operating system designed to work in everything from PCs to supercomputers. No longer, UNIX promised, would the computer industry be a Tower of Babel, where one company's machines wouldn't "talk" to a competitor's. Now, not only would all UNIX machines in one market be able to talk to one another, but they would enable the user to become upwardly mobile, to "port over" (translate) applications from an older, slower machine to a higher-performance new one. That appealed to customers, because it meant that for the first time they could save money by mixing and matching computers from different companies, rather than being trapped in the product family of a single supplier.

Unfortunately, the many competitors in the computer industry interested in UNIX didn't exhibit the same attitude of cooperation that they wanted to see in their computers. For much of the 1980s, while less ecumenical operating systems prospered and proliferated, the members of the UNIX world squabbled amongst themselves. Thus, although UNIX had been invented in the 1960s at AT&T's Bell Labs, as late as 1988 it was still doubtful that it would ever be generally adopted. The greatest hope of the computer industry threatened to become its greatest fiasco.

Then, almost miraculously, the boiling world of UNIX suddenly cooled and gelled. The many competitors, who just months before were at each other's throats, were holding hands and cooing. They hadn't given up their fight, but only agreed to make UNIX the site of the war.

The computer industry now had a universal operating system . . . well, not quite universal, as it didn't cover all of the desktop world, but even that day could be seen on the horizon. UNIX, which advertised itself as multiuser (it worked well in networks), multitask (it could perform multiple jobs simultaneously), and multivendor (it worked on a lot of different companies' computer platforms), was now predicted to grow 25 percent each year well into the 1990s. That meant $25 billion in revenues already by 1992—a figure as large as the entire personal computer market.

Clearly, that in turn meant a rich reward for anyone able to find the hardware to take best advantage of UNIX. But such hardware would also have to be blindingly fast to handle not only the complexities of UNIX, but also the demands of the new user interfaces and applications software that would arise from it.

As is often the case in electronics, the answer not only existed, but had been waiting for years in a semidormant state. RISC, for reduced instruction set computing, had been around as an idea without portfolio for more than two decades. In the early 1970s a team of IBM researchers under John Cocke had actually built a RISC computer, the model 801. Introduced in 1975, it was a business failure. But it was a technical success, not only proving that RISC worked, but training a generation of RISC fanatics, like Skip Stritter, John Massouris, and John Hennessy, who would eventually make their dreams real at firms such as MIPS.

The appeal of RISC, as opposed to complex instruction set computing (CISC), used on most computers of every size, was that it controlled the number of built-in instructions with which the computer worked. This might sound limiting, like trying to build a language with only ten letters. But to RISC designers the problem was just the opposite; to continue the analogy, CISC machines were using not only the twenty-six letters, but also several dozen complete words and even sentences, and lugging this bloated alphabet around was beginning to slow the computers' "thinking." Thus, RISC was a return to elegant simplicity, and with it would come greater speed and cheaper design costs.

Certainly one didn't have to look far for evidence of overcomplexity in CISC computers. In the early years of electronic data processing, memory was often the most expensive part of the computer. It was therefore most cost-effective for computer designers to hard-wire as many instructions as possible in the computer's core processor so the instructions wouldn't have to be stored in the precious memory. So, the CISC paradigm was set by the late 1950s, and the computer industry, in keeping with its historic style of being innovative in the details and conservative with underlying principles, made complex instruction sets the heart of everything from mainframes to home computers for the next three decades. The instruction sets became ever more complex as well. For example, the modern Digital Equipment Corporation VAX, the quintessential CISC large computer, has more than three hundred built-in instructions.

A comparable RISC computer could duplicate all of the functions of the VAX with less than fifty instructions. How? By the addition of a second element, called the compiler. Go back to our alphabet analogy. If you are going to limit your alphabet, but still be as lucid as before, you had better develop a strong vocabulary and a powerful knowledge of grammar to translate complicated statements into simple ones. In a RISC computer this critical, yet ancillary, function resides not in the central processor, as it does in the CISC machines, but in software memory. And that is the key to the speed of RISC: The very basic processing tasks, operating within the limited vocabulary, can scream through the central processor, and then, out of the way until needed, the more complex operations can be called up and used.

Because the hardware and software are more detached, RISC designers can focus more on the hardware architecture of the processor, adding performance without necessarily adding complexity. That in turn means, as Hewlett-Packard computer systems group vice-president Willem B. Roelandts told *Business Week,* that RISC technology should advance computer performance by 50 percent to 75 percent annually at a given price, compared to 30 percent annual gains with conventional computer designs.

Further, because most of the instructions are in the compiler and not the central processor, customers may choose the composition of the compiler. MIPS, for example, offers its customers a catalog of programs for its compiler that ranges from database management (from Oracle and Relational Technology, among others) to math and science (Mathematica) and from automated design to networking.

Separating hardware from software and putting most of the burden for complexity on the software also means that RISC chips are easier and quicker to design than their CISC counterparts. According to industry analyst Alice K. Leeper of Dataquest, "a new RISC generation can be designed in just a year to eighteen months, rather than the three to five years it takes with CISC." This is because the processor itself is essentially hard-wired (as opposed to also being programmed, or "microcoded," with CISC), so it can be constructed of simple, fast circuits, such as the popular gate arrays manufactured by scores of young new chip houses in the United States and the Far East. The sole task of these circuits is to perform "load-and-store" operations under the control of a sophisticated program that establishes the hierarchy of that stored memory.

An analogy here might be to a race car engine. The block of the engine is essentially simple: a half-dozen or more cylinders holding pistons attached to a crankshaft. The pistons have only one task: to move up and down at a fast rate. Everything else on the engine—carburetor, alternator, distributor, clutch, exhaust pipes—exists solely to make sure that those pistons accomplish their task and that the result of their efforts is usable somewhere else (to turn the wheels).

The theory behind RISC is the same. At the heart is the processor, containing several million high-speed circuits. The trick is to construct the right systems to get raw data to the circuits and pull processed information out of them in a manner that keeps them operating at full performance while doing the overall job required.

Designing these support systems has been the hard part of making RISC technology real. In theory each circuit in a perfectly run RISC circuit could perform one instruction per cycle of electrical power running through it. Some theorists predict that RISC circuits may someday even achieve multiple instructions per cycle.

But how to feed such an enormous processing hunger? Traditional input and output technologies would be the equivalent, respectively, of trying to put out a raging house fire with a garden hose and catching a rainstorm in a bucket. For that reason, the perfection of RISC would always be constrained by the ability of its designers to develop adequate processor support.

The search for adequate peripheral systems to the RISC processor has led to a growing catalog of support circuitry offered by firms such as MIPS, including registers, cache memories, and pipelines.

While all computer processors have registers, the holding cells for data about to be processed, in RISC technology not only must these registers be fast and flexible, but there also must be a lot of them—up to nearly two hundred individual register locations, compared to less than fifty in a typical CISC processor.

Another crucial peripheral is cache memory, in which the incoming data are queued up. Cache memory may be the most crucial of all the support systems in RISC, because if designed inefficiently, it creates an effect similar to sucking on a flattened straw: the flow of information into the processor slows to a trickle.

Finally, there is the pipeline, which moves instructions from the compiler to the processor to explain the work that must be done. So fast must these pipelines work in RISC that they now not only feature multiple stages (to overcome potential stalls in the instructions being pumped through), but also carry their own built-in intelligence to maximize efficiency.

The description of RISC and its peripheral systems may make it sound as though the processor would consist of so many boxes, motors, and plumbing fittings, but in reality the system consists of a hundred or more semiconductor chips soldered onto a foot-square printed circuit board. This board then is mounted into a larger metal enclosure, where it is interlinked with the displays, disk memory, keyboard, printer, and all of the similarly complex systems it will control in the resulting computer.

From this brief outline of the technology, it should be apparent that while the RISC business is not especially challenging for a computer maker or semiconductor company to get into, being successful at it is far more difficult. To use the race car analogy again, the outcome of the race is not judged by the horsepower of the engine or the design of the car body or the record of the driver. All that counts is which car crosses the finish line first. And that depends upon which car consistently drives the fastest.

In RISC this consistent quickness is measured in mips. And to squeeze out the maximum mips to beat your competitors, you must start with the right array of processor circuits. You must also have the right number of registers and a sufficiently sophisticated cache memory and a smart, high-speed pipeline. On top of that, you must have ported over enough popular programs to your compiler to meet the routine needs of your customers.

And then, having achieved the maximum speed, you must line up enough important computer makers to use your particular RISC technology in their products so as to make your version the industry standard that your competitors must match.

Only when all of that has happened do you have a shot at victory in the RISC Grand Prix and the riches that will come as a result. And riches might be too conservative a term: Dataquest, for one, predicted that the RISC processor market alone would enjoy a compound growth rate of 151 percent well into the 1990s, to reach $350 million by 1992, and that that number was just a fraction of what could be made from RISC-based computers, file servers, and other systems.

At the time of its IPO, MIPS Computer was further along this business path than any company in the world and claimed to be the world's biggest RISC supplier. It also claimed to have the fastest RISC processors, which blistered along at 20 mips, with a 55-mips machine waiting to roll onto the track.

But then, in order to survive MIPS had to be in this leadership position. MIPS was also the world's only computer company completely dedicated to this new technology. By choice, the company had inextricably linked its fate with that of RISC.

With all these apparent advantages, why wouldn't the computer industry plunge into the new technology of UNIX and RISC? Because, despite its futuristic and adventurous image, the computer industry is at heart conservative about fundamentals.

And there is good reason for this. Computer makers do not operate in a vacuum. They have customers, and those customers have strong expectations. One of the most important of these expectations is compatibility between generations. When a customer buys a computer, be it a personal computer or a supercomputer, he or she expects that the next generation of that machine will still be able to talk to the older model and use its software.

After all, whether one spends $2,000 or $2 million on a computer, one does not want to see that system orphaned two years later by a new machine. Furthermore, especially with the higher-end computers, customers may spend as much as ten times the hardware price on the purchase or design of software. Rather than abandon this software, many customers who might upgrade with a compatible replacement will stay with the older machine if the new generation is not compatible.

The problem created for computer makers by this expectation was first encountered in the early 1960s when IBM set out to replace the landmark IBM 360 mainframe with the new generation 370 series. Today it is universal throughout the industry: How can the computer maker balance the competitive advantages of embarking on an innovative product with the heavy, albeit lucrative, anchor of a huge, installed customer base using its last generation machine?

IBM, for example, chose to stick with its existing base. And, while no one could ever claim that Big Blue has been a failure over the last two decades, it would also be hard to dispute that this reactionary approach has kept the firm from the huge revenues it might have enjoyed with a more dynamic approach to such emerging new markets as personal computers and workstations. In fact, IBM has at times turned its back on billion-dollar industries out of a desire not to antagonize its loyal customers.

Other computer companies have taken a different approach toward their installed base—but always at their peril. Apple, for example, faced with an aging but wildly successful product, the Apple //, that didn't lend itself to the more sophisticated new applications, chose to embark on a new computer that featured an innovative but wholly incompatible operating system and user interface: the Macintosh. The Mac turned out to be a runaway success, but not without cries of betrayal by loyal // users (especially in education, where the earlier computer was a standard) and even internecine battles within Apple between the competing product teams.

Now consider UNIX and its claims to be the panacea for computer incompatibility. Sure, many of the customers might like to be less restricted in their computer purchases, to be able to buy the best-performing box without having to worry about how it will interconnect with the others it already owns. But is that advantage worth the cost of throwing out years of software investment and employee training?

For the high-end computer business, where longer strategic views tend to hold sway, it apparently is worth the cost. That explains the great success of UNIX in the workstation and mainframe industries. Also, in those markets the perceived added complexity of UNIX is not a serious problem.

But in the personal computer market, by far the largest installed base of computers, it is a different story. In this industry UNIX had made little headway, having sold, by the time of MIPS's planned Going Public Day, just 200,000 copies. Compared with the more than 30 million personal computers running MS-DOS (the Microsoft operating system for IBM-compatible PCs) and the more than 2 million more Macintoshes running the Apple Mac operating system, the number of UNIX users represented little more than a rounding error. Worse, of these 200,000 UNIX users, nearly all were in the high end of the market, in multiuser office computers that could just as easily be included in a higher market categorization. In other words, UNIX might be a universal operating system in theory, but it was not in application. And, until it created a major presence in personal computers, it risked losing an entire generation of young programmers.

That is not to say that UNIX was doomed to be forever shut out of the PC world. One critical advantage in future competition against other operating systems is that UNIX operates in a 32-bit format, that is, it handles information in blocks of 32 bits, the same as mainframe computers, workstations, and some of the newest personal computers. The 32-bit format is considered vital for the future in that it is the only format to date capable of dealing with such emerging applications as high-level graphics (like full-motion video) and speech recognition. MS-DOS, by comparison, is only 8-bit. Its successor, OS/2, is still 16-bit, although Microsoft promised a 32-bit version by 1991. This gave UNIX a brief window of opportunity if enough software designers were willing to develop software for it. But, by the end of 1989, despite hints that many software companies were doing just that, few observers believed UNIX would have the decisive impact it needed. And that, in turn, meant that RISC technology, which had effectively hitched itself to UNIX, was all but shut out of the PC market as well.

The loss, at least temporarily, was by no means fatal to RISC. After all, the rest of the computer industry was equally enormous and in many ways more receptive to technological breakthroughs. It alone could provide enough growth potential to keep companies like MIPS expanding at the limits of their capabilities through the turn of the century.

But like UNIX, RISC faced a well-entrenched competitor, one defended by an immense installed base of customers.

Before defining this competitor, it is useful to understand that RISC technology is an embodiment of the 80-20 rule in computing. This rule says that 20 percent of a computer's functions are used for 80 percent of its tasks. Because RISC was designed to be very good at that 20 percent, from the beginning it has been perceived by computer designers and users as a niche technology, designed for specific applications. In other words, while RISC processors are seen as good in computers used for distinct applications (such as scientific research, engineering design, or professional networking in such fields as law and medicine), it may not be as appealing in wide-ranging general applications such as retailing, banking, and airline scheduling. RISC manufacturers dispute this, and they may be right, but, once again, we're back into the subjective.

A more objective factor is protection of investment. The cost savings offered by RISC are, for many potential customers, dwarfed by the millions, even billions, of dollars those customers have spent on software over the thirty-year rule of CISC. Do you throw out all that work and convert to UNIX just to save a few pennies per mips with RISC?

And even those pennies have been a matter of dispute. Some RISC doubters have jokingly claimed that mip really stands for "meaningless index of performance." CISC manufacturers have claimed that many of the performance specifications for RISC are made in controlled settings, that in real-life applications the gains for the new technology are comparatively marginal, perhaps no more than a 50 percent improvement—not enough to justify the cost of replacing a user's current investment in software.

Like UNIX, RISC faces its biggest challenge in the personal computer market. Here, CISC processing is so much a part of the very notion of what a personal computer is, it is hard to imagine extricating it. The Intel CISC 80x86 family is the most successful microprocessor design in history, the 16-bit 80286 and the 32-bit 80386 virtually defining what an IBM-compatible computer is all about—and selling tens of millions of these devices in the process. On top of that, at the time of MIPS's Going Public Day, Intel had introduced the 80486, a high-powered CISC microprocessor with processing power claimed at 15 mips, in league with the best RISC processor. And 80486 customers didn't have to throw out all of the software they'd developed for the early members of the Intel 80000 family.

And Intel wasn't alone. The other great microprocessor maker, Motorola, had sold millions of its PC/workstation processor, the 68030 (designed in part by one of MIPS's founders, Skip Stritter), and was getting ready to introduce its next generation CISC machine, the 68040. Obviously, the CISC establishment wasn't going to take this assault from upstarts without a fight.

In this fight RISC companies had certain advantages. One, already noted, is price. For example, at the time of its going public, MIPS's top-of-the-line processor, the R3000 25-mips processor, sold for $200, $600 with all of the support chips. At an estimated 20-mips performance in a VAX computer, this amounted to $10 per mips for the processor, $20 per mips for the whole chip set. By comparison, the new Intel 80486 cost $1,000 just for the processor and $1,200 for the chip set.

But even this apparent pricing edge was not decisive. For one thing, the resulting computers, priced at, say, $10,000 for RISC and $20,000 for CISC, may not have a sufficient price differential for a customer to justify replacing all that software. What's more, CISC processor makers such as Intel have enjoyed such huge volumes that they can slash prices to the point where their cost per mips is equivalent to RISC. Of course, they don't want to do this, and the fact that the price-cutting process had already begun by the time of the MIPS IPO suggested that RISC had scored a small, but important, victory by redefining the economics of the entire microprocessor industry.

A second victory for RISC, the one more than any other responsible for the huge interest in the MIPS IPO, was the growing number of important computer manufacturers adopting RISC for their systems.

In the modern world of high technology innovation is no longer sufficient. The world is full of entrepreneurs with brilliant new ideas. Survival and success come with standardization. Unless a critical mass is reached in the number of influential users of that new technology to make it a de facto industry standard, that great idea is doomed. By the end of 1989 RISC, despite the many obstacles, seemed to be approaching that turning point.

The process of standardizing RISC got off to a fast start. First, there was the IBM RISC project. Then, starting in 1982, Hewlett-Packard began to investigate RISC. Thus the industry's two most influential companies suddenly deemed this new technology, if not yet practical, at least interesting.

In 1986 IBM finally announced the first commercial RISC computer, the RT/PC workstation. Underpowered, it wasn't a big seller, but its influence was wide.

Then in 1987 Hewlett-Packard introduced its RISC-based Spectrum computers to rave reviews. As was often the case, HP's timing was impeccable, as the market's strong response to the Spectrum machines helped save the company's computer operations from financial disaster during the collapse of the minicomputer market a year later. Now, suddenly, the big boys weren't just talking RISC; they were selling it.

That same year, Sun Microsystems, the leading light of the workstation boom, announced its first RISC product. At the heart of this machine was a new proprietary RISC architecture that Sun labeled SPARC.

The chip industry, never one to miss a new market opportunity, also was racing to implement its own RISC designs. Most of these came from semiconductor firms left out of the big CISC microprocessor boom, such as Advanced Micro Devices, Inmos, Fairchild-Intergraph, and VTI. However, none would make an enduring presence in this market either.

The final important player to arrive on stage was MIPS; and, in mid-July 1988, in the most important week yet in the brief history of RISC, both MIPS and Sun announced that they would offer their respective RISC architecture for license to other computer makers. Both companies had recognized that for RISC to succeed it must become pervasive and that they could not accomplish that task themselves. Rather, they would have to give their designs away to prospective competitors in the hope that the market would grow large enough to accept them all and in the belief that they were cleverer than the competition they were about to create.

The battlefield was now set and the key suppliers identified. By the end of 1989 Sun would claim to be the world's largest supplier of RISC-based computers, those machines accounting for nearly all of the company's revenues. MIPS, having lined up more large licensees, would be close behind. And HP, still keeping its RISC architecture proprietary to its own machines, would claim the highest industry revenues from the sale of RISC computers.

It was this rapid galvanization, combined with the industry-wide agreements on UNIX, that gave RISC makers hope in their struggle against CISC. They had a long way to go. According to industry watcher In-Stat, Inc., in 1989 the total number of RISC processors shipped for use in computer central processing units was less than 500,000, compared with more than 13 million CISC processors. But In-Stat also predicted that RISC would grow faster than CISC in the early 1990s, reaching 2.5 million per year by 1992, compared with 19 million CISC. Even more important, RISC would increasingly dominate high-end computers; Dataquest predicted that by 1993 61 percent of all workstations sold around the world would be RISC.

That was a start, enough to capture the attention of the big CISC players. In a validation of the arrival of RISC as an emerging standard, Intel and Motorola introduced their own RISC processor families, the i860 and 88000, respectively, and seemed to be moving toward the notion of a hybrid computer central processor that would use both CISC and RISC processor chips.

This was not to suggest that either Intel or Motorola would ever consider abandoning CISC altogether—not with that installed base or with their current control of the personal computer processor market. Rather, they were just the latest in fifty years of shrewd industry leaders in electronics, keeping their hand in any potential technological contenders to their throne and co-opting the best features of the competition.

This co-option worked both ways. In an effort to be acceptable to the CISC customer base, the RISC industry also had done more than its share of compromising. For example, in an effort to ease customer costs in the porting over of their software, many RISC suppliers had begun to add extra instructions until, by late 1989, many of the so-called RISC chips actually sported larger instruction sets than the so-called CISC processors of a decade before.

So, it seemed, the upstart architecture for computer processors, despite all impediments that the chip and computer industries threw at it, was going to make it as a new industry standard. But in the process it would be changed and compromised and end up in many cases only slightly distinguishable from the established technology it had set out to replace.

That process of synthesis has been the history of the electronics industry. It will also very likely be its future. But the history also teaches that with the acceptance of a new technology, the small pioneering firms are typically overrun as big established firms move in to prospect the field. In this corporate bloodletting (''shakeout'' is a more polite term) at best only a couple of the original firms survive and grow to become major players. They do so, as Apple did when IBM crashed into the personal computer market, by being exceedingly clever and by having sufficient size to outlast the inevitable revenue and profit shocks.

At the time of its Going Public Day, MIPS Computer was about to close a $100 million year. In agriculture that level of sales would make a company a major player. In computing it wasn't enough to make MIPS a blip on the radar screen. And the big boys were on their way. In early 1990 IBM was expected to take a second shot at the RISC market with a new computer workstation code-named Rios. The shakeout was about to begin.

That meant MIPS, to survive the pending adolescence of its industry, would have to be shrewd enough to devise a new kind of business organization that would make the company look big long before it was.

MIPS believed it had that model. The business organization for the 1990s. As Going Public Day continued, it seemed that investors thought so, too.

CHAPTER 3

Holding the Bag

DAVE LUDVIGSON never planned to be here. Now he was the man responsible for one of the most publicized stock offerings in recent business history.

Early in the morning of December 21, at the same time Bob Miller was driving up the Peninsula to San Francisco, Ludvigson, MIPS's 39-year-old chief financial officer, was racing toward the same location. He had reached his home, in the Contra Costa County city of Pleasanton, at midnight, after having seen Latta off and cleaned up some final work at Bowne printers.

He got up at four and was driving through the starless darkness over the Oakland hills and across the newly repaired Bay Bridge. He still felt a little uneasy crossing the bridge's center span—like everyone else he remembered the frightening image of the car pitching over the edge—but it was a hell of a lot easier than driving halfway down the Bay and crossing over at the Hayward-San Mateo Bridge . . . or worse, as he had done in those chaotic days after the October 17th Loma Prieta quake, taking a crowded BART train under the Bay at 3 A.M.

Boy, what a week it had already been. And then the ups and downs of the last two days. A month before the experience had been exhilarating, a definite improvement over the deathwatch work Ludvigson had known earlier in his career presiding over the dismemberment of Memorex. He had said, ''You know, not many people get to take a company public, so from that standpoint it's exciting. To me, in fact, taking the company public is one of the easier things I've done here at MIPS because it's such a defined project. There's a very definite set of things you have to accomplish.''

42

Taking a firm public, Ludvigson had claimed, was a matter of "going into this tunnel, locking everything else out and just, clunk, focus right on it. You have to go from here to there in a certain amount of time. That's it. That's your objective. That kind of thing is easy to do."

But that was before the killing road show had bounced him to every corner of the world, before a second month of living on four or five hours sleep each night, and, most of all, before the eleventh-hour battles with the SEC that had almost killed the entire offering.

At the beginning of the process of going public, Ludvigson had lowered his voice to a near whisper and said, "If we have to pull this offering, it will mean we may never make it." Worst of all would be if the company itself was the cause of the failure: "I'd rather that if we fail it's because the market went down two hundred points rather than that the company didn't make its revenue and profit targets in the fourth quarter and had to withdraw."

But, in the end, the offering had been put at risk not because of a failure by MIPS or the NASDAQ stock exchange, but rather by the company's success, by the surfeit of press attention the IPO had attracted. Was it fair to be punished for that?

Come on, Latta, you're our last chance. . . .

Miller had warned about the unexpected, but even the pros had been stunned by the last few days. The SEC was supposed to come back with questions, but each iteration was supposed to get increasingly precise—not launch off into a whole new line of interrogation.

This was Dave Ludvigson's first IPO. "When I was hired by Miller and Jobe, they said, 'Oh, by the way, you're going to take the company public. But don't worry, we'll help you a lot. We'll be there. We'll go out and do the selling; you just take care of the numbers.' "

Now, here he was, driving into San Francisco to the Morgan Stanley office on the morning of what was supposed to be Going Public Day, the biggest event of his career, and yet no one, much less Dave Ludvigson, knew for sure it would happen.

Ludvigson had never dreamed of running an IPO. But for that matter, he had never planned to be an accountant either. With his blond hair and custom shirts, he looked like a young midwestern executive, the kid from the right family in town seen at all the best parties at the country club. Indeed, Ludvigson had spent his time in country clubs, but that was only because his father, a high school math teacher and football coach, had chucked it all to become a resident golf pro.

Dave was born in northern Minnesota, a cold little town called Ely near the Canadian border "at the end of the road" where his dad taught school. When he was 10, the family moved to Chicago, where his father, in search of a longer golf season, had found another teaching and coaching job. In short order, Ludvigson's father went full-time pro at a nearby club.

Dave dreamed of attending the University of Illinois and majoring in the arts. But he was a mediocre high school student, and good SAT scores weren't enough to get him into the university's liberal arts school. But, like his old man, Dave was a good golfer; it was that skill on the links, thanks to some help from the golf coach, that at last made him an Illini—but in the business school, which had lower requirements.

Ludvigson played on the team for two years, then quit. "I was on the team, but I didn't play much. One of those burdens of great potential never realized, right? Very honestly, though, golf there was pretty big time stuff; you had to put a lot of time and effort into it and I just had too many other interests. Like chasing women. And I wasn't a scholarship player, either, so I had to work tending bar, delivering pizzas, doing everything I could and going to class.

"I also went through one of those phases where I switched majors every semester. So eventually I looked around and I was at the end of my junior year saying, 'Jeez, what do I do now? I have to figure out a major so I can graduate. Okay, so what do I have the most credits in?

" 'Accounting.' Clunk. So I graduated in accounting.

"Luckily, I found college pretty easy, actually. It was interesting, but it wasn't really that challenging. . . . But what I couldn't figure out was what I really wanted to do with my life. I had spent four years trying to figure that out. I had good grades—a B-plus, A-minus kind of thing—so I was successful.

"For a while I thought I wanted to go to law school. I took the LSAT and scored very well, like ninety-seventh, ninety-eighth percentile. But then I realized I wasn't ready to sign up for three years of law school. Nor was I ready to go to work. Therefore, I thought, 'Jeez, maybe I ought to get a master's degree.'

"At first I thought maybe an M.B.A. Then I found I'd have to retrace a lot of my steps through subjects I'd already done. So I signed up for the master's in accounting program—partly because they paid me, including tuition and fees, to be a teaching assistant while I was going to school. It was a lot of fun."

The future was being defined, though Ludvigson at the time didn't know it. "I was one of the few guys in business school that spent time in the computer lab. I was always interested in systems-oriented sorts of things, so I spent time in statistics, operations research, linear programming, those kind of things. The irony was that the school was known as a CPA factory. But I didn't do any of that stuff. Instead I went off and did cost accounting, managerial accounting, systems, really kind of an individual studies program."

Ludvigson also got married during this time, and suddenly the days of hiding in college were over. He laughs as he remembers, "Yeah, that's the reason I still don't have a Ph.D. or a law degree. If it was up to me, I'd still be in college. But Jennifer finally said, 'Look, you've really got to get a job.'

"So, I had some pretty good offers. I finally went to work for Price Waterhouse because they not only offered me the best deal, but they also allowed me to do what I thought I wanted to do, which was to get into consulting."

The first job at Price Waterhouse was in Chicago. In the evenings Ludvigson studied for the CPA exam "though I wasn't too interested in that stuff. The first time I took the exam I passed a couple parts of it. But it took me a long time to pass the whole thing. I just could never get very psyched up to do it.

"What I was interested in was [computer-based management information and accounting] systems. So I started talking to people at Price Waterhouse. And they said, spend two years on the audit staff and we'll train you, and then we'll let you go off and do systems projects consulting.

"So, I spent my two years on the audit staff, went into the consulting world, and spent seven more years there."

Four of those seven years were in Chicago and the next three in South Bend, Indiana, where Ludvigson started a consulting practice. Those two periods in his life still define Ludvigson, from the MacNelly Cubs opening day cartoon in his office to his regular use of Notre Dame coach Lou Holtz in his analogies about leadership and management.

"[South Bend] was my first experience in hiring people and going out and selling consulting engagements, completing them, delivering them to the client, and collecting the bills. At the time it was a lot of fun."

It was also at South Bend that Ludvigson met his mentor, an older Price Waterhouse veteran named Tom Buck. "He was a descendant of

Captain John Smith. I always found that intriguing, but he pointed out to me that no one picks his relatives, that he also had family members in Kentucky who'd been put in prison for various crimes. . . . Tom was a sort of maverick at Price Waterhouse. Tom's view was, 'Don't show me what's in the books. Tell me what the business problem is and let's figure out how to solve that problem. The accounting answer or the consulting answer will flow from what the right business answer is.'

"So he was real pragmatist. Tom taught me a heck of a lot about how to approach business problem-solving. But, like I said, he was a maverick. He was one of those guys that would show up at the partner meetings once a year and have all of these really good points to make and nobody wanted to hear them because he was so controversial. He really believed in saying it like it was. And that's why he was in South Bend. Forever. In fact, he retired there a few years ago.

"But then, in South Bend, when I was six years in [at Price Waterhouse], I started thinking to myself, 'I really ought to do something else.' I was getting a little bit tired of doing the same things over and over. I finally decided the problem was that I was in a small office and that I really needed to return to the big office to figure out whether it was just the environment that I was having problems with or whether it was my whole career at Price Waterhouse.

"I also had another reason for wanting to go to a big office. Blumenthal was in the process of rising to power at Burroughs and wanted Price Waterhouse to do some extensive consulting engagements. Well, in the end, the firm picked me to be project manager for those assignments and I moved to the Detroit office. I was there for a year and a half, and then went to work for Burroughs. The guy who hired me was the corporate controller, Dave Rynne, who's now CFO at Tandem Computer."

It was an exciting time to be at Burroughs. Blumenthal was moving fast, trying to turn the company around after it had spent a bruising decade competing with and slowly losing ground to IBM. The job Ludvigson was offered was in San Diego. He took it, but grudgingly, moving his now family of four (two daughters) to the West Coast.

"You make a decision when you're in a large corporation as to how important is your personal life and location and how important is career. And at that time, for me, career was very important. Still is. So I knew the thing to do was to work my way back to the corporate office [in Detroit] and start moving up the ladder."

No sooner did he accomplish that than Ludvigson realized that he hated being at the corporate office and hated his job. "I told the company I was unhappy being in Detroit and, secondly, that I was unhappy being a finance guy. I wanted a line operation position. Somewhere outside of Detroit. I mean, if they wanted me to run a sales office, I'd do that. If they wanted me to run a manufacturing plant, I'd do that. Inside, I knew I'd just always wanted to be an operations guy, that I'd just defaulted into finance. I wanted to break out, and I'd been trying to do that for a long time.

"As it turned out, I got a handshake agreement with the executive office to take a line job, to come back to California and run a division. But then, Paul Stern, who was president of Burroughs at the time, called me in and said, 'Gee, we've got this very significant problem at Memorex and we're really in a turnaround situation. We're losing money and we really need somebody to go out there and fix it. You're one of my guys. I know that we have this commitment for you to do something else, but I'd really appreciate it if you would go out and run the finance operations of Memorex and get this thing straightened out.'

"Well, you don't say no to the president of the company. So, my bid to leave finance fizzled and I came out to Silicon Valley as VP of finance and business development for Memorex."

Memorex at the time was an open wound. Once one of Silicon Valley's highest fliers, a driving force in the tape business, it had collapsed in the late 1970s under poor management and misguided entries into the wrong computer memory systems markets. A potentially saving merger with Amdahl Computer in 1980 had failed and the company slowly withered through the decade, finally being bought at a cut rate by Burroughs in 1981.

But even that price turned out too high for this husk of a company. And when Ludvigson arrived at Memorex in May 1980 to join general manager Phil Dawber, the firm was already bracing itself for a two-week shutdown in June to save costs.

"When I got there Dawber was working on a pitch he was going to make to the executive committee of Burroughs that we buy Storage Technology [of Louisville, Colorado, once Memorex's biggest competitor and which had tried to buy Memorex two years before]. His theory was that the combined volumes and resulting economies of scale would yield profitability.

"Well, I argued that absolutely the wrong thing for Burroughs to do was to stay in the peripherals business; that really this whole place ought to be shut down.

"What finally convinced Phil was my doing a little profitability analysis that said if we did everything right, we'd see some amount of profit—it figured to about 5 percent of revenues. And that was it, with everything right. So, it was going to cost $400 million to $500 million to buy Storage Technology. And we asked ourselves, if we were Blumenthal running Burroughs, in the computer systems business, what would we do with [half a billion dollars]? We wouldn't buy peripherals, that's for sure. In fact, we'd buy some communications company, or another computer company.

"And so we put together a pitch for the executive committee. It was really funny, because in an hour it went from a pitch to buy Storage Technology to a pitch to shut down Memorex and sell the whole thing. The key was that Phil had a real analytical kind of mind—where he just looked at [my proposal] and said, 'Yeah. Absolutely right. It's the thing to do. Let's go.' "

But in winning that argument, Ludvigson essentially talked himself—and several hundred other Memorex employees—out of a job.

Putting a large company, no matter how enfeebled, to sleep is a long process. In Memorex's case it took nearly a year and a half. And that was just to sell off Memorex's distribution system and cut back on operations, which initially was all of the proposal to which Burroughs would agree. Being an attendant at this corporate deathwatch was not a pleasant business.

"It was a year of once-a-month layoffs. Cut and lay off, cut and lay off. You work just as hard doing this as you would running a successful company, but with the added thing that it's all downhill.

"It's very emotionally draining; and at times it got to be very difficult. One thing that kept us occupied was planning how we thought we could make [Memorex] into something else, or at least make some money for Burroughs. You always develop a salvage plan—and at least that reduces some of the pain of the current chop, chop, chop.

"As it turned out, it was a good plan, because when the Sperry merger came along [to form, with Burroughs, Unisys] we were able to come quickly to closure on selling a piece of the business and generate some cash for the new company."

It was at the beginning of the Memorex evisceration that Ludvigson was first contacted by MIPS. The possibility of moving from a company in extremis to one still experiencing birth was appealing, but the timing was wrong. Remembers Ludvigson, "We were going into this sale mode and after that I quit talking to people [about jobs] because once I get going on something like this I get very project-oriented. I always feel the need to complete the project."

Because of that timing, Ludvigson wouldn't join MIPS for several more years. In the meantime, the last rites completed and Memorex suitably interred, Ludvigson left his family in the Bay Area and spent six months in Bluebell, Pennsylvania, at the new corporate headquarters of Unisys. There, he handled the dispositions of excess properties and plants—in other words, selling off all the properties of Burroughs and Sperry made redundant by the merger.

Ludvigson loved being the de facto vice-president of real estate, wheeling and dealing with hundreds of millions of dollars worth of property and buildings. "It was a deal a day. Lease, shut down, combine. I thought it was a lot of fun."

But there were other responsibilities as well, forces countervailing to the ambitions of this self-professed career man. The family was still back in Silicon Valley.

"We had sold our house because we were down to the point of 'It's summertime and where are the kids going to school?' I promised my wife—the first and probably the last time I'll promise her on something like this—that by the end of June I'd make a decision on what I was going to do. At the time we were either going to come to Philadelphia and stay at Unisys or move to London, where the new Memorex, headquartered there, wanted me to do all their external financial stuff."

Instead, Ludvigson quit Unisys, returned to Silicon Valley, and joined Systems Industries, a computer peripheral maker, for a year as chief financial officer.

Why that choice? "It gave me a reason to stay here. I really hadn't wanted to leave the Valley, because in the Bay Area you not only have everything from a living standpoint but from a working standpoint as well. It's just a matter of being in the mainstream here long enough to get acclimated to the community. I figured if I could do that and get plugged in, I could stay here for a long, long time."

CHAPTER 4

The Company That Wasn't There

Here's a riddle. What company designed integrated circuits for others to make, makes computers for others to sell, and sells software that others have developed? If you answer Chips and Technologies, Convergent and Computer Associates, we'll give you partial credit. But we're thinking of just one company, not three: MIPS Computer Systems, the company that is likely to have a spectacular growth year by going public in the near future. We don't envy the underwriters standing between MIPS and wary investors, because in structure and strategy, this company is like no other we follow.

—*Technologic Computer Letter*, October 1989

TO BE A SUCCESSFUL START-UP COMPANY in the modern international world of high technology is to draw upon yourself a host of furies—new start-up competitors that have attracted big venture money by pointing at your success and offering to copy it; troubled mid-sized companies trying to stay alive by shifting into your newly created business; opportunistic foreign competitors that exist by copying emerging technologies at a lower price; and, worst of all, multinational electronics giants that keep tabs on all up-and-coming businesses, wait until they reach an interesting size, then crush them with a combination of large-scale manufacturing, high-powered promotion, and far-reaching distribution channels.

Yet, every year, thousands of entrepreneurial teams try to survive this onslaught. Hundreds manage to find funding, some from venture capital and some from friends, relatives, and second mortgages on their homes.

Not surprisingly, the fate for most is oblivion.

MIPS did not intend to fail. It had already come too far in its brief existence, too many dreams and lives were wrapped in the company's story for it to end now. The company had nearly succumbed once because it had not had the right survival strategy and had misjudged the lethal nature of the RISC business. It had cost the company its founding management team. The new team would not make that same mistake.

Only a veteran executive staff, like that formed by Bob Miller, could have attempted the revolution in organization that MIPS began to exhibit in late 1988. A less experienced team with the same idea would have likely been told by the board of directors to knock it off or simply been purged.

But venture capital had put a lot of money into MIPS. More than that, it recognized the fundamental value of the MIPS RISC architecture. It was simply too good to lose. And finally there was Miller himself, not your typical president of a $100 million company. So, the board and its venture capital members listened to the plan. Why not? A desperate situation requires radical solutions. Anything would be better than where they were. And, the MIPS business model was born.

The challenge MIPS had to overcome was straightforward. How could it survive in battle with all of its potential competitors and imitators and still grow to the defensible size?

One option, that of hiding in the wing, sneaking its technology onto the stage, and then stepping into the limelight only when it had gone too far to be stopped, was out. Amdahl had pulled off that strategy in mainframes and Compaq in portable computers, but that was against IBM, which seemed not to care (or, given antitrust risks, didn't dare to care) about markets until they reached a billion dollars in size. The RISC business was something else entirely, with already too many players and too much publicity for any company to try to take center stage undetected.

The only other way then was to go all out, to create enough market presence in a short time to make it more appealing for potential competitors to work with MIPS than against it. Achieving that, without overextending and exploding the company in the process, was the heart of the plan.

In traditional business models the correct strategy for growing a firm is to stake out a niche market in which the firm has, almost from the start, dominance and then to serve that market through increasingly sophisticated customer support and an unmatched understanding of the market's distribution channels. This creates product and company identification, builds customer loyalty, and erects both obvious and subtle barriers to market entry by competitors.

If this niche market is of sufficient size to meet a company's near-term growth needs, then the proper procedure is to begin increasing profitability by "verticalizing," that is, expanding the company's operations backward into product manufacturing (if that work is being contracted out) or a step further into component manufacturing—or even further into processing the raw material of its products. Verticalization should also go forward as well into the distribution channels, ultimately replacing distributors and retailers with the creation of the company's own stores.

This verticalizing, when done right, cuts out intermediaries on both sides of the company and puts the profits those intermediaries would have made into the company's own coffers. Theoretically, these added gains are useful for several reasons besides enriching company executives and investors. They provide the capital needed to research and develop new products to keep the company ahead of the competition. Also, the added margins serve as a cushion the company can cut out if competition heats up and it must cut prices to maintain market share. Finally, and just as important, these added profits can fill a war chest to finance the company's ultimate "horizontalization" into new niche markets, where the process begins again.

The most extreme examples of this traditional model for business expansion existed in the first half of this century. Take Ford. It verticalized to do everything from pouring steel at its Rouge River plant to building the cars to selling them through Ford-owned dealerships to helping customers finance their purchases. The big Hollywood studios of the era were also highly verticalized, from having the stars under contract to showing the films in studio-owned theaters.

Antitrust regulations and the complexity of contemporary business have made such vertical business constructions all but impossible in modern America. Most companies recognize their inability to match the expertise found in their suppliers, distributors, and retailers and choose not to compete with them. Equally, contemporary consumers are not as brand loyal as their predecessors and have grown accustomed to piecing together their own finished products and systems rather than depending upon packages from a single source.

Nevertheless, this traditional business model still dominates the businesses of the world. Even T-shirted electronics tycoons subscribe to its principles. Even when the company looks like an ashram and the president speaks in Zen koans, the strategy of the business itself is usually as conservative as its buttoned-down counterparts: Focus on a single market, establish a loyal customer base, and expand the product family. Stick to what the company knows, verticalize but don't overextend on capital investments, protect the technology, defend the home market, and constantly look for new markets to attack.

MIPS, and this is what intrigued industry watchers and business philosophers, essentially threw out the traditional model and, in the view of the old model, set about committing corporate suicide. It was only after the new model worked that outsiders began to spot precedents for what MIPS had done, to recognize it as the culmination of trends that had been under way in the electronics industry, especially in personal computers, for years.

Here's how the MIPS model works. If you find it confusing at first, you aren't alone. Even experienced executives are puzzled the first time they see it. By the end of this discussion it should be clear.

Structurally, the firm is not one company but three: a technology developer, a hardware builder and seller, and a software provider. The first, the technology company, is holder of the MIPS RISC architecture patents. Until 1987 this first company was also a manufacturer, contracting out the manufacture of its processors to overseas and domestic semiconductor "foundries." Like other chip firms, MIPS quickly discovered that these foundries, perpetually distracted by other contracts, were simply not reliable enough to serve as the basis of a fast-growing company. So, MIPS provided an incentive for reliability by switching to a licensing agreement by which the resulting "semiconductor partners" would not only provide MIPS with parts, but could also (after paying MIPS a royalty, of course) sell those chips on the open market.

The idea worked brilliantly. At the time of its Going Public Day, MIPS had three giant semiconductor partners—Sony Corp. and NEC Corp. of Japan and Siemens A.G. of West Germany—and three domestic semicustom chip house partners—Integrated Device Technology, Inc., LSI Logic Corp., and Performance Semiconductor Corp. All but latecomer Sony were producing MIPS chips in volume, not only filling MIPS's needs but those of MIPS's computer licensees.

The second MIPS company builds and sells hardware, from printed circuit motherboards stuffed with chips to powerful workstations and special computers, called servers, designed to be used with multiple terminals. The workstations, named by the company *RISCstations,* ranged in power in late 1989 from 12 mips to 20 mips. The servers, called *RISCcomputers,* ranged from a 12-mips version designed for desktop networks to a 20-mips Enterprise server designed to perform all the processing needs of a small company. Waiting for an early 1990 introduction was a 55-mips server.

Prices for these products ranged from $17,000 to $40,000 for the workstations and $15,500 to a newly announced $500,000 top-end model for the servers. With price-performance ratios continuing to plummet, MIPS expected to be able to offer a 25-mips workstation for just $7,000 by 1991.

Except for a few university sales, MIPS sold all of this hardware either through original equipment manufacturer (OEM) deals with large computer customers by which the customers would put their logos on the MIPS machines or through value-added resellers (VARs), which would package these products into larger systems for sale to specialty markets.

While MIPS built some of these products itself, most were built under license by other manufacturers, including Sumitomo Electric Industries of South Korea, Silicon Valley's Loral Rolm Mil-Spec Computers, Nixdorf of West Germany, and, most notably, Kubota of Japan, which also, at the time of the IPO, owned about 20 percent of MIPS.

The third MIPS company is in the applications software business— buying and porting over key programs in CISC to MIPS's RISC architecture to support customers of the other two MIPS companies. This is to help overcome the problem, described earlier, of the shortage of available software in UNIX and for RISC.

Almost from the beginning, even before the Miller era, MIPS recognized that it had to prime the pump by doing some of its own software porting work on key programs in order to attract both key hardware customers and third-party software developers who would then work with the MIPS RISC architecture. Traditionally, this is a Catch-22: Third-party software developers don't want to work on programs for unpopular hardware products, and customers won't buy hardware products unless they are backed by sufficient software.

MIPS escaped the catch in 1986 by forming a subsidiary called Synthesis, backing it with what was at the time very precious capital, and setting it to work designing key basic programs such as RISC compilers and windows—stuff nobody else would be willing to do.

Apparently the plan worked (though Synthesis didn't and was absorbed back into MIPS in mid-1989). By Going Public Day the company was busily signing on third-party designers (nearly a hundred by the first week of December) and had nearly three hundred software programs available on its architecture. The company's goal was to have several thousand such programs by 1991.

According to the MIPS model, the three companies each have a distinct and defined role in the success of the larger firm. Royalties from technology licensing provide capital inflow, hardware sales generate revenues, and software acts as a pull on the market. All very neat. And by Going Public Day, each segment was making its contribution: Software accounted for 11.9 percent (the target was 12 percent), technology 26 percent (17 percent target), and hardware 62 percent (71 percent target).

By now the reader has probably been struck that running a combined hardware, software, and semiconductor chip business would be tough for a $10 billion company with 75,000 employees, much less a $100 million firm like MIPS with just 600 people. IBM does all three. So do Hewlett-Packard, half a dozen Japanese giants, and, to a lesser degree, Motorola, Texas Instruments, and Apple. But these are all big, established companies. MIPS had been on the scene for just four years—and the first two years didn't really count. How could Miller and team possibly make such a wide-ranging tripartite structure work?

One clue can be found in George Gilder's book about the semiconductor industry, *Microcosm*. According to Gilder, power in that industry comes not from greater control but from less control of the forces shaping the market. The key to long-term success is not gradually to subsume all of the processes that create and sell a chip, but to bring maximum value to bear upon one's point in the chain. This works, Gilder suggests, because proliferation of a new technology is everything, and this can happen only if numerous participants are driving that technology into general use, searching out new applications, perfecting old ones, and discovering untapped markets.

MIPS, which arrived at its model independently from Gilder's theorizing, could be said to be the first company to stake its corporate life on that idea. Other tech companies had gone partway down this path. Certainly in the personal computer industry many firms packaged components from suppliers, licensed software, and then sold the resulting products through computer chains. But none had carried the process of diffusion as far as MIPS.

When describing the MIPS model, terms like vertical and horizontal almost have no meaning. Though reality had demanded a few compromises, MIPS was basically a company with no front end, no back end, and a supposedly impossible horizontal reach for its size. Using traditional measures, MIPS might be in less control of its business than any company of its size in history. It was, by the old business books, the quintessence of corporate impotence.

Yet, if corporate growth and profitability are the ultimate measures, then MIPS was one of America's fastest-growing firms at the turn of the decade. It was also among the most profitable, having at midyear 1989 an extraordinary $24 million cash balance.

Sociologically, MIPS was a runaway success too, having less than a 5 percent turnover in a business community where employee loyalty is virtually nonexistent and annual average employee losses hover around 20 percent. Plus, despite the chaos normally associated with doubling employment in just two years, the ratio of revenues per employee had still climbed from $100,000 to $250,000, and company executives privately talked about topping $300,000 per employee.

The same was true in technology. Not only was the MIPS architecture rated by outside experts as among the best in RISC, but by Going Public Day MIPS claimed that it held the dominant market position in RISC workstations and would hold the same leadership in UNIX computers within two years.

The final accreditation of this revolutionary new model had come financially. Not only was MIPS about to close out on a $100 million year, but it was on the brink of, in the words of more than one stock analyst, "the most eagerly awaited technology company stock offering in years."

MIPS had recognized that for its new model to work, the company would have to keep advancing the state of the core RISC processor technology itself and to place itself quickly in the middle of a number of giant corporations many times its size and act as a sort of traffic cop, signing up licensees that didn't directly collide with one another, making sure the semiconductor partners manufactured sufficient quantities to meet the market's needs. In theory, MIPS could have licensed its semi-conductor partners to sell their chips to its computer licensees and then just sat back and waited for the flood of royalty checks. In part, that is exactly what MIPS did—which explains the source of all the cash. But Miller and team caught on early that simply acting as a remote licensor was ultimately self-defeating.

For one thing, if MIPS didn't push the technology forward, its lic-ensees would, until they wrested control away. Also, if MIPS didn't participate in the actual marketplace, if only in a minor way, it risked losing touch with end-users' real needs and losing its computer licensees to more practical technologies. And there was money to be made in building boxes as well—60 percent profit margins in some of the work-stations and servers—so why not build them? And lastly, and this was rarely admitted at MIPS, more personal factors were at work as well. Miller, Boesenberg, Jobe, Vigil, and the others had spent their profes-sional lives building and selling computers. That was where the excite-ment was, and they weren't about to sit around and endorse royalty checks, no matter how lucrative it might be.

It took every day of the two years between Miller's arrival and the Going Public Day to construct the organization. At the front end, as noted, were the semiconductor partners. Specifically, in 1987 and 1988 the three U.S. semiconductor companies and Siemens were licensed to manufacture MIPS's processors in CMOS (complementary metal oxide semiconductor), a semiconductor manufacturing process that results in chips with low power consumption. Under the terms of the agreement, MIPS could not sign on any new CMOS semiconductor partners until January 1993. These partners were required to meet MIPS's processor needs, but were also free (with royalty payments to MIPS) to sell to MIPS's computer customers.

In 1989 MIPS added the two Japanese semiconductor partners, NEC and Sony, and licensed them to manufacture the company's designs in ECL (emitter coupled logic). By MIPS's Going Public Day neither firm had yet reached production stage, but both were expected to be shipping within the year. Until then the company was relying on a small domestic firm, called Bipolar Integrated Technologies, Inc. (BIT), to soon begin producing these chips. MIPS planned to add other ECL semiconductor partners in upcoming months.

According to the agreement, these firms supplied MIPS with the processors MIPS needed for its proprietary workstations and servers. In addition, the semiconductor partners were free to sell additional MIPS processors on the open market for a royalty of approximately 10 percent of sales price. Implicit in this agreement was that the semiconductor partner would devote its energies to fulfilling the demands of both MIPS and the marketplace (in fact, only LSI Logic manufactured a competitive RISC chip). Also implicit was that MIPS would continue to advance the architecture and keep at the forefront of the industry. MIPS proved this commitment by devoting 18 percent of its revenues to product development in 1989 and a staggering 28 percent the year before.

The MIPS RISC processors fabricated by the semiconductor partners were sold in one of three forms:

- As chip sets, usually sold directly by the semiconductor partners to computer companies;
- With a full complement of supporting chips emplaced in a printed circuit board, usually sold by MIPS to computer makers wanting to enhance existing products;
- And as part of MIPS's proprietary workstations and servers.

To help close a deal with potential customers, all three formats ran MIPS's growing software library, thus explaining the company's heavy investment in the Synthesis subsidiary early on.

By Going Public Day the top executives of MIPS had logged millions of miles over the previous eighteen months flying around the world pitching computer companies on adopting the MIPS RISC standard. In September 1989 alone, Bob Miller logged 60,000 miles flying to and from Europe, landing in a new city every five waking hours, lining up deals. Backing these visits was an increasingly skilled team in MIPS's legal department under Joe Sweeney. At that point in the company's history, nothing was more important than lining up customers, and MIPS scoured the world looking for them. Only with a sizable number of these corporate users adopting MIPS RISC could MIPS have any hope of seeing its architecture become the industry standard.

Kubota had been the first, in late 1987, and Miller had been willing to give away a fifth of the company and a board seat to get Kubota's capital ($25 million), manufacturing, and a first big name on MIPS's customer list. In the fall of 1988 came the big coup: Digital Equipment

Corporation (DEC), one of the world's leading computer makers. DEC wanted the rights to MIPS's technology for use in its own proprietary products. It got them and 5 percent of MIPS's stock (and warrants for 15 percent more) for $15 million.

The DEC deal was the breakthrough MIPS needed. First, it helped legitimize MIPS as a contender against the established leadership of its primary rival, Sun Computer's SPARC technology. Second, it trained the MIPS team in structuring future licensing deals. It was also the last time MIPS gave away equity to a licensee. From that point on, customers would be able to buy only products, not a piece of MIPS.

After DEC, the deals came quickly, as MIPS management and the legal team scattered to every part of the globe. By Going Public Day the company had nailed down deals with more than fifty corporations and institutions. The nature of these deals varied with the business of the customer and its particular needs. For example, there were distributors (Kubota), laboratories and universities (Stanford, Cal Berkeley, Texas A&M, Rice, Lawrence Livermore Lab, Sandia National Laboratories), and value-added resellers (American Airlines, Hitachi-Zosen Information Systems, Racal-Redac). There also were big tech and aerospace customers looking to license RISC for use in their own products. These included Boeing, DEC, Kodak, GE, Lockheed, Sony, Nixdorf Computers A.G., Northern Telecom, Rockwell, Tandem Computer, Silicon Graphics, TI, TRW, and Westinghouse. (With Tandem, MIPS also signed an agreement making it the official service and repair company for all MIPS workstations and servers.)

Some of the biggest deals, however, were with the OEM customers, those selling MIPS workstations and servers as part of their own larger systems. These included Groupe Bull of France, Control Data Corporation, Nixdorf Computers, Pyramid Technology Corporation, and Sumitomo Electric Industries, Ltd. It would be these customers, as well as a few of the technology clients, that would serve as the tiny MIPS's giant phalanx driving into the computer marketplace.

Through September 30, 1989, MIPS had sold approximately 2,500 computer systems and subsystems to nearly 250 customers worldwide. These products had found use in fault-tolerant transaction processing (as in banking), communications controllers, computer-aided design, three-dimensional graphics, and defense systems.

One of the last big deals before MIPS's IPO was also the most portentious. In signing the technology agreement, Sony announced it intended to base its new workstation line—the leader in Japan—on MIPS architecture. But more than that, Sony added that in the future it intended to stuff its MIPS chips into commercial products, perhaps including future, more intelligent generations of VCRs, Walkmen, and Talkmen.

There it was. If Sony did what it said, RISC technology would at last escape the confines of the high-end computer and its dependence upon UNIX. Even the personal computer market for which it had long lusted would shrink in importance next to 100 million or more VCRs and portable music players. And if RISC made that breakout, it would be in the MIPS version. It was a prospect so enormous and awe-inspiring that even Bob Miller lowered his voice when speaking of it.

One well-known fact about revolutions is that no one can predict how they will end.

In creating a new kind of corporate organization at MIPS, Miller and his crew seemed to have discovered a way for a small new firm to have the impact of a large established one. On Going Public Day the plan seemed nearly flawless.

But the brilliance of the strategy might be short-lived. As MIPS was sailing on a new course through uncharted waters, its future was undivinable. It might capsize or run aground a month hence, its strewn wreckage serving as a warning to other companies interested in imitating its model. Or, in another three years MIPS might grow to the $1 billion company it fully expected to become, a year after that arriving as one of the youngest members ever of the Fortune 500.

Whatever the future, MIPS was now locked into its strategy. There was no way of backing out of the complex licensing arrangements it had constructed. Company executives could only try to identify the looming, shadowy threats waiting ahead of them—and hope they could navigate around them in time. There wouldn't be much time to react, as MIPS was racing forward as fast as a company could go.

MIPS believed the greatest internal and external challenges to its long-term success to be competition among its customers and partners, an unstable and immature market, and managerial problems created by growth.

MIPS, by design, existed in an almost perpetual balancing act between opposing forces. The DEC investment was countered by Kubota's. There were the six semiconductor partners. The value-added resellers competed not only with one another but conceivably with MIPS's own hardware. The original equipment manufacturers and technology customers collided with one another in certain markets and perhaps one day, though MIPS tried to stay out of their way, with MIPS's own hardware sales.

Such balances of power are inherently unstable. At the time of the IPO the pie was big enough for everybody to have a piece. But when a crunch comes, as it always does, companies tend to fall back on the old model and verticalize to maintain their profit margins. Would MIPS find itself crushed between its computer customers moving downward and its semiconductor partners moving up? There would still be royalties, but would that be enough for the giant MIPS of two or three years hence?

Success was equally fraught with potential friction. For now, MIPS could quietly sell its own hardware to customers not served by its OEMs. But as MIPS grew, could it still play this niche game or would it have to begin competing with its own giant computer licensees? And what kind of chill would that put on those relationships?

For all of its success, the MIPS RISC architecture was not yet the industry standard. And RISC itself remained, for now at least, a high-performance niche technology, representing just one third of the entire $6 billion workstation market in 1989. UNIX, the horse RISC was supposed to ride to glory, had also yet to achieve the universal acceptance expected for it.

In other words, the market was still unstable and immature. The race was not over yet, and Sun SPARC had enjoyed a head start. And even if MIPS RISC outdistanced SPARC, there was an even more frightening potential challenger. All that would be needed to trip up MIPS RISC would be for IBM to choose a different RISC architecture for its impending workstations. Director Bill Davidow also feared the dark horse: an unexpected new competitor that would outdo MIPS on performance. In a business still mips-obsessed, that would be disastrous.

MIPS's third great challenge was internal. It was currently on one of the great ramp-ups in Silicon Valley history. Over the previous two decades, every other firm that found itself in this enviable position—Intel, Apple, Tandem, and even, in the months before the MIPS IPO,

Sun Microsystems itself—has eventually stumbled, discovering that it could no longer manage the chaos created by explosive growth.

Thanks to its innovative business model, MIPS had forestalled this day of reckoning by essentially remaining just the small core of a company. But, to reach $1 billion, there would be no escaping the managerial nightmare of rapid personnel hiring and training, communications foul-ups, and lack of coordination that inevitably followed. Intel had found itself frozen in warfare between older employees and a new coterie from Texas Instruments. Apple had hired so fast that employees had spent weeks waiting to be told what their job requirements were. Sun was currently circling confusedly as it tried to replace a failing management information system. What would MIPS's weak point be?

The best firms always reach this hurdle, and the great ones learn to regroup and, wiser, move on at a more prudent pace. The rest simply collapse. MIPS's management was as experienced as that of any firm its size in Silicon Valley history. But did it have the flexibility to cope with a company beginning to gnaw on itself?

There was one other potential flaw to the trend-setting new MIPS model of business organization, one more apparent to outsiders than to those within the firm. It was the heavy dependence of this type of organization on the person at the top.

All start-up companies rely heavily on the chief executive. One reason is that the CEO is also typically the founder. This is especially true in electronics, where that same individual is often the chief scientist and the only true entrepreneur as well. But even in the traditional start-ups, a CEO operates as the first among equals.

The MIPS model was different. From the beginning the company was structured like a multidivision giant corporation—only the controlling superstructure of a giant firm's bureaucracy wasn't there. Instead, there was only the CEO trying to satisfy with limited resources the often competing needs of the company's distinct hardware, software, and research operations.

That suggested a hidden dimension to the MIPS model. Just as MIPS could be seen as a tiny company around which orbited chip companies, distributors, and giant computer firms, so could MIPS itself be seen as a host of managers, engineers, and assembly workers orbiting around the solitary figure of Bob Miller. That meant that the MIPS business model wasn't just helped by a veteran CEO and management team, but that it probably couldn't work without them. A weaker chief executive or a younger, more ambitious management team, and a MIPS model company would tear itself to pieces.

This fundamental and unstated aspect of the MIPS model implies something else as well. It is that ultimately the most important duty of the company is to keep the CEO alive and on the job.

And it was in this most crucial task that MIPS nearly failed.

CHAPTER 5

The Pitch

THERE WAS NO PRECISE DAY on which MIPS decided to go public with its stock. That event had always been in the company's business strategy, somewhere out in the future when all requisite corporate characteristics were in place.

"I think there's always been the understanding here that MIPS would go public," Ludvigson would recall in late November. "In the year and a half since I arrived here, I've regularly made this ritual presentation of what's required for the company to go public and where we are against that set of benchmarks. Bob [Miller] and I called it the 'red light/green light.' We'd look at the list and figure out how many of these requirements we'd achieved—green light; and how many we hadn't—red light.

"And then suddenly one day we seemed to have all green lights. These included company readiness, market receptivity, requirement for capital funding. There were also a number of judgmental kinds of factors, like, did we now need to be seen as a real company in the eyes of our customers? See, public companies are seen as 'real' companies, private companies aren't. Those were the kinds of things we looked at.

"One thing we didn't get was a lot of pressure from any of our investors to take the company public. It was more our feeling that we were at that point, that it was time."

The biggest "red light," both Ludvigson and Miller later admitted, was MIPS's software business, until then the wholly owned subsidiary called Synthesis.

"For a variety of reasons, we just could not make Synthesis work alone, and decided we really had to clean that up and fold it into the company and get it into working order. Once we'd done that we felt we were ready to go. Profitability was increasing. We had some level of predictability in our business results. We had our business units going well. Our products were on target. . . .''

Thus, one of the most important decisions in a company's history was made almost automatically and without fanfare at the end of the CFO's quarterly presentation.

Recalls Ludvigson, "It was not a monumental occasion. It was just sort of in the context of the business of the day. I think probably Miller and I were talking in his office and decided, 'Well, it's starting to look pretty good. I think we ought to put together a plan.' "

The company had already picked one underwriter for the deal, Cowen & Company, where one of MIPS's founders and current directors, Robert Wall, was currently a partner. MIPS had begun to look at underwriters when, before Ludvigson's arrival, it had casually estimated the date for going public at sometime in early 1989. Ludvigson, despite his lack of experience in IPOs, intuitively knew this was premature and had intervened.

"I said I think it ought to be September or October 1989. Not the first quarter. I said, 'The company's not going to be ready. We're not going to know enough. We're not going to have enough revenue. We're not going to have enough profitability. We're going to need some more time.' "

Ludvigson felt that the nature of his position required him to express contrary opinions: "I view part of my job as being like the teeter totter. When it looks like all the momentum is going to one side, you add a little weight to the other side to bring things back into balance. That's the job of the CFO. I tend to take the contrary point of view, even if I don't believe it, just to test and push and make sure we're thinking twice and not doing something out of impulse."

But he also saw practical reasons for objecting to the early date. "I really felt the company wasn't ready. We had poor budgeting mechanisms. We had very poor forecasting. We didn't understand the balance sheet. We couldn't predict the results. And we didn't have all the talent here yet. It was pretty gruesome. . . .

"And I'd had enough experience reporting surprises. I don't like doing it because it gets very personal. You've got your customers, your shareholders, calling up and saying, 'But Dave, I thought you said that it was going to be like this and now it's like that.' How do you say, 'Well, the engineer that was working on that particular product screwed it up and we couldn't ship it'? The investor doesn't really care about who screwed it up. You're the one who delivers the news and so it becomes very personal.

"So eventually I moved Bob to saying, 'Yeah, you're right. Probably the end of the third quarter.' At which time, to keep the balance, I moved it to early 1990. So we had this thing going for a while about timing."

That disagreement would continue, the date of Going Public Day vacillating back and forth between the end of 1989 and the beginning of 1990, until that day in October and the meeting in the boardroom when the estimable attorney Larry Sonsini at last set the date.

By then, even though the final date was just decided upon, the IPO process was already well down the track. The green light may have glowed feebly in the meeting between Ludvigson and Miller the previous spring, but it quickly cast giant shadows across MIPS and the firm it had chosen as lead underwriter, Morgan Stanley.

There is big money in underwriting an IPO: a 10 percent commission on the value of the stock sale. With the value of MIPS going public an estimated $75 million to $100 million, there was a lot to be made. And that didn't count the good publicity accruing to the underwriter handling the biggest tech stock offering in nearly a decade, certainly the biggest since the 1987 market crash.

That's why when the Morgan Stanley equity team drove down from San Francisco to MIPS headquarters on May 2, 1989, it came ready to put on the most elaborate show that computer graphics programs and laser printers could devise. The presentation, made by the Morgan Stanley team of Richard Fisher, president of Morgan Stanley Group, Inc., W. Carter McClelland, managing director of the technology group, William Osborne III, managing director for equity capital markets, Carol Muratore, principal for equity research, Frank Quattrone, principal of the West Coast technology group, and Steven Strandberg, associate in Quattrone's group, took two hours. With slides and a hundred-page report clad in a blue plastic ring binder with gold lettering, Morgan Stanley set out, in its words, to "Communicate our enthusiasm for MIPS's business and prospects." The MIPS and Morgan Stanley logos appeared in the lower left and lower right corners, respectively, on every page in the report. The copy was printed on a block of gray scale blending from dark to light going down the page. All pages were turned sideways, with the top at the ring holes. There were also a few heavier sheets showing bar charts and pie charts in color. As most were about international Morgan Stanley operations, they likely were shipped in from a company office overseas for the occasion. The first letter of every noun, verb, adjective, adverb, as well as some prepositions, was capitalized. This was no doubt meant to give the printed matter an air of authority and force, Corporate Emphatic the style might be called, but it created the cluttered effect of reading an early eighteenth-century manuscript—Daniel Defoe as West Coast technology group associate for equity research.

Morgan Stanley laid out its case in four sections. First, it made the point that Morgan Stanley was a major force in technology IPOs in the United States. It illustrated the point with charts showing corporate growth and key recent IPOs and newspaper quotes. Second, it attempted to establish that it was a far better performer than its archrival, Goldman Sachs, with nose-to-nose comparisons on market making. Third, it claimed to understand MIPS's business and goals. This was the first non-boilerplate section; it curiously attempted to explain to company executives what the company did. Fourth, it announced that it already had a plan for taking MIPS public.

The last was the most interesting section, as it provided a preliminary map to the territory that Miller, Ludvigson, and the rest of the MIPS team were about to enter.

The section began with a list of objectives for the IPO.

The first objective, Morgan Stanley said, was to "Maximize Value of Proceeds, While Insuring Good Aftermarket Trading Performance." Put simply, this meant MIPS should, not surprisingly, want to get the most money for its stock not only on Going Public Day, but in the market trading in the days and months afterwards.

The second objective was more subtle: to (with normal capitalization) "Establish a broad, institutional shareholder base, with 5 to 7 key major investors and a large amount of unsatisfied demand to provide ongoing support for the stock price." What this meant was that Morgan Stanley wanted to build a strong foundation in MIPS stock by lining up some big institutional investors (pension funds, insurance companies, foundations, mutual funds) to scoop up most of the available MIPS stock on Going Public Day. These investors would not only lend cachet to MIPS stock, but would also remove some of the long-term volatility in its pricing and trading.

The second part of the objective was also important. The goal of a successful initial public offering is not only to sell stock to the right people, but also not to sell it to everybody else. In the best scenario, the stock, widely publicized, becomes a lust object not only for the big boys in the market, but also for private individuals, retirees, and small-time players. It is this pent-up demand and the queued up "buy" orders that give a young stock its early impetus upward and create for it a self-perpetuating reputation for rewarding its investors.

Left unsaid was that this "unsatisfied demand" can also be a sucker's bet when the institutional investors, watching this demand drive up per share price, unload their holdings and take the profits. The small investors, finally able to acquire their desired stock, get to ride it down. Embittered, they unload the stock . . . and the big investors step back in at bargain-basement prices.

The remaining IPO objectives were of secondary importance: to promote MIPS in international markets, consistent with the firm's future business strategy; to develop a collection of market makers and stock analysts to track and trade MIPS stock; and to build a positive impression for MIPS in the investment community "as an Exciting, Innovative, Global Company Through an Innovative and Dynamic Marketing Program" in order to grease any future stock offerings by the company.

The second part of the section on the plan to take MIPS public detailed what Morgan Stanley saw as characteristics of the MIPS offering. It would be 5 million shares, priced between $15 and $20, to yield revenues of between $75 million and $100 million. Of these shares, no more than one-third would be "secondary," that is, not new shares but sold by existing shareholders. Furthermore, Morgan Stanley preferred that none of these secondary shares would come from MIPS's board of directors, no more than 10 percent of any manager's ownership position, and as little as possible from outside investors and ex-employees. This was to remove any questions from the minds of new investors that MIPS's top people were cashing out as early as possible.

To drive that point even further home, the Morgan Stanley team also proposed a "lockup" structure. This structure would limit the number of founders shares sold by any holder in the first 120, 180, and 240 days and would also help minimize the number of secondary shares sold on Going Public Day.

A final feature would be a so-called "green shoe." This gave the syndicate a set period (usually thirty days) in which to purchase an additional number of shares, typically amounting to 15 percent of the original offering. In a hot deal implementation of the green shoe helps to maintain an orderly market for the stock. Needless to say, it also makes more money for the underwriters.

The next page of the section listed Morgan Stanley's proposed syndicate structure for the MIPS IPO. Syndicates are created because no single underwriter is willing to accept the risk associated with a major public stock offering. Internationally, there also are intervening factors such as varying securities laws. In the proposed syndicate, Morgan Stanley & Company held the top position as global coordinator. In the United States Morgan Stanley acted as the lead, backed by forty-five other firms. In Germany, Deutsche Bank held the top position, followed by Morgan Stanley GMbh and six "co-managing" firms. In Switzerland, it was Union Bank Switzerland, followed by Morgan Stanley SA, Swiss Bank Corp., Credit Suisse, and then six co-managers. Finally, for the rest of the world, syndication was led by Morgan Stanley International, followed by six co-managers.

Next in the section the Morgan Stanley team laid out where key U.S. institutional investors were located, categorized by type of investment—computer systems, software, and specialty semiconductors, the three industries in which MIPS could be seen to fit. Not surprisingly, perhaps, New York topped all three columns, with investments of $2.74 billion in computers, $1.58 billion in software, and $1.7 billion in specialty semiconductors. In each category the next place was only one-quarter the size of this investment.

The lists reflected both the orientation of individual communities and the presence of key institutions. For example, Hartford, Connecticut, hardly a center for the chip industry, was the sixth largest investor in specialty semiconductors, reflecting no doubt some key investments by the insurance industry. Other unexpected cities included Baltimore (sixth in computers and software), Lansing (ninth in computers), Pittsburgh (ninth in software, tenth in chips), and Kansas City (tenth in software).

The expected locations were there, of course. San Francisco was second in computers, fourth in software, and fifth in chips; Boston third in computers, second in both software and chips. Still, the geographic diversity of investors in U.S. technology companies was a reminder that the effects of the electronics revolution were not confined to the famous enclaves such as Silicon Valley. The life insurance premiums of Midwest farmers and the pension payments of steelworkers in Pennsylvania and government employees in Michigan had played a key role in the rise of high technology to become America's largest manufacturing industry.

The next three pages of the plan finally got down to the trench work of going public. The objectives of a wide shareholder base, an international high profile, and a body of analysts and market makers all would be served, if properly done, by that most visible of events in going public: a road show.

The schedule for the road show was an astounding display of computer logistics and modern high-speed transportation. The three MIPS executives tagged for the tour team, Miller, Ludvigson, and marketing vice-president Chuck Boesenberg, looked at the itinerary and swallowed hard. All experienced business travelers, still none had ever attempted anything as ambitious or potentially debilitating as this. Nearly 30,000 miles in one week! The travel alone was awesome enough, but on top of that, there were the speeches, presentations, meetings, and interviews, most of which would be done through the fog of sleep deprivation and jet lag. How could anyone survive something like this, much less do a good job and run a company at the same time? Impossible.

The domestic schedule consisted of visits to seven U.S. cities: New York, Boston, Chicago, Minneapolis, Los Angeles, San Diego, and San Francisco. In each city nine key investors would attend the presentation, three from each of the three categories. For example, in Minneapolis the First Bank System, the Lutheran Brotherhood, and Norwest Corp. would represent computers. In Chicago Kemper Financial Services, Stein Roe & Farnham, and American National Bank & Trust would represent software. In San Francisco, the last stop on the tour, the software investment trio would be Husic Capital Management, Associated Capital, and the California State Retired Teachers Association.

In addition to the domestic schedule of presentations there would also be live television interviews (through the satellite-based Institutional Research Network) to pick up key investors not on the tour itinerary, such as First Interstate in Denver, State Farm Mutual in Bloomington, Mellon Bank and US Steel in Pittsburgh, Aetna Life & Casualty and Travelers Corp. in Hartford, and the State of Michigan in Lansing.

And that was the easy part. The international road show circumnavigated the world, bouncing among the major cities of the Northern hemisphere: Tokyo for Mitsubishi Trust, Sumitomo Trust, and Nippon Life; Frankfurt; Geneva and Zurich for, among others, Lloyd's Bank; London; Edinburgh; Paris.

The financial SWAT team proposed by Morgan Stanley for this global assault included not only the trio from MIPS of Miller, Ludvigson, and Boesenberg, but also a quartet from its own offices: Carter McClelland, Frank Quattrone, Carol Muratore, and Steven Strandberg. Representatives from MIPS's strategic partners would join the team when it reached the partners' headquarters. In Tokyo that would be NEC, Kubota, Sony, and Sumitomo; in Europe Siemens; in Minneapolis DEC; and in San Francisco Tandem.

Morgan Stanley next presented possible timetables for the IPO. The first scenario began June 12, just six weeks hence, and aimed at a Going Public Day of October 9, 1989. Another began January 8, 1990, and closed April 9, 1990. In between was the timetable Morgan Stanley desired, the one it titled "The First Deal of the 1990s."

It was that title that sold MIPS on Morgan Stanley. It proved that Morgan Stanley understood the private thoughts of Miller and his executive team. There was also an element of luck and timing. Recalls Ludvigson, "We were spending too much of our time listening to underwriters and investment bankers. Pitch after pitch after pitch. And you can't say no nicely unless you've made a decision. So we made a decision."

So, Morgan Stanley got its client and its calendar. In the end it would also nearly lose its reputation as well.

That middle calendar presented in May 1989 outlined the hurdles MIPS would have to vault in its race to Going Public Day:

September 11 First organization meeting.
Thereafter Drafting of prospectus/legal due diligence [background check] on the firm.
November 13 MIPS's audited nine-month financials available to include in the prospectus.
November 20 File S-1 (the red herring and other documents) with Securities and Exchange Commission.
January 1 Receive SEC comments on S-1, incorporate amendments.

January 8–15   Road show.

January 22   Set the pricing for the stock, based on perceived value, demand, price-earnings multiples of comparable firms.

January 29   Closing. Going Public Day.

As it turned out, MIPS squeezed the drafting/due diligence interval to just over a month, filing the red herring on November 7, two weeks before the anticipated date. Then, in an effort to go public before Christmas, the SEC comment period, pricing, and the road show were all piled atop one another. The road show itself began November 29, finished its international leg on December 8, and ran the U.S. tour through December 14, ending just days before the revised Going Public Day.

It was a strategy that made even the Morgan Stanley hyperkinetic schedule seem sedate. A strategy of a piece with the hard-charging style of Silicon Valley, perfect for a gutsy company that had made itself an industry leader in just two years.

But it was also a strategy that allowed no room for errors or delays; not by MIPS and not by any of the other players in the game from Morgan Stanley to American and British airlines to the Securities and Exchange Commission to Nature herself.

Unfortunately, not everyone was willing to play his or her assigned part.

CHAPTER 6

Red Herring

THE FIRST ORGANIZATIONAL MEETING for the MIPS IPO took place on September 1, 1989. Already MIPS was beginning to outrun the Morgan Stanley calendar.

Attending were representatives from Morgan Stanley and Cowen, MIPS executives, and a host of attorneys for all sides, including Sonsini for MIPS.

"It was real informal," remembered Ludvigson. "We met in the [MIPS] boardroom. There must have been thirty people there, so it was kind of crowded. We talked about the major issues of the deal and we put together a schedule. Morgan Stanley brought a list of issues that we talked about. And Sonsini led the schedule development."

It was at this meeting that the January IPO date was ratified, though it was soon to be pulled forward into December on Sonsini's recommendation.

The organizational meeting served as a starter's pistol. The attendees would then separate and recombine in various groups at various times, all rushing the process toward the finish line fifteen weeks away.

The first, and ultimately most important, step was the preparation of the prospectus. This document, in its incomplete red herring form, lacking pricing information and dates, would be the vehicle MIPS would have to ride through the Securities and Exchange Commission. The SEC would scrutinize every word of narrative, every number in the pages of balance sheets and consolidated statements, every referenced legal tussle and stock option.

Like the annual reports that follow, prospectuses are always positive. To the naive, they always present a vision of the company too perfect for the two-fisted world of corporate life. Even the best companies are sued by embittered ex-employees over wrongful termination or by former executives demanding a larger golden parachute. Huge chunks of stock are often given away in the early days of the firm to the least likely people—landlords, office equipment providers, headhunters—all in a desperate effort to preserve precious cash flow. Once the company is finally flush, loans are often made to the founders to help them try to restore some of the private lives they've lost. For some it is already too late, and thus sometimes the list of leading shareholders also includes angry ex-spouses.

All of these skeletons emerge from the past to rattle their bones on the pages of the prospectus. Experienced readers quickly find them out and point to them for all the world to see. It only takes one such stigma, if sufficiently egregious, to turn a young firm's dream of going public into a living nightmare.

No one understands this more than the individuals assigned to write the prospectus. That's why it is typically a team process: the company's best writer, someone from the finance department, the corporate attorney, a representative from the lead underwriter, and, frankly speaking, anyone who has done one before. What this means is that probably the most important document in the history of a company is written by a committee, only some of whom fully understand that document's contents.

This, of course, is the perfect setting for acrimony, if not downright mayhem.

"The hardest part," said Ludvigson in the middle of writing the prospectus, "is reconciling everybody's views. We've got disparate views and we've got different agendas. We've got investment bankers who have to market and sell the deal. We've got the company wanting to tell its story. And we've got lawyers who want to make sure that the document's factual, accurate, doesn't lead investors to the wrong conclusions, and all that stuff. So there's a real tug of war going on.

"On top of that, you've also got a lot of very bright people who don't really understand your business. And still, you've got to be factual not only in the things that are in the document, but you've also got to be sure all the right things are in the document—that you've made all the important points you wanted to make."

The key to any such group writing is the first draft. Typically, it is the best shot by the most qualified individual in the group in terms of business knowledge, legal acumen, and writing skill. With a good first draft as a foundation, the process then becomes filling, excising, and correcting. A rickety first draft can doom even superior subsequent work to an eventual crash.

The task of writing this first draft fell on Joe Sweeney, MIPS's general counsel. His entire career seemed targeted for just such a role.

Sweeney, 41, grew up in Connecticut, the child of two high school teachers. In an effort to give his son the best education, the elder Sweeney took a job as an instructor at the aristocratic prep school Choate. That got Joe a scholarship for the school's tuition, which otherwise the Sweeneys could not have afforded.

The humiliations of class distinction were comparatively minor, but having a father who was an instructor there and having parents living a few yards away didn't make school easy for Joe. "If I had to do it over again, I would never do that," Sweeney would say. "But I didn't have much choice. At the time there were no arrangements among the various prep schools permitting the children of teachers to attend other schools."

He remembers a certain hostility from some of his fellow students: "They didn't take it out on me, but there was some residual resentment that I was there and my father was there and maybe I would get some special treatment. Actually, it was just the opposite. I got treated [tougher] just so it wouldn't be viewed as favorable treatment."

Upon graduation Sweeney chose Harvard over nearby Yale. "I wanted to go to a college that was far enough away from home so I wouldn't be visiting every weekend or my parents wouldn't be visiting every weekend. And that would be in a big city so there would be more social activities. Yale was too close to home. And New Haven isn't nearly as interesting a city as Boston is."

Sweeney started out pre-med, but soon concluded he didn't want to spend his college afternoons in a formaldehyde-reeking lab. So he switched over to liberal arts, graduating with a degree in government. While at school he worked at various times in a dining hall, as a YMCA swim instructor, and with high school kids on basketball and weight lifting. In his junior and senior years he worked for future Senator Barney Frank, then executive assistant to the newly elected mayor of Boston, Kevin White.

In his senior year, having been exposed to public life, young Joe Sweeney decided he wanted to go to law school. Boston University accepted him. During the next three years, while still in law school but before passing the bar and setting up in private practice, Sweeney worked in the U.S. Attorney's office, working primarily with the major crime and drug enforcement units. As he recalls it, the U.S. Attorney's office in Boston was "a very political situation," which was congruent with Sweeney's own budding political ambitions. But Sweeney found that seeing politics close up had actually soured him on the process. "I decided that I, as an individual, did not want to attempt to become an elected politician for a number of different reasons."

Nor did he want to stay with the U.S. Attorney's office. Though he didn't know it yet, he was an entrepreneur in the making: "What I wanted to do was get into litigation, get into private practice. And I decided the best way to do that was to go with a small firm—because if you start at a big firm you generally wind up spending several years being an apprentice. You start off in the library. You graduate to carrying somebody's bags. Then the third step, maybe after you've been doing this for a number of years, is to actually get to do something yourself.

"I didn't want to take that route. So I went with a small firm where I knew I would get some hands-on experience and responsibility fairly quickly."

Very quickly indeed. Eighteen days after being admitted to the bar he found himself in a courtroom. "The first jury trial I ever saw from beginning to end was the first one I ever conducted myself."

Soon, Sweeney was handling personal injury cases, securities work (the slowdown of the stock market in the early 1970s after the 1960s boom had resulted in a lot of litigation), and some pro bono criminal work. Thanks to some key cases, he drifted into specializing in construction litigation, Jones Act work (sailors injured on ships), and suits under the federal employees liability act (railroad workers injured on the job). Initially, Sweeney handled a lot of plaintiffs; later, as his reputation grew, he found himself increasingly hired by insurance companies. He stayed in private practice for eight years, from 1973 to 1981.

In time, "I decided that I didn't want to spend the rest of my life doing litigation." It was not for lack of love for the courtroom. "There's nothing more invigorating. No. That's not a jazzed-up enough term. You're really on fire when you're in front of a jury because you're hanging out there and everything's up to you—your strategy, your tactics, what you're saying, how you're saying it, how you ask questions, how you handle people, in what order you do things. Absolutely everything you do affects the result."

So why quit something he enjoyed so much? "It's a little bit of an oversimplification, but I decided ultimately that rather than being in a recovery mode—which is what litigation usually is because the events have already occurred and you're trying to sort things out and make right what was wrong—I wanted go more into the creation side. Contracts and doing deals and conducting business.

"Having made that decision, I looked around for an opportunity and took a job with Data General."

At Data General Sweeney was essentially put in charge of domestic litigation. After a couple years of litigating he fulfilled his original goal in joining the firm by moving over to the corporate side, working on technology licensing, mergers, and acquisitions. "All the general corporate things. After a couple years I was running that side of the house."

One of the people Sweeney met during his six-year stay at Data General was Bob Miller. "We had talked about his coming out here and going with MIPS. Some time after that he and I talked and he offered me this job.

"At Data General I got a view of and experience with a very different world than I'd experienced in private law practice in Boston. It was something that really interested me and I was having a lot of fun with. In many respects the natural extension of what I was doing at DG was to go off with a start-up and see what we could do."

Still, Sweeney would admit later, moving to California was "a wrenching change. No question about it. I'd grown up in New England and lived most of my life there." His parents were now dead, but Sweeney had always been close to his sister "and having 3,000 miles between us is not conducive to lots of contact." Furthermore, he'd become engaged while at Data General; his fiancée, a Ph.D. in chemical engineering from MIT, was in charge of Data General's mergers and acquisitions. It would be ten months before she could move to California.

Sweeney hit MIPS running. There wasn't any choice; partnership agreements were waiting. Looking back, Sweeney would see the red herring process as less demanding than the early days at the firm. "When I first came here I was working even harder than I am now. I'm probably averaging between 60 and 90 hours a week now. Back then I was averaging closer to 90 almost all the time. Before my fiancée arrived, I was putting in seven days a week."

They were married in November 1988. By March she was pregnant, due in early December 1989. Thus, as Sweeney would ruefully joke, including the IPO, he had two babies due at the same time.

"The pace has unfortunately been a running joke—or an open sore, depending upon how you look at it—because when I first came out here, I flew out on a Sunday with Bob Miller and started work the next day, Monday. And on Tuesday, the second day, we had a board meeting. On Tuesday afternoon, Bob Miller, Skip Stritter, and I got on a plane and went to Japan and spent a little over a week there starting negotiations with Kubota—on what turned out to be almost a company-saving financial arrangement. We also did some initial prospecting on what has turned out to be one of Bob's biggest strategic coups: the semiconductor partners.

"That was my first week at MIPS. And we've been going from big deal to big deal ever since. It's been a never-ending series."

With the MIPS IPO Sweeney faced a challenge as great as any in the company. With the imminent arrival of a baby already shattering his normal habits at home, he also now had to draft the prospectus, while still directing (and participating in) negotiations with new corporate strategic partners. If he fell down in either job task, he could severely wound the company, and at the same time his heart was home with his pregnant wife.

Nevertheless, "Sweeney did a helluva job getting a good first draft to us," said Ludvigson. "He did it the right way, too, by getting each operation in the company to contribute copy on what it did, then supplementing that with existing literature. It gave us a great start."

Then the editing process began. Writers of corporate financial documents, be they prospectuses, annual reports, or quarterly earnings statements, must quickly learn to drop pride of authorship because, by the time the document has been edited, revised, and vetted by a dozen or more blue pencils, it rarely retains a single sentence of the first draft. Authorship-by-committee is very efficient at assuring that a document is free of errors, improper connotations, and ambiguous phrasing. It also creates works that are inevitably dull, anonymous, and austere.

The MIPS prospectus was no different. And that was exactly what the firm desired. The goal of the writing team was neither to entertain nor to inspire, but to be accurate, complete, and fast. Hence they chose Sweeney, who, it was properly believed, could circumvent early delays and mistakes in the drafting process by bringing both corporate and legal points of view to the first draft.

Said Ludvigson, "A lot of times the investment bankers or the lawyers themselves write the first draft. But I don't understand how you can be successful with that approach.

"What we went through was almost a pendulum. First, the company [through Sweeney] wrote its view of the business. Next Morgan Stanley edited that, then went through their own diligence efforts, where they tried to understand the business and comb through all the records and other details. In doing that, they found items they wanted put in, so we took those things and rewrote the document—this time with more of the marketing perspective they wanted.

"Then the pendulum swung over to the lawyers. And they crashed the document in terms of taking everything out of it that made MIPS sound like it was actually a decent company. They put in all the negatives and took out all the superlatives.

"Then we pulled it back to what was probably the middle. So there was a lot of give and take, needless to say."

The noticeable edge in Ludvigson's words arose from what is always the most disputed part of any prospectus, the so-called *Risk Factors* section. Preparing the rest of the document is usually straightforward. The front of the prospectus, containing a summary of the stock offering, a description of the firm and its history, an explanation of company technology, products, and markets, and biographies of board members and executives, requires little more than fact gathering and editing. The back pages, containing the many financial documents and legal matters, are all but untouchable, the province of the corporate auditors and attorneys. The combined disputes over these sections, perhaps sixty pages, rarely equal those over the one to three pages describing the risks to the firm's future success. Not only can the IPO itself be threatened by the inclusion of a few injudicious words in this section, but, just as important, the exclusion of some words may ultimately be the most damning evidence in some future class action suit by shareholders, angry that they were not warned of this risk in advance.

As one might imagine, choosing what goes into the risk factors section and how it should be phrased often divides the prospectus writing team into opposing camps, with the company representatives on one side, the lawyers on the other, and the underwriters and everyone else dancing in between. Aggravating this battle is the inevitable postponement in writing this section till last, when nerves are frayed from exhaustion, stress, and a growing furor at home.

Something like this happened with the MIPS prospectus. In the beginning, thanks in large part to the Sweeney draft, all went comparatively smoothly. According to Ludvigson, "It was all very workmanlike. We had some very good people working on this and they had the ability to compromise. We didn't have anyone who was an especially rigid personality. Frankly, I would have killed them. I would have thrown them out.

"So, as it worked out, everyone's opinion was respected. There was a lot of give and take; a lot of balance. The Wilson, Sonsini guys were on our side so they were fairly easy to control. I think if the counsel on the other side of the transaction had viewed himself as an adversary rather than a party to the transaction, things could have been very, very difficult. But I thought that Alan Dean [partner in the New York law firm of Davis, Polk & Wardwell], who was Morgan Stanley's counsel, had, for a lawyer, a pretty good business perspective. So, when he brought up a legal point, I always found it had a lot of substance.

"I think the other thing we had going for us was that Sweeney and I really believed in the full-disclosure approach. We have such a good company here, with so many strengths, that we didn't have any problem being extremely opinionated about the things we thought were issues and the things we didn't think were issues. The underwriters or the lawyers would say, 'We think this is an issue,' and I'd say, 'Well, yes, but that's not the issue. You don't understand. Here's what the real issue is. Let me explain it to you. Here's how we're doing it and here's why. Here are the interrelationships. And here's the thing you're really after.' "

That was at the beginning. Then, on October 17 a two-mile stretch of the Loma Prieta fault in the Santa Cruz Mountains, just fifteen miles southwest of MIPS headquarters in Sunnyvale, shifted several feet. The resulting 7.4 Richter quake, the Great San Francisco Earthquake of 1989, did no real damage in Sunnyvale or, more specifically, to the three MIPS buildings, although they were more than twice as close to the epicenter as the heavily damaged sections of San Francisco and Oakland. But the quake did paralyze the Bay Area for weeks, disrupting commuting patterns and traumatizing local residents.

Bob Miller was on a plane flying home from a meeting with DEC in Boston. "I was listening to the preliminaries to the World Series when the Mutt and Jeff announcers start saying to each other, 'Holy shit! Did you feel that?' Then I start hearing the news reports that the Bay Bridge has collapsed and things are so bad in the South Bay they can't broadcast any reports from there.

"I knew enough about going public to expect the unexpected. But I didn't think it would be an earthquake." Miller spent that night sitting in the Denver airport.

Back in the traumatized Bay Area, most businesses, by unspoken agreement, simply shut down. Employees, staying home to deal with everything from simple insomnia to completely demolished homes, trickled back into work over the next week, sometimes to disappear again as crises at home demanded it. For the next month the entire Bay Area seemed to operate in a daze. Many commuters spent extra hours trapped in rerouted gridlocks. Parents tended terrified children afraid to sleep in their own beds. And every time a lull allowed the citizens to forget momentarily the events of October 17, an aftershock would bring the memory back with sickening vividness.

Afterwards, MIPS estimated that it had lost, through power outages, attenuated commuting times, jammed telephone lines, and employee absences, the equivalent of at least two full days of business. That was bad enough for a fast-moving company trying to prove to the world its prospects for growth and stability. Far worse was the effect of that lost time on the going public process. The schedule had left no room for such a delay. As Miller would say in late November, "We still haven't made up for those two lost days."

Now a superhuman effort was needed to go public before Christmas. The screws began to tighten on the prospectus team, and on no one more than Dave Ludvigson, as he arose at 1:00 A.M. to catch the crowded 3:00 A.M. BART train under the bay and its broken bridge to Bowne printers in San Francisco. The risk factors section still lay ahead, and with just two weeks left to finish the entire red herring, the current gentility of the writing team would be put to the test.

CHAPTER 7

Risky Business

IT IS IN THE NATURE of a business, especially one still in its entrepreneurial start-up stage, to be optimistic about the future. The odds are so great against any new company's succeeding that even to consider the downside risk would be to abandon the enterprise. In order to go on, to sacrifice their careers and personal wealth to the dream of their own company, entrepreneurs have to believe that they can wrestle with Fate and win two falls out of three.

"The strange thing about the red herring," said Joe Sweeney later, "is that it's used as a marketing document. That's the purpose of it supposedly. But the real purpose is to describe the company and minimize risk. So it winds up something you hopefully use as an insurance policy. The one thing that securities plaintiff lawyers look at when they think of suing is the prospectus. Did it fail to describe some material event or transaction or situation? Or did it describe some material event in a misleading fashion?"

That's why, in preparing the prospectus, the risk factors section is so painful. The company has overcome so many seemingly impossible obstacles to reach this point; now to have to personally and publicly admit everything that can go wrong in the future is like admitting for the first time the possibility of defeat. The company authors find themselves wanting to put an addendum on every printed paragraph: "Sure, this *might* happen, but come on, look at all the worse things we survived in the past! Compared to them, this is nothing, nothing at all." Or, "Okay, we admit this is a *possible* risk, but if you knew as much about this business as we do, you'd know this kind of thing couldn't happen in a million years."

Meanwhile, the underwriter and its attorneys are taking the opposite view. They don't want to queer the offering either, but they also don't want to be accused of misrepresentation. And, of course, sitting in the background, ready to second-guess every word in the section, is the Securities and Exchange Commission, trying to be diligent in its role of protecting the public from con artists and securities fraud.

The SEC has good reason to be careful. American business history is filled with stories of corporations conning innocent investors by hiding bad news, hyping marginal advancements into major breakthroughs, trading on inside information, and pumping up stock values with false leaks just before management cash-outs. Home-Stake, Ivan Boesky, Equity Funding, the S&L crisis, all examples of securities fraud or incomplete financial disclosure, have filled headlines for the last two decades.

And these are just the more notorious examples. In her research for the 1984 book *Wayward Capitalists,* author Susan P. Shapiro studied more than 500 securities violations during the previous quarter-century and concluded that two-thirds involved misrepresentations by either stock issuers or brokers—and that more than half of those occurred during a stock offering.

Some of the cases Shapiro cites are bizarre, such as the evangelical preacher and gospel singer/pilot/oil promoter friend who hopped around the country in the mid-1960s selling stock in a Wyoming oil lease only to "good Christians." They raised nearly a half-million dollars from unsuspecting investors.

Or the president of a chemical engineering and electronics firm who pledged $10 million of his stock as collateral for $4 million in loans—then had his company advance money to several of its subsidiaries to buy the company at inflated prices to keep value high. On some days, as much as 86 percent of the trading in this stock consisted of these purchases.

Most disclosure problems, however, are less flamboyant, though often more costly: the company that predicts a rosy future, only to see profits disappear the next quarter; the CEO who confidently announces a major new product, only to have the introduction date slip by a year. This is the gray area of disclosure. Did the company intentionally falsify information to pump up the stock price? Was it simply fooling itself? Or was the eventual disaster out of its control?

To punish the obviously criminal acts and to sort out the more subtle cases has been the role of the SEC since its creation out of the Securities Act of 1933—which in turn was a product of the dismay over the 1929 Crash and its exposure of questionable securities dealings. In the subsequent years, growing stricter or more complaisant depending upon the era and the Commission chairman, the SEC has continuously refined a complex "disclosure philosophy" to protect investors against the latest forms of duplicity or stupidity.

As *Nation's Business* magazine wrote in June 1988, "the SEC wants a full description of the company, its operations and the securities being offered. The regulators also want a detailed financial statement certified by an independent accountant. And the SEC also wants to know the backgrounds of those who are in charge."

But even that kind of disclosure could be something of a striptease. The magazine continued: "Factors in a company's past sometimes preclude it going public, and investment bankers have backed out of deals they felt were legally suspect or ethically unpalatable.

"If a few indiscretions were grounds alone to abort a new stock offering, however, many firms would be unable to go public. The trick in these circumstances is to convey just enough information to comply with disclosure rules without shouting, 'Here's our dirty laundry.' . . .

"For example, a prospectus issued by a consumer-electronics firm in Fort Lauderdale contained a veiled reference to a federal investigation into the source of the company's start-up capital. The inquiry revealed that the money used to start the company in 1974 had come from the illegal profits of a drug smuggler now serving a prison sentence." Nevertheless, the SEC approved the document and the company's stock offering was oversubscribed.

MIPS had no such skeletons in its closet. But nobody knew what it would take to set off the examiners these days. Predicting how the SEC might react to the go-go 1980s just ending had lately been a hobby of American industry. For the writing team at Bowne it had become a vocation.

Exhausted and under the gun, the MIPS prospectus team began work on risk factors. (The unfortunate combination of "risk" and "RISC" made the document, as the reader no doubt has already noticed, one of the most homophonic prospectuses in recent years.) The meetings now stretched from eight o'clock in the morning until ten or later every night.

Happily, Bowne printing was accustomed to this kind of struggle. Meeting rooms were available all night, with meals and beverages on call at all times. Day after day the team wrote, negotiated, rewrote, and proofed, working its way step by step through the section.

Ludvigson, a congenial, soft-spoken man, was not one to raise his voice. But as he saw one weakness after another in his company identified and probed, he grew increasingly angry. "I didn't yell, but I took a rather snide, cynical approach. I would tell the lawyers from time to time that they had managed to turn what I thought was a pretty darn good company into a piece of shit—and now who in the world would ever want to buy into it?"

Bob Latta tried to explain the conservative phrasing to Ludvigson by calling it "the German shepherd in the doorway," referring to his own dog, Mad Max. "I told Dave that I have that German shepherd in the doorway because when a burglar comes to my house and sees Mad Max, he decides it's easier to rob somebody else's house. The risk section serves the same purpose: to convince any hungry attorneys to look at somebody else's stock offering."

Later, during one of the more bitter writing sessions, Ludvigson turned to Latta and said, "Mad Max just pissed all over the prospectus."

Interestingly, the one MIPS executive who sided with the underwriters was Miller. Just two years before, he had made his own risk analysis of MIPS before joining it. Moreover, as the man at the top, he had a more complete sense of the strengths and weaknesses of the firm than anyone else, and with typical shrewdness, he was anxious to display the worst faults before any outsider discovered them.

"Dave and I switched roles on this," Miller said afterward, "and I think it was because I had more experience in this area. One of the advantages of having been at Data General was that I must have been deposed [that is, had to give a deposition in a lawsuit] at least seventy-two times. So now, whenever I look at a document, I always ask myself, 'What's the asshole lawyer sitting across from me going to be asking me about this document? And how well am I going to be able to defend what's in it?'

"There's nothing that's more fun than, when they start in on you, to say, 'Well now, if you'd refer yourself to page 2, we listed that as a major risk. Maybe your client should have read all the prospectus and not just page 27.' And that really gets to be delightful.

"I looked [at the risk factor section] with the idea that someday I might have to use it when some jerk who bought fifty shares decides this is the way to really make some money through litigation and hopefully a settlement. So, I'm all too happy to load up the risk section. In fact, if it had been up to me—and the investment bankers talked me out of it—I would have stamped every chart in the prospectus with 'This is not a forecast or a projection of future performance' and let some asshole, who is going to the road show just in the hope of someday being able to sue the company, swallow the poison pill early.''

Miller, sitting in his office just hours before leaving for the international road show, continued more philosophically, ''You see, you can't talk about reward without talking about risk. I always tell people that if they want a solid 8 percent return with no risk, there's a place called Bank of America just across the street. But if they want the potential for 20 percent returns but with risk, it's a company called MIPS. My feeling is there are always people who think they can make an investment with a guaranteed high rate of return. But there's no such thing, at least not since junk bonds.

''So that's why, if it were up to me, the risk [factor section] would be three times as long.''

As it was, at three single-spaced pages and more than three thousand words, the section was remarkable in its candidness. As perhaps Miller secretly knew, the sheer brazenness of MIPS's admissions may have countered any doubts in the minds of potential investors. After all, would a company be this open if it wasn't awful damn confident in itself?

In the end the team identified a dozen potential risks to MIPS's long-term success.

Some of these were little more than boilerplate. For example, one risk was MIPS's ''Limited operating history and operating results,'' that is to say, even though the company was doing great, it was still early in the game. Another was ''New product offerings,'' which noted that in MIPS's new line of products, one, the top-of-the-line 55-mips RC6280 Enterprise Server, was as yet being manufactured only in prototype quantities and could still fail. A third such boilerplate risk was ''Fluctuations in quarterly performance,'' which pointed out that a substantial portion of the company's revenues in a given quarter came during the last month of that quarter, so that if shipments were delayed or orders not received, the company might show disproportionately high expenditures for that reporting period.

Other risk factors of this type included "Management of growth," which reminded that MIPS was growing like Topsy and such growth put a strain on every corner of the firm, from management to materials. There also was "No prior public market, possible volatility of stock price and dilution," which fulfilled Miller's desire to post a warning to potential future shareholder litigants. And finally, a reminder that 12.75 million shares held in lockup on Going Public Day could theoretically go on the market within 240 days and could thus undermine the market value of MIPS stock.

A second set of risk factors dealt with the unproven nature of MIPS's revolutionary business strategy. One noted that "Adoption of the company's proprietary RISC architecture by major computer system manufacturers is critical to the company's success." A second reminded readers that MIPS relied upon third parties, including the five CMOs and two ECL semiconductor partners, as well as a mob of OEMs, VARs, system integraters, and distributors ("some of whom currently offer competitive products") to build and market MIPS's products. Here, the company admitted, the danger was of lost interest: "There can be no assurance that these third parties will commit adequate manufacturing or marketing resources to the Company's products."

A third strategic risk lay with the availability of application software to run on MIPS's servers. Here is the entire entry: "The Company does not develop application software for its products. As a result, customers must either develop or purchase software to address their particular application needs. Adoption of the Company's RISC architecture will depend, in part, upon the continued development and availability of application software for its products, including the modification of existing software packages for use with its products. Although a number of third-party application software vendors have made their software available for use with the Company's products, there can be no assurance that the number of software offerings will be sufficient to support customers' application needs."

To computer cognoscenti, these words were a reminder that even a terrific product can die a slow death if the software industry refuses to design new software or port over old software for it. A perfect case of this was Atari, its superb Amiga struggling to obtain enough applications programs to keep it viable in the face of the more established Apple Mac and IBM PC families. Without the right applications software even the best computers were little more than expensive glowing boxes. And software designers gravitated to the market; after all, that's where the money was. That's why MIPS had tried to prime the pump with its adoption of UNIX, with its creation of the Synthesis subsidiary, and with its current race to fill its RISCware catalog with as many different and far-ranging applications programs as possible.

The fourth strategic risk went to the very heart of the MIPS business model. Under the single word "Competition," MIPS reminded potential investors, in case they hadn't yet caught on, that the company was operating in an "intensely" competitive market characterized by rapid change. Furthermore, MIPS was going up against giant firms many times its size, armed with vast resources MIPS could never match. In other words, one false move in the next three or four years and MIPS could be crushed like a bug.

Yet, despite their apparent fierceness, none of these warnings created as much apprehension or acrimony among the authors of the prospectus as the one Ludvigson nicknamed the "BIT factor."

To the inexperienced prospectus reader, this item, after the warnings of potential annihilation and stock price collapse in the other items, might seem inconsequential. But to the men in the meeting room at Bowne printers, it took on gigantic proportions.

Entitled "Single source components," the item pointed out that certain parts and components used in MIPS products were available from only a single supplier. Most of these were peripherals and communications controllers used in all MIPS systems products, and, in a pinch, substitutes could be found.

But one all but irreplaceable chip, the ECL R6000 microprocessor used in MIPS's flagship new RC6280, was produced only by Bipolar Integrated Technologies, Inc. (BIT), a tiny, privately owned, six-year-old chip house in Beaverton, Oregon, which also had an agreement to supply RISC microprocessors to MIPS's archenemy, Sun Microsystems.

Sure, the software library might not reach critical mass, or the giant computer companies could decide to attack, or the management team might collapse under the strain of hyperbolic growth. But those problems were nearly metaphysical in the short-horizon world of techno-business. But the BIT factor, now that was something different. It was both proximate and imaginable. BIT encounters yield problems or a design bug or undercapacity or any one of a million things, and suddenly MIPS cannot build its top-of-the-line product. Now *that* was something an investor could honestly worry about.

It was a measure of how seriously the team took the BIT factor that this entry became the longest of the risk factors. "We arm wrestled a lot on that one," said Ludvigson.

Such a tense atmosphere can turn ugly quickly. But the group, experienced team members all, knew enough to sublimate any animosity or frustration into nonconfrontational channels, such as humor. As always, the guy with the pen, in this case Dave Segre of Wilson Sonsini, was the butt of much of this. He soon gained the nickname Ernie.

Said Ludvigson, "I started calling him Ernest Hemingway because every time we gave him a revision to the document, the document came back looking very different from what we'd told him to do. So I began accusing him of doing a Hemingway on me—you know, creative writing. Eventually, we just called him Ernie. It was a good way of dealing with a pressure situation by using some humor."

In the final sprint to completion, beginning Tuesday, Halloween, the team was at Bowne from dawn until late at night. Now it took everything to keep tempers in check. Ludvigson's challenge now became the lawyers from Davis, Polk [Morgan Stanley's counsel].

"Alan Dean was the Davis, Polk guy. They're back in New York, the underwriter's counsel, so they went back and forth a lot day after day. At various times I dealt with three different guys, but Dean was the main one, and Richard Truesdale [who had just appeared in the book *Barbarians at the Gate*] the second. They did an interesting Mutt and Jeff, the two of them. Alan was the pragmatic businessman and Richard was the legal eagle, so it was sort of a good guy/bad guy routine—and they had it down pretty well.

"Then Alan left. The rest of us were at the printer for four days, but Alan missed the last day. So, when I came in that last day I said, 'Okay Richard, I want you to put on your Alan Dean hat today—because now that he's not here, you're gonna have to carry the business mantle and take that really positive, constructive view that Alan had.' So later, when he gave me a hard time I just kept reminding him that he had to rise to the occasion.

"You just got to let off steam in ways that let people be critical without making it real personal."

At this point Ludvigson had been working on the prospectus continually for a month. Prior to that, he had been in France helping with the negotiations with Groupe Bull, an OEM customer. During all this time he was depending not only upon MIPS to continue performing in such a way as to make it a viable IPO prospect, but also upon his own staff to keep the financial operations of the firm running. In effect, for six weeks, almost since the earthquake, he had been operating on the MIPS prospectus detached from the company itself.

Now was the moment of truth. On Thursday, November 2, standing in the Bowne meeting room, he placed a call to Miller. "I said, 'Okay Bob, we've got a couple of issues left. We need your help on them. Here they are. And, oh, by the way, tell me the fourth quarter is going okay. I haven't had a chance to look at it in several weeks.'

"Miller laughed, 'Don't worry about it. We've got it under control.' "

Ludvigson had the time to make that call because a few minutes before he had called off the original plan to file the red herring the next day, Friday.

"The perfect timing for us would have been to file the document on Friday. We were actually working to that. But I called it off for a variety of reasons. But we always had contingency plans in place—that way we could run on the edge while knowing in the back of our minds there were alternatives."

The team worked through Friday, then adjourned for the weekend to catch some sleep and reintroduce themselves to their families. Ludvigson, already bothered by the many moves he'd put his two children through over the years, as well as his long absences, was pleased to find they'd warmed up to the current project. "I think they got a real charge out of it. I even spent a couple hours one night explaining to my daughter the difference between the New York Stock Exchange and the National Market System and between a specialist system and market system. She's a freshman in high school and she's really intrigued. She thinks it's just fantastic."

Monday was a marathon session, a hard drive to this interim finish line. As the hours passed, the team argued, negotiated, agreed, and drafted the final passages. On hand were Ludvigson and Sweeney from MIPS and representatives from Wilson, Sonsini, Cowen, Morgan Stanley, and Davis, Polk. Lunch and dinner were brought in.

At two o'clock in the morning on Tuesday, November 7, the team completed the SEC filing for MIPS to go public. "We were all exhausted," recalled Ludvigson. "We found some beers in the refrigerator and sat down and popped a few."

Ludvigson, 39 going on 60, left Bowne at three o'clock, nineteen hours after he'd arrived, and rode BART home. He reached his front door as the dawn was beginning to glow.

Meanwhile, John Sandler from Wilson, Sonsini had left early the previous evening for Washington and the SEC with all of the backup documentation in support of the filing (the S-1). The next morning, Bowne electronically submitted the S-1 document itself, essentially the material of the red herring. Bowne then printed from this information a mock-up version of the red herring in blue ink (a "blue line" in printing jargon).

Tuesday, after a few hours sleep, the team reconvened and edited the blue line copy. This session lasted until eleven that night, when the final draft of the red herring was handed to Bowne, which immediately went into production.

By Thursday 45,000 copies of the red herring were on their way to Morgan Stanley, Cowen, and the supporting syndicate of underwriters for worldwide distribution.

Back at MIPS at last, in his spare office decorated with little more than a framed MacNelly Chicago Cubs cartoon on the wall, Ludvigson was tired but ebullient. "We did it. Now it's bottom of the ninth, two outs."

But getting that last out would turn out to be harder than the entire game before it.

CHAPTER 8

Signs and Signifiers

THE FINISHED MIPS PROSPECTUS in its red herring version was, at least in format, identical to thousands of corporate prospectuses that had come before it. Eight and one-half by eleven inches, center-stapled, glossy front and back covers, several dozen pages of thin, white paper covered with dense verbiage and numerical tables, all in eyestrain-inducing 9-point type.

The cover featured in the upper left-hand corner, in red ink, the title: PROSPECTUS (Subject to Completion) Issued November 7, 1989. Running down the left side, in the same red ink, was the 98-word red herring warning noted earlier.

Centered at the top of the cover page was the announcement of "4,750,000 Shares." Directly below that was the MIPS logo—which looks like the symbol for some new three-blade Gillette razor—and beneath that, in smaller type, the words COMMON STOCK.

Under that, in microscopic 7-point type in the shape of an inverted pyramid, was a notification that of the 4.75 million shares MIPS was offering, 3.75 million would be offered in the United States and Canada by U.S. underwriters and 1 million more in the rest of the world. Of the 3.75 million domestic shares, 2.5 million would be sold by the company and 1.25 million by the selling shareholders. Next came the announcement that this was an initial public offering: "Prior to this offering, there has been no public market for the Common Stock of the Company. It is currently anticipated that the initial public offering will be between $14 and $17 per share." And finally the notification referred the reader to discussions on each of these items in the prospectus.

Beneath this block, in larger type, was a single ominous line that must have pleased Bob Miller: "THIS OFFERING INVOLVES A HIGH DEGREE OF RISK. SEE 'RISK FACTORS.' "

That completed the upper half of the cover page—not the flash and glitter one might expect from the cover of a best-seller. The lower half of the page, however, did contain the securities world's version of a mystery story.

First, more ominous words: "THESE SECURITIES HAVE NOT BEEN APPROVED OR DISAPPROVED BY THE SECURITIES AND EXCHANGE COMMISSION NOR HAS THE COMMISSION PASSED UPON THE ACCURACY OR ADEQUACY OF THIS PROSPECTUS. ANY REPRESENTATION TO THE CONTRARY IS A CRIMINAL OFFENSE."

Then a shift into italics, and the unknown: *"Price $ a share. . . . If all such additional shares are purchased, the total Price to Public, Underwriting Discounts and Commissions and Proceeds to the Company will be $, $, and $ respectively. . . . It is expected that delivery of the certificates for the shares will be made on or about December , 1989, at the offices of Morgan, Stanley & Co. Incorporated, New York, N.Y., against payment therefor* [not a typo, but financial term meaning 'in exchange for'] *New York funds."*

Thrilling and illuminating stuff; all the blanks waiting to be filled, interestingly, following SEC approval and therefore *after* the stocks would actually begin trading. The only figure listed, "a 30-day option to purchase up to 712,500 additional shares" by the U.S. underwriters, the green shoe, came as a footnote.

At the bottom of the cover page were the titles of the two chief underwriters, Morgan Stanley & Co. and Cowen & Company. Finally, in the lower left-hand corner, was the most tantalizing mystery of all, the unfinished date "December , 1989."

Like the subsequent annual reports it inaugurates, the prospectus is a document steeped in ritual and protocol. It is deadly dull to the inexperienced reader, and it is meant to be, bloodlessness being a desirable state in corporate finance. But to the initiated, every phrase and every number is fraught with deep and multiple meanings. Tellingly, those sections most interesting to the naive reader are often dismissed by securities sophisticates as meaningless fluff; while those hair-splitting footnotes and eye-glazing tables of numbers passed over by unpracticed eyes are endlessly scrutinized, analyzed, and gnawed upon by professionals. These tables, the experts know, hold the ugly truth about the company. These musty corners of print and passages of false cheer hold that single fact that can expose the very soul of the firm and reveal its most sordid secrets.

(At a time when academic semioticians and deconstructionists tear apart comic books and sitcoms in search of textual signs and signifiers to explain our "post-modern society," they do not seem to have noticed that securities and investment analysts, stockbrokers, and astute pensioneers have been engaged in this operation for decades. Arguably, a financial document such as a prospectus probably contains far more information about the multiple ways in which language is used in modern daily life than an entire season of "Who's the Boss?")·

The second page of the prospectus, devoted primarily to the table of contents, was almost entirely boilerplate. In addition to some standard warnings to investors to inform themselves about the contents of the prospectus, it said, in so many words, that nothing said about the IPO beyond what is in this document can be "relied upon as having been authorized by the Company, by any Selling Shareholder or by any Underwriter."

This may protect the company against investors, but it cuts both ways. Should any company executive (or, to a lesser degree, any other employee) or any underwriter make public remarks that diverge, especially on the positive side, from what's in the prospectus, there will be hell to pay to the SEC. Underwriters can be thrown out at the last minute, and the company itself may suffer the cost of a painful delay in going public.

The second page also contained another notable warning, all in foreboding bold-faced capitals (reduced to regular type here for readability): "In connection with this offering, the underwriters may over-allot or effect transactions which stabilize or maintain the market price of the common stock of the company at a level above that which might otherwise prevail in the open market. Such stabilizing, if commenced, may be discontinued at any time."

In other words, the numbers of shares announced on the first page are only an estimate; don't trust them.

Pages three and four contained the prospectus summary covering the nature of the company, the nature of the stock offering, and company financials—topics to be discussed at greater length in the rest of the document. The language in this summary is a first glimpse of a literary style that will characterize the next sixty-eight pages.

This style, which might be called prospectese, features soft, formal, beseeching verbs (seeks, believes, derives, delivers, intends), countered by vainglorious terms (leading supplier, industry standard, significant changes, breakthroughs). Sentences are inevitably long, often without adverbs or multiple clauses, but typically with at least one embedded list.

Here's an example from page five: "The Company seeks to establish its RISC architecture as an industry standard by licensing its architecture, microprocessor designs, and system software to leading semiconductor and computer systems manufacturers, as well as by selling fully configured computer systems, subsystems, and board products of its own design.''

When Ludvigson and Sweeney sat down with the underwriters and lawyers, they immediately adopted the rules that govern this style not so much by desire, but by default. Legal documents such as a prospectus are not designed to entertain, much less to edify. Rather, they are written to be complete and not to cause any unnecessary trouble. Begin with these two criteria, stir in a handful of lawyers and accountants, and you inevitably end up with the soporific tones of prospectese, in which each sentence, though it contains entirely new information, sounds exactly like the one that came before it.

The second page of the prospectus summary contained the summary consolidated financial information, a half-page condensation of the company's income statement over the past five years and balance sheet over the last twelve months, followed by a half-page of italicized support copy. It is on this page that experienced readers found their first clues into MIPS.

For example, according to the condensed income statement, the company had no revenues its first two years—not unusual for a computer company. But this was followed by an awesome take-off: $7.8 million in 1986, $13.9 million in 1987, $39.4 million in 1988, and $70.1 million for the first nine months of 1989. That's nearly 300% growth each of the last two years, trending toward a $100 million finish for 1989.

Meanwhile, the company did not turn a profit until the last year, having lost $9.0 million in 1986, $10.5 million in 1987, and $3.7 million in 1988. For the first nine months of 1989, MIPS was at last in the black for $592,000, or 3 cents per share—not a lot, but a sufficient profit for a young firm to go public.

The condensed balance sheet showed that the company had, as of September 30, 1989, $40.5 million in working capital (a strong position, no doubt from the royalty stream from licenses) and total assets of $81.1 million.

The second half of the page, the block of italics, suggested other questions to be investigated in upcoming pages by the astute reader. Here was a listing of which outside entities had their hooks on MIPS stock. According to the copy, Kubota had warrants for 150,000 shares of preferred stock, and, if the U.S. underwriters were to exercise their full over-allotment, up to 1.2 million shares of common stock. Similarly, Digital Equipment could buy up to 3.4 million shares of common stock, and the exercise of that option would enable Kubota to buy 962,450 more shares. Then, there was preferred stock, to be converted to 191,278 shares of common stock, owed to some company called Synthesis Software Solutions that had merged with MIPS. Also, 20,000 shares of common pledged to Stanford University and 85,714 shares of common owed to Sumitomo Electric Industries.

This information suggested a company that had sold off pieces of itself to a couple of giant corporations, probably as part of a licensing or manufacturing agreement. The clever reader would certainly have to look into this further. Also, what was the history of Synthesis? Was it an independent firm bought by MIPS? Or, was it a spin-off that was brought back in? And why? And what was this Stanford connection— just some loyal alum on the founding team or a vulnerable licensing agreement?

The answers to these and other questions provided in the rest of the prospectus had cost Dave Ludvigson many nights of lost sleep, but still they would not satisfy the most demanding analysts and rich investors. That was the purpose of the road show.

Pages 5 and half of 6 were devoted to a description of MIPS itself, not any easy task given the revolutionary nature of its organization. In fact, this section was the first serious attempt the company had ever made to state succinctly what it did. It turned out to be a salutary experience, according to those involved.

Next came the section on risk factors, the one that had led to so many late-night arguments at the printer. While its formidable length (it ran to page 9) might have worried small investors, that same completeness provided a certain comfort to analysts. After all, it suggested that the company both recognized its weaknesses and was honest enough to discuss them.

The risk factors section was followed by a "Use of Proceeds" section, which essentially said MIPS would spend the money from the stock sale on anything it wanted (or, in prospectese, "will be used for working capital purposes, primarily to finance accounts receivable and inventories, and to acquire capital equipment" and "to acquire businesses, products, or technologies complementary to the Company's current business"). Until then, the money would be handed over to Steve Bennion to invest in short-term paper.

The next section on that page, "Dividend Policy," was just forty-four words. It was a statement that MIPS, like most high-tech companies, had no plans ever to pay cash dividends on its stock. MIPS was never going to be a stock held to produce an income for pensioners and trust fund babies.

At this point, the narrative was temporarily interrupted by nine pages of tables and footnotes—capitalization, dilution, selected consolidated financial data, and management's discussion and analysis of financial condition and results of operations. These were sections lay people ignored and experts shredded for hidden prizes.

On page 18 and for the next seventeen pages, MIPS attempted to explain its business, organization, products, customers, partners, and competitors. The need to compress all of this information into such a limited space apparently imposed some literary discipline on the writing team, for here the prose is terse and active, even though it is often bewilderingly dense with product names and acronyms. For example, this was the complete text on the operating system used in its microprocessor chips and RISC compilers:

"The Company's microprocessors and compilers were designed to run with the Company's RISC/os operating system. This operating system, which is binary compatible across the Company's systems, is based on AT&T's UNIX System V.3.2 operating system with University of California at Berkeley's BSD 4.3 extensions. Support for AT&T's UNIX System V.4 release is planned. RISC/os, comprised of over 1.1 million lines of software code, has been globally optimized using the Company's C compiler.

"The RISC/os operating system supports advanced development utilities such as source-level debuggers and performance profilers. RISC/os supports the Company's graphical user interface, a native implementation of the X-window standard, and incorporates OSF/Motif, an emerging standard user interface for UNIX. RISC/os includes the TCP/IP high level networking protocols and Network File System ('NFS'), a networking standard for UNIX systems.''

No point in asking why the authors felt compelled to elucidate NFS, but not TCP/IP (transmission control protocol/internet protocol, a UNIX networking standard) or OSF (open systems foundation). Obviously, those who should know would know, and everyone else should just trust his or her stockbroker. Still, this cryptic copy says something both about gathering raw material from engineers and about the arcane world of technology. The MIPS prospectus may have had the same format as a prospectus from a supermarket chain or a clothing manufacturer, but what resided within that format often appeared to the inexperienced reader to have come from an alternate universe.

Other subsections in this part of the prospectus included a two-page table of applications software packages designed by other companies to run on MIPS's architecture (''RISCware''), a partial list of the heaviest hitters among the 250 customers using a total of 2,500 MIPS computers and subsystems, and, in keeping with the current business vogue, a section on customer service and support:

''The Company believes that the quality and reliability of its system products and the ongoing support of such products are important elements of its competitive strategy. The Company's customer service organization includes hardware engineers, software engineers, training specialists, and administrative support personnel who provide a variety of services including sales assistance, system installation, hardware maintenance, software upgrades, documentation support, and training.''

The section went on to point out carefully that MIPS's sales, service, and support operations domestically employed 148 people in 21 locations in 15 states and internationally consisted of 58 people in 9 offices in Canada, France, Germany, Japan, Korea, Singapore, and the United Kingdom. Note that the ratio of sales to support staff was not mentioned. Further, MIPS took pains to add, it maintained a twenty-four-hour, toll-free telephone support center and offered a ninety-day warranty (and various repair contracts) on its system products. Finally, and most important for the customer, there was the agreement with Tandem Computer, by which the Silicon Valley giant provides on-site field service for MIPS customers in North America. After a decade of

Japanese predations, that was how a U.S. tech company made obeisance to customer service.

The final pages of the section were a reminder of why, despite the need for capital, companies often hesitate before going public.

One of the advantages of being a private company is privacy. You can tell snoopy reporters to go to hell. You don't have to worry about facing some political activist who holds two shares and stands up at an annual meeting to ask why you are doing business with some vicious country you didn't even know bought your products. Your hirings, firings, salaries, and perks are your own business. And, outside of a few basic items of tax and payroll information, you don't even have to tell your business to the United States government.

It's a nice deal, if you can maintain it. Just ask the Mars family or Newhouse or Bechtel, to name some of America's largest privately owned corporations. It takes teams of people at *Forbes* and *Fortune* months just to estimate the wealth of those companies and their founders.

But, take a dime from venture capitalists or offer stock options to management and you have put your company on the path to going public. Do a good job building the company and the reward for your success is to be forced to stand naked in print before millions, your failures of judgment exposed, private loans revealed, and intimate matters like your salary and net worth exhibited for all the world to see.

And the prospectus is just the start. For the rest of the company's life (unless, usually after some disaster, it manages to buy back all its stock and turn itself private again) it will have to perform a financial fan dance once every three months in its quarterly earnings statement and a full striptease once each year in its annual report. No longer will the company be able to tantalize and conceal as it performs behind its veils; from that point on, the hard truth will be exposed before the devouring eyes of strangers.

It is not surprising that company executives look for alternative ways to raise money. About the time the MIPS team was preparing its prospectus, the *Wall Street Journal* ran a series of articles on the risks associated with an IPO. It told the story of Roger M. Buoy, the president of computer game maker Mindscape, Inc.

As is required by the SEC, Mindscape's prospectus included Buoy's salary of $180,000 per year. "The day before, even my mother didn't know my salary,'' the *Journal* reported Buoy as saying. "The next day, everybody knew."

Then, Mindscape's stock collapsed, falling from $10 per share on Going Public Day to just 75 cents. "I went through absolute purgatory," Buoy told the *Journal*. "What we really needed was encouragement, but I spent many hours on the phone with shareholders who just wanted to vent their hostility."

"Such are the vicissitudes of selling stock to the public," the *Journal* concluded. "It is the dream of many entrepreneurs, surely—almost a rite of passage in American business life. It provides a badge of status, a source of cheap capital, a means of putting a value on the founder's fortune and a perfect prelude to acquiring other companies.

"But going public carries risks. In an era of hostile takeovers, it means a potential loss of control of the enterprise. It is expensive and time-consuming. More than anything, going public means that a once-private company must conduct much of its business in the open, and if business turns down, as in Mindscape's case, the whole world is watching and booing—or so it seems. Even when things go well, the newly public company has to disclose much that was previously secret."

Much of what the *Journal* said applied to MIPS as it moved toward its own Going Public Day. The company was more likely to overheat from too-rapid growth than to suffer a downturn in the near future, and hostile takeovers are rare among technology companies because most of the assets reside in people's heads. But certainly the matter of expense and time was dead-on. And, as the reader of the prospectus turned the pages, the issue of public exposure grew until one could almost hear the groans of the MIPS board of directors.

Take the bottom of page 31, where MIPS was forced to announce that its research and development expenditures were $7.3 million in 1986, $8.8 million in 1987, $12.9 million in 1988, and $13.3 million for the first nine months of 1989. Setting aside the high up-front expenditures expected in start-up, the final figures showed that MIPS was spending nearly 20 percent of revenues on R&D, suggesting that the MIPS business model, forced as it was to stay one step ahead of its "partners," might suffer from endemic low profitability. That wasn't something shareholders might appreciate.

A section on manufacturing recapitulated a matter discussed in the risk factors section: MIPS's dependence upon a single source, Bipolar Integrated Technologies, for the key R6000 chip in its flagship RC6280.

This is an admission of vulnerability that companies don't like to make to themselves, much less to competitors, customers, and everybody else who sees the prospectus. Nor can this sort of publicity be particularly helpful in future in negotiations with little BIT itself.

In fact, one can almost picture MIPS (or Bob Miller, if one can believe his brave words) swallowing hard and then speaking through gritted teeth the for-want-of-a-nail words of this section: ". . . BIT is a private, venture capital-financed semiconductor manufacturer which has yet to achieve consistent profitability. The Company plans to reduce the exposure associated with this single source by increasing its inventory of the R6000 as available. While the Company has licensed its ECL microprocessor technology to NEC and Sony, neither manufacturer has commenced production of these devices. If BIT were unable to supply sufficient quantities of R6000 devices, it is likely that the Company would experience a delay in developing an alternative source . . . a reduction or interruption in supply or a significant increase in the price of one or more components would adversely affect the Company's operating results and could damage customer relationships."

The opening of the corporate kimono continued in the section on competition. If there is one thing companies don't like to do, it is name their competitors. It's one of the earliest lessons public relations people give their executives. One reason is that it gives unnecessary publicity to those competitors, especially if they are very small (it may make them seem more threatening than they are) or very large (it reminds the reader how daunting the task really is). Such lists also may include a name or two an analyst or customer hasn't considered. Finally, especially when the company is being pejorative about the competition, to be delicately vague ("Some of our competitors choose to . . .") instead of specifying names looks less petty.

But not so in the prospectus. Here the names of the opposition are listed in all their terrifying glory. Suddenly spunky little $100 million MIPS, the hero of the opening sections, begins to look tiny and fragile against such reseller market competitors as Data General, Hewlett-Packard, and Sun Microsystems; such end user market competitors as HP again, IBM, Sun again, and Unisys; and such microprocessor competitors as HP and Sun for a third time, Intel, and Motorola. Of these multibillion dollar firms, some, like Intel and Motorola, are legendary innovators, and others, like HP and IBM, are among the world's most admired and enduring companies.

If that doesn't scare you, the prospectus seems to be saying (one can hear Miller's voice), just read the next paragraph: "Many of the Company's direct and indirect competitors are major corporations with substantially greater technical, financial, and marketing resources and name recognition than the Company. Many of these competitors have a much larger base of application software and have a much larger installed customer base than does the Company. There can be no assurance that the Company will have the financial resources, technical expertise or marketing, distribution or support capabilities to compete successfully in the future."

Have you got it yet? the prospectus seems to demand, it's a goddamn tough business and at any time any one of these behemoths could smash us flat, so you, Mr. and Mrs. Dilettante Investor, don't go buying this stock thinking it's some sort of ticket to tycoonship.

Still don't believe us? Okay, then try this line: "The Company expects substantial additional direct and indirect competition." In other words, the better we do at this, the more big boys like the ones listed above are going to be chasing us. Still want to buy?

Now that it had described the onslaughts, the prospectus tried to show how MIPS could defend itself. One means was legal, the protection afforded by patents and copyrights. That was the subject of the next section, "Proprietary Rights." But, though MIPS agreed it "currently holds several United States patents and international patents, registered trademarks, registered [chip design] mask-work rights and copyrights," as well as having several more of each in the works, it rightly reminded readers that "because of the rapid pace of technological change in the industry, its technical expertise, innovative skills and the management ability of the Company's personnel may be more important to its business than protection of its proprietary information."

All of the dross and plumage of the earlier sections have now been stripped away. Suddenly, in two short sections ("Employees" and "Facilities") MIPS can at last be seen for what it really is: a little California company with 548 employees, 54 of them overseas—206 in marketing, sales, and related customer support services, 187 in research and development, 91 in manufacturing, and 64 in administration. They are housed principally in two locations, an 85,000-square-foot building in Sunnyvale with a lease that will expire in 1996, and a 65,000-square-foot building in Santa Clara with a lease that will expire in 1992. The rest of the company is scattered in thirty small offices around the world.

The company that through one side of the lens seemed to represent the future of American computer technology and business organization, through the other side appeared but a tiny and battered raft in a stormy sea of commerce, its handful of passengers clinging to one another to survive.

Yet, somehow, each of them believes that together they will conquer the world.

CHAPTER 9

The Back Pages

THE FULL EXPOSURE of going public came home to the management of MIPS in the second half of the prospectus.

It began with the section on management. First came a list of the company's directors, executive officers, and key personnel, giving their full name, age, and title.

Though such a list might, at first blush, seem benign, it came freighted with emotional baggage. For example, there was the matter of age, often a touchy subject in a community as youth-oriented as Silicon Valley. According to the listing, the oldest executive, Jake Vigil, at 53 was one year younger than the senior member of the board, Bill Davidow. The youngest senior executive, co-founder and chief scientist John P. Hennessy, was a year older than the youngest director, venture capitalist Grant Heidrich, an astonishing 36. That Hennessy and Heidrich had been there at the beginning of MIPS six years before was testament to the truth of the saying that Silicon Valley was built by children. They were merely the latest in a long line of junior empire builders that stretched back to Jobs and Wozniak at Apple, to Bob Noyce at Intel, all the way back to Bill Hewlett, David Packard, and the Varian brothers during the 1930s.

Another sensitive issue in the preparation of such a list was the matter of inclusion. Who should be on the list?

Obviously the board of directors belonged there. It included Davidow, venture capitalist, author of two best-selling books, and former Intel senior vice-president; Heidrich and his partner at Mayfield Fund,

F. Gibson Myers, Jr.; Samuel H. Fuller, vice-president of research at Digital Equipment; Francis Lorentz, chairman and CEO of the French computer giant C. M. Bull (subsidiary of Groupe Bull); Nohisa Matsuda, Kubota's manager of the Office of Computer Business; Jimmy Treybig, the shrewd cowboy founder and CEO of Tandem Computers; and Robert Wall, another MIPS co-founder, the company's first president, then chairman and CEO of Presentation Technologies, Inc., currently a principal in the venture capital firm R. T. Wall & Co., and, since the beginning of 1989, a partner at Cowen & Company investment bankers.

The experienced prospectus reader would learn a lot from this impressive list of directors. Heidrich, Myers, and Davidow would be self-explanatory: a directorship is one of the prizes venture capitalists get for their money, so they can hold a sword to management's neck in case any quick executive decapitations are necessary. The presence of Matsuda, Fuller, and Lorentz suggests that some of little MIPS's biggest corporate partners and investors wanted to have some control over the company's fate. Treybig is important enough to have been invited on merely for his presence, but his acceptance, the skilled reader would say, may have had something to do with the MIPS-Tandem service deal. The long-time Silicon Valleyite would also know that both Davidow's and Treybig's names are on the original Tandem low-fault computer patent—a clue to who did the inviting.

Finally, there was Wall, early enough on board with MIPS to be considered, for the purposes of the prospectus, a founder, but no longer with the company. John Massouris, a member of the original founding trio, was in the same position, but he wasn't on the board of directors. Perhaps the difference lay in Wall's position with an investment firm. And it could hardly be a coincidence that of all the investment banking firms in the country, only little Cowen was teamed with giant Morgan Stanley as the principal underwriters of MIPS's IPO.

So, the directors were necessarily included in the management list, as were chairman, CEO, and president Miller, executive officers Boesenberg and Jobe, and senior vice-president Vigil. But who were the "key personnel"? The choices made for the prospectus can be as telling as the May Day figures atop the Kremlin Wall; observers can spot rising stars and the newly purged. As there is only one IPO prospectus in a company's history, making the list becomes vital to fragile executive egos.

MIPS charted a safe course by including all company vice-presidents in alphabetical order. That list consisted of Joe DiNucci, 48, marketing for the entry systems group; John Hime, 41, marketing for the system products group; Ludvigson; Walter Pienkos, 43, administration; Tom Rohrs, 41, manufacturing; Chet Silvestri, 41, marketing for the technology products group; Edward "Skip" Stritter, 42, development programs; Sweeney; Larry Weber, 42, software development; and Hennessy, 37, chief scientist.

It seems a straightforward list, though a company insider might note some interesting choices. For example, strictly in terms of management and span of control, lone wolf Stritter would not be considered a true vice-president. But he was a company founder, the largest individual shareholder, and, most importantly, the amanuensis of MIPS—hence, he makes the list. Hennessy's inclusion is similar, though he was even less involved in the day-to-day concerns of the firm, as he was a full-time professor at Stanford.

The executive striptease reached its climax in the next subsection on management, the material on executive compensation. As with Mr. Buoy of Mindscape, here was the awful moment when the top guys had to yield up their most private secret. They did it by the book, listing only the five most highly compensated officers of the firm:

Bob Miller	$311,863
Bill Jobe	564,086
Jake Vigil	211,277
Joe Sweeney	131,311
Skip Stritter	130,485

Almost as interesting as the names on the list were those not included. Sweeney on the list and Boesenberg not? Was this due to Sweeney's being a professional negotiator, having more seniority in the firm, getting less stock than Boesenberg, or having come from a higher-paying job? And why was Jobe's pay so much higher than Miller's? What did the others make? For now, the prospectus added only that all nine executive officers as a group (it didn't say which nine) made a total of $1,809,272 per year.

But there were footnotes to the list, and skilled readers know that much about the daily dealings of a company can be gleaned from the follow-up pages to the brief list. For example, in the footnotes one could discover that Miller's salary figure did not include $250,000 in relocation loan forgiveness under a deal Miller had made when he first signed on with the company. Conversely, Jobe's figure had been greatly swollen by $405,417 in a bonus deal based upon how much revenue he'd brought in. That suggested a base salary of $158,669, a figure more commensurate with those of his peers.

The next two pages (40 and 41) addressed a pair of sensitive topics to a modern corporation, "Limitation of Liability and Indemnification Matters." In an era in which the attorneys of disgruntled shareholders have grown increasingly effective at piercing the corporate armor to go after company directors, so much so that serving on a board has become less appealing to worthy nominees, such a move was not surprising.

According to this subsection, which more accurately could have been titled "Warning to Sleazy Lawyers Hunting for Deep Pockets," MIPS had "adopted provisions in its Articles of Incorporation that limit the liability of its directors for monetary damages arising from a breach of their fiduciary duty as directors." Not only did MIPS indemnify its directors and officers to the full extent possible under California law, but actually had adopted provisions "broader than the specific indemnification provisions contained in the California Corporations Code"— including covering them against liabilities that arose not just from willful misconduct but merely from holding the job, advancing their expenses in any legal proceedings, and taking out for them directors' and officers' insurance.

The longer subsequent section addressed two stock plans, one for directors, executives, and consultants ("1985 Stock Incentive Program" or "Option Plan") and the other for the rest of the company's employees ("Employee Stock Purchase Plan"). According to the first, which was, as with most young companies, used as a carrot in recruiting experienced managers, a total of 7.4 million shares of common stock were to be handed out according to rules set by the board. These stock options would take four years to vest fully, 25 percent of the shares becoming exercisable after the first year and 6.25 percent more every quarter thereafter. Thus, executives would be signing on to the firm for a four-year hitch.

Combined with riders on valuation and term, this was a standard plan. What caused some trouble with the SEC was the subsequent announcement that the company had recently amended the plan to provide options to nonemployee directors to buy up to 6,000 shares of common stock at the time they joined the board. Further, the text continued, as of September 30, 1989, options for 1.8 million shares had been exercised, and options to purchase 4.2 million more were outstanding at a weighted average exercise price of $2.125 per share. That left just 628,565 shares available for future option grants.

So, announced the prospectus, in October the board had increased the number of shares in reserve under the plan by 800,000 and expected that move to be rubber-stamped at the annual meeting in November, that is, being a private company, at what would be little more than another board of directors meeting.

This was diddling with the stock a little close to Going Public Day. MIPS knew it and awaited any explosions emanating from Washington.

By comparison, though it also would have to be approved at the November annual meeting, the employee stock purchase plan was out of a textbook: 500,000 shares of common stock, to be purchased by full-time (more than twenty hours per week) employees through payroll deductions, and priced at 85 percent of the lower of the two fair market values of the stock at the beginning and the end of each offering period. And so, in one of the smallest subsections of the entire prospectus rested the hopes of more than five hundred MIPS employees. Eight dry sentences stood for all those dreams of a new life, a home, a family, even of salvation.

Grander, if not necessarily more profound, dreams could also be found on this same page. They hid in a table listing the stock options granted and exercised by the company executives. Here was the Silicon Valley of fantasy. For example, Miller, three years on the job, had the right to buy 200,000 shares at a weighted average exercise price of $2.03 per share. He had exercised 108,000 of those shares, worth $324,000, plus another 150,000-share option he'd be able to exercise between the printing of the prospectus and the planned Going Public Day. Thus, if the company's stock opened at a not unlikely $15 per share, Bob Miller would see his net worth jump by nearly $4 million by breakfast. And if, in future days, as seemed likely given the market response, MIPS stock cleared $20 per share, Miller would be more than $5 million richer, just from his existing options. And that was only the beginning; by mid-1992 he'd be able to exercise 300,000 shares more.

The next largest fortune to be made was by Bill Jobe, already sitting pretty from his bonuses. Jobe had been granted 84,000 shares for just $1.29 weighted average per share. He had exercised 127,000 shares—nearly $2 million if MIPS stock went out at $15. Vigil had exercised 68,000 shares on 94,000 granted at $1.30 per share. Sweeney had exercised 19,500 on 25,200 shares at $1.70.

Skip Stritter had exercised 11,500 on 31,200 at just $1.17 per share, the low valuation a reward for having been with the firm from the start. But that handsome figure of $470,000 if the stock opened at $15 per share was pocket change compared to the money Stritter would make from the founder's stock he held from the original divvying up of the company, from the days when MIPS was three guys sitting around a back booth in a Palo Alto coffee shop. As these shares didn't have to be reported in the prospectus, Stritter was spared this revelation.

As for all thirteen of the company's executive officers, the table reported that total options of slightly more than 1 million shares had been granted at a weighted average exercise price of $1.96 per share. Of this total, and not counting new options that would mature in the upcoming two months before the IPO, 478,249 shares had been exercised. So, again assuming an opening price of $15 per share, MIPS's management team would see at least $7.2 million in new wealth and conceivably $15 million or more.

Not bad for a team whose average tenure with the company was less than two years.

The next four pages of the prospectus addressed "Certain Transactions" dealing with other disbursements of company stock. The relationships with Kubota (up to 20 percent of the firm, with MIPS having first rights to buy back any shares put up for sale) and DEC (approximately the same deal) were described in greater detail.

Then at last came the first full description of what had happened to the software subsidiary Synthesis. According to the prospectus, in April 1988 Synthesis was formed "to procure, market, port, and support certain third-party application software for use on the Company's RISC architecture and to arrange for porting by third parties of other application software through sharing the cost and results of such porting efforts with groups of the Company's computer system customers."

To accomplish this, MIPS issued to itself 4,000,000 shares of Synthesis common stock to be used as royalty payments to third parties, as options for Synthesis employees, and, most of all, to finance the operation of this subsidiary. For the last, 2.2 million of these shares were sold, at $1.20 per share, to venture capital firms already investing in MIPS, as well as to some of MIPS's semiconductor partners (as a growing library of software would help the sale of their MIPS RISC chips). Among the investors were Kubota for 312,500 shares and Mayfield Fund V for 500,000 shares. The Synthesis board had five members: Miller, Myers, Jobe, and two others tellingly not named.

In July 1989, according to the prospectus, "it was agreed that the operations of Synthesis would be discontinued" and some of its operations folded back into MIPS. By October 1989 "an acquisition agreement was executed" and, following the November annual meeting, Synthesis would be merged back into MIPS through a share exchange of one share of Synthesis Series A preferred stock for .0872727 share of MIPS Series F preferred stock.

So simple, so equitable, so discreet. As if the spin-off and merger had been planned from the start; as if the decision to erase Synthesis from MIPS's history had been decided with a gentlemanly handshake. But the experienced business watcher would know that no such experience is easy for the parent company or the spin-off. Rather, they are typically characterized by acrimony and recrimination. So what was the real story? Had Synthesis been a strategic mistake by MIPS management, or had it been a good idea badly executed by the Synthesis team? And who and where were those other two Synthesis board members, no doubt also being former officers of the now-defunct spin-off?

For these questions, the prospectus had no answers. It mentioned, 20 pages later in a note in the financial statements, only that an unnamed officer of Synthesis still held a warrant to purchase up to 200,000 shares of Synthesis common stock at $2.00 per share. Perhaps the parting had not been so friendly after all.

The next subsection in "Certain Transactions" described how, in April 1985, MIPS had pledged to give Stanford University's School of Engineering 20,000 shares of company stock, or its cash equivalent, to establish the MIPS Computer Systems Fund. Needless to say, for this windfall of $300,000 or more, Stanford could thank its own Professor John Hennessy.

(Given the close relationship between high-tech companies and university research laboratories, such gifts are, not surprisingly, comparatively common. Unfortunately, almost as common is for the recipient university to watch this pleasant surprise evaporate as the philanthropic corporate giver disappears into Chapter 11.)

Finally, concluding "Certain Transactions" was the section dreaded by management and loved by gossip-mongering employees and voyeuristic company watchers. Information on Certain Management Contracts was expected to validate the rumors the staff had always heard about the boss, to show how far the company had to go to land certain key execs, and, in the most entertaining and illuminating prospectuses, to provide a shocking glimpse into how certain key managers, noted for their organizational and financial skills, had made a mess out of their private lives.

In the MIPS prospectus most of the comparatively benign skeletons were the many gifts the company had to dangle before potential executives before they would agree to join what was then a foundering firm. Others were a reminder of how the lifestyle demands made on executives often precede the pay-off for their efforts, forcing them to go hat in hand to the company as if it were a loan agency.

For example, in April 1987, to land Miller, MIPS made him a $1 million interest-free loan "in order to defray the costs of relocating to the Company's geographic area." That explained the Millers' grand home in Woodside. According to the deal, the note would mature in April 1991 and Miller would have to apply 50 percent of his proceeds from any sale of his holdings of MIPS common stock. However, that day might not come, as the agreement also called for one-fourth of the loan, $250,000, to be forgiven by the company for each year Miller remained with the company. That rule, in turn, was modified in October 1989 to provide full loan forgiveness 240 days after the closing of the stock offering—no doubt in recognition that the half a million or so debt remaining was chicken feed if Miller really could turn the company around and take it public with a total valuation of $400 million.

The section revealed another term of acceptance in Miller's employment contract. This was a noninterest-bearing bridge loan of $700,000, no doubt to get him through the transition out of Data General and into MIPS. By October 1988 this loan had been repaid and was replaced by a $1.3 million line of credit secured by a MIPS certificate of deposit in a bank at prime rate. During the eighteen-month guarantee, MIPS would assume all interest payments and bills owed by Miller by taking it off the annual $250,000 "forgiveness" of the original relocation loan. Miller could also pay off the line of credit, if used, by a 1989 amendment that let him sell up to $1.3 million of his shares in company common stock up to 240 days after the IPO.

(By the end of September 1989, according to the prospectus, Miller had burned up just $205,000 of the credit, and MIPS had made interest payments of $14,000 in 1988 and $75,000 in the first nine months of 1989.)

Next up was Jobe. In November 1987 he'd been loaned $100,000 by the company at 9 percent interest. By December 1988 he'd paid off the loan.

Finally, to get Chuck Boesenberg, in February 1989 MIPS loaned the executive $450,000 interest free in return for a promissory note due February 15, 1993. Boesenberg secured the loan with a $100,000 lien on his house and agreed to use 50 percent of any proceeds of MIPS stock to retire the loan. Conversely, Boesenberg's employment contract also called for the payment of a bonus of $475,000 to be paid out in approximately $10,000 per month installments over the next four years. These payments were to be applied to the loan. Thus, Boesenberg was essentially given a $450,000 signing bonus.

But that deal was later amended to end the bonus payments twelve months after the IPO, leaving Boesenberg to use his new wealth to pay off the balance of the loan, which, as of September 30, 1989, stood at $370,833 and would apparently stand at the end of 1990 at about $120,000.

All in all, a comparatively mild "Certain Transactions" section—just a few signing bonuses and bridge loans, what one might expect from a company with such a veteran management team. None of the juicy stuff sometimes encountered in prospectuses of wilder, less disciplined start-ups—company yachts, divorce settlements, questionable payoffs to litigous former employees, stock options to mistresses, company "gardeners" who work at executives' houses. But for as sober and conservative a group as the MIPS "over-the-hill gang," no doubt what was there was more than enough.

The next major section, principal and selling shareholders, was essentially a full-page chart followed by a page of footnotes, listing every major investor, director, or executive who planned to cash out at the IPO. Analysts scrutinize this chart to see if any company insiders, individuals in a position to know any nasty truths about the future of the company, are choosing this first possible opportunity to cut and run.

The MIPS selling shareholders chart gave observers something else to chew on. It looked like a textbook example of how to build investor confidence by giving the impression of satisfaction and optimism. Among Kubota, Mayfield, DEC, Miller, the board of directors, and the officers of the company, none was selling a single share of stock. The shares to be sold column was a series of dashes, as each shareholder's equity was dutifully diluted by the new shares: Kubota's from 20.73 percent to 17.03 percent (not counting the options it might choose to exercise), Miller's from 1.6 percent to 1.32 percent (with the same exclusion), and all fifteen directors and officers from 6.88 percent to 5.65 percent. (Note how the number of directors and officers changed throughout the prospectus according to reporting requirements.)

Morgan Stanley had wanted as small a figure as possible for in-house shares on the block, and it got its wish. In fact, as Miller noted in his road show presentation in San Francisco, the number of available shares for sale had continued to fall in the month after the red herring prospectus had been printed.

But officially, on this November 7, 1989, the selling shareholders were all second-tier investors that had been part of the venture syndicates funding the creation of MIPS. Many were selling now under the rules of their investment funds. The biggest of these exits would be by Chancellor Capital Management Group, which planned to sell 494,588 shares out of a total of 683,493, thereby reducing its stake in the firm from 4.25 percent ownership to just 0.96 percent. Assuming that the Chancellor Fund had invested approximately $1 million in the company five years before, and that the stock at IPO would sell at $15 per share, this investor would see about a $6.5 million profit—and still have about $3 million more left to sell.

Next biggest were all banking venture funds: Security Pacific Capital Corp. (to sell 184,800 out of 358,597 shares); Citibank, as trustee for the United Technologies Corporation Pension Fund (159,635 out of 220,606); and Gibraltar Trust (157,144 out of 217,164). The expected profits these institutions would see would be especially welcome in the current banking environment.

Less anxious, or driven, to sell, were the venture funds. Institutional Venture Partners Fund III, which held 791,944 shares, was selling only 42,578 shares. Merrill Pickard Anderson & Eyre Fund III was selling only 40,000 shares out of 475,610 it held. (The Roman numerals suggest both the age of the venture firm and the youth of MIPS; the Mayfield investment in MIPS was Fund V.)

For the astute market watcher, this table, with its loyal investors, combined with the positive articles in the press, showed that MIPS, a company all but unknown two years before, had all the ingredients to be the first hot IPO since the Black Friday. Probably not an Apple Computer—MIPS was still too small and didn't have a universally recognized product—but perhaps hot enough to signal the return of tech stock IPOs. Much would still depend upon the SEC and the state of both the stock market and the economy in the weeks ahead, but everything seemed to suggest that more than just a few personal fortunes were riding on MIPS's Going Public Day; scores of other young technology firms would be waiting, watching closely to see whether Miller and crew would stumble and fall into a bloody heap or soar into the air on gossamer wings.

The remainder of the prospectus was the grit and bile of stock data, underwriter boilerplate, and pages upon pages of company financial statements.

Entering such a labyrinth without a deep personal or financial stake in the company's future is deadly. Thus, for our purpose, we will address only a few important items . . . and briefly.

Beginning on page 48 was a section offering a description of capital stock. It basically noted that MIPS had an authorized capital stock of 100 million common shares and 10 million preferred shares. Of the common shares, 16.1 million were outstanding, held by 246 shareholders. After the IPO the number outstanding would jump to 19.6 million—which, at $15 per share, would give the company a valuation in common stock of about $300 million.

The preferred shares had been offered in six series, A through F, and, upon the closing of the IPO, these shares would be converted to common stock and a new class of 10 million preferred shares would be authorized. The new class of shares would be insurance against company takeovers by outsiders or disgruntled future shareholders. At present MIPS had no plans to issue any of these new shares.

Of the nearly 20 million outstanding shares of common stock, according to this red herring prospectus, 4.75 million would be available for sale on Going Public Day (remember that number dropped to just 4.5

million by mid-December as some of the sellers held back). However, the prospectus warned, of the remaining 14.8 million "restricted" shares, 5.2 million would be available for immediate sale, and ninety days later 7.5 million more could come on the block. The rest, about 1.9 million shares, would be available for sale as their various two-year holding periods expired, which would be sometime between April 1990 and November 1991.

This was one of those warnings sufficiently extreme to encompass any real-life scenario that could possibly happen. In truth, were 5.2 million more shares, held by MIPS employees, executives, directors, and investors, suddenly to come up for sale the day after the IPO, all hell would break loose. Trading would probably be suspended as the stock's value shriveled to pennies. Faced with this miserable valuation, sell orders would be recalled. Meanwhile, the SEC would probably begin an investigation for securities fraud against the company directors who had falsely pumped up the IPO value in order to cash out. Huge fines and prison terms might be the eventual outcome.

Once again, what MIPS was really protecting itself against was a shareholders' suit. There was ample precedent. The company might experience a reversal in its fortunes. Due to increased competition, profits might fall. Employees, having a more acute sense of the problem than outsiders, might decide this would be a propitious moment to cash out their options. The sudden cascade of shares on the market, combined with a recognition by analysts that company employees were cutting and running, might cause the stock price to collapse. Meanwhile, shareholders reading the stock tables in a farmhouse in Topeka or an office tower in Pittsburgh would be left with dark and litigious thoughts about what went wrong.

MIPS wanted even less than the shareholders for such a scenario to play itself out. But if it did, some lawyer for MIPS, perhaps Bob Latta or Joe Sweeney, would stand before each plaintiff in turn, wave page 49 of the prospectus, and ask if he or she had read the section on "Shares Eligible for Future Sale."

The narrative at last petered out in a heap of boilerplate—of twelve paragraphs, five began "Pursuant to the Agreement between U.S. and International Underwriters"—describing the legal responsibilities of the two principal underwriters, Morgan Stanley and Cowen. A final subsection noted that the pricing of the stock would be based upon "sales, earnings, and certain other financial and operating information of the Company in recent periods, the future prospects of the Company and its industry in general, and the price-earnings ratios, price-sales ratios, market prices of securities, and certain financial and operation information of companies engaged in activities similar to those of the Company." Not to mention any disputes between the underwriters and the company, intuition, a golden gut, and what the stock market would bear.

Closing out the copy, standing like Cerebus at the entrance to the pages of financials, was the report of the independent auditor, Ernst & Young. Dated October 27, 1989, it announced that Ernst & Young had audited MIPS's 1987, 1988, and (three-quarters) 1989 balance sheets, statements of operations, cash flows, and shareholders' equity "in accordance with generally accepted auditing standards," including checking for material misstatements and examining, on a test basis, evidence supporting the entries in the financial statements. Ernst & Young found these MIPS documents "in conformity with generally accepted accounting principles."

Analysts know better than to bet the ranch on such a pronouncement, but private investors might not. For example, they might not realize that such "reports" certify only that the financials conformed with standard accounting principles. If the company president wants to put every member of his family on the payroll, that's okay. If the chairman wants to declare his yacht a sales office, that's okay, too, as long as it is properly noted.

And that's only the most obvious limitation of the auditing report, one that can be spotted by a diligent peruser of the subsequent tables. But what if a nefarious company chooses to lie to the auditor? Well, with any luck, that will be discovered in one of the test searches for supporting documentation. But what if those documents themselves are fraudulent? Such deception falls under the purview of the regulations covering securities fraud and is not the responsibility of the auditor. In other words, caveat emptor.

At last, after fifty-five pages of print, medium and fine, the prospectus closed with fourteen pages of financial tables. Here the sinew and muscle of the company, lives and passions, feuds and dreams, were reduced to tabulations of numbers.

On the back cover of the prospectus, in 1-inch tall type, like a last assertion of corporate selfhood after three score pages of vivisection, was the MIPS logo and name.

The 45,000 copies of the red herring prospectus, Dave Ludvigson's youngest child, were stuffed into envelopes and mailed throughout the world. The potential investors and analysts were already sharpening their scalpels.

CHAPTER 10

Dissection

ONE SUCH DIVINER of red herring entrails was Robert Herwick, senior technology analyst for Hambrecht & Quist in San Francisco. Several hundred institutional investors would base their decision on whether or not to invest in MIPS largely on his opinion.

Herwick's preferred technique for reading a prospectus was to make a quick pass through it upon receiving it at the office, hopping from page to page pursuing specific strengths and weaknesses of the company as they emerge. Then, that night at home, with a glass of his favorite Chardonnay, he carefully analyzes each page of the prospectus from front to back.

Herwick admitted looking forward to the arrival of the MIPS prospectus for several reasons. First, "quite candidly, H & Q had competed for the [underwriting] business. I wasn't involved in that, but as the analyst covering the company soon left, it fell upon me to cover MIPS."

Just as important was the attention the MIPS IPO was receiving. "There was a real warm-up in the media. That was no accident, of course, but still you couldn't help knowing that the deal was coming. Also, a lot of people who tend to invest in technology anyway were aware of MIPS because a number of companies that had been fairly successful were using the MIPS technology—Silicon Graphics being an excellent example. Also, Digital Equipment had adopted the MIPS technology, so anybody who was a technology investor or interested in technology already knew about MIPS at this point. They were also aware that this was a chance to invest in a major player in RISC processing.

"So, everyone knew what [MIPS] was about, and that tends to create a greater sense of anticipation."

Heightening this excitement was the novelty of the offering itself, coming as it did following the long fallow period for technology IPOs after the 1987 market crash. "There had been a number of successful technology offerings on the order of $10 million to $20 million before this. And, in fact, the success of these and the strength of the technology sector in general I think created the opportunity for MIPS to go public. It was the first big technology IPO in quite some time. It wasn't the first of the wave, if you will, but it certainly was the first big one in the wave.

"But even the size of the deal wasn't the most important thing— except maybe to the investment bankers. Rather, it was that investors were excited by the opportunity to invest in a new company doing important things."

Herwick had done his own preliminary research about MIPS by talking to the company's customers and attending presentations for earlier rounds of private financing. Now he was ready to take a close-up look at MIPS, and that would come from the prospectus. "So, when it finally hit my desk, it was like 'Gee, here it is. So what is this company really all about?' "

Herwick read the cover page with an astute eye. "The first thing you look at is right on the cover at the very top. You ask yourself, 'How many of these shares are being sold by the company and how many are being sold by investors or management or some other entity? And to the extent that there is a high percentage of sales by venture capitalists, that may bother you a little bit. But if you see a large number of shares being sold by management, that is even more bothersome. See, I think every public market investor appreciates that the venture capitalist's role is to fund the company prior to the IPO and that their pursuit of liquidity is understandable. That's their charter. But for management to be selling is a real red flag because theoretically they should have a longer term commitment to the future of the company.

"The fact that MIPS's management was not selling I think sends a message to investors that, yeah, the management team is going through some changes, but there clearly is not a sense of urgency about selling stock to the point they'd sell it on the deal. They're obviously going to take their chances along with us in the public market."

Next Herwick did some computing in his head based upon the proposed offering price. Too high a price might instantly end his analysis:

"Let's see—$14 to $17 isn't very meaningful. So, let's look at the financial summary on page 4 and kind of eyeball the valuation. Hmmm. This company will have roughly 24 million shares . . . and at $17 that's going to a valuation of a little over $400 million on a company with annual revenues of about $100 million. Hmmm. Four times sales. That's not outrageous, but it's high for a hardware company.

"Now, you can also see that in the last nine months they've earned 24 cents [per share] from continuing operations. And that means probably that they're not going to do much better than 35 or 40 cents for the year—and that means, at least on a 'trailing' twelve months' earnings, that we're being asked to pay a multiple that's rather high.

"So what we've got here is a company with rapid growth, which is attractive, but also a company where the valuation on revenue is a little high and where the valuation on historic earnings very high. So now I say to myself, 'Hmmm, this is not being given away.'

"So now I need a better feeling as to what their earnings will be. And that means I've got to turn to . . . page 16. That's where they lay out the quarterly financials. From that I can get the most recent quarter and a clearer sense of the trends in earnings growth and revenue growth. Okay, and what I see here is that while year-to-year revenue growth is quite striking, in recent quarters product revenues haven't been quite so dramatic."

The first question has now arisen in Herwick's mind: How much of MIPS's success has come from licensing (technology revenues) and how much from the sale of company products? Too much of the former could mean a sudden drop-off in profits in the near future, and, as a result, suggest a vulnerability in the company's long-term strength as a manufacturer.

"Okay, what I see is that it's the technology revenues that have continued to grow very rapidly. Now that's basically pure profit; there's little direct cost in that. The good news is that I can now see how the company's level of profitability can continue to improve rapidly, and that means higher levels of earnings. The one bit of mystery I still have is just how much the company thinks it can earn in the next year. That's why the road show will be important. The syndicate is going to have to give an estimate of MIPS's earnings for the next year and provide a good justification for it.

"So now, let's say I assume their projections for the next year and the times-earnings multiple I'm being asked to pay is in line. There is still the fact that this is technology revenue, which is to a large extent nonrecurring revenue that is fueling the growth in earnings. Subtract that off and you see a different story. Look at the September quarter. Technology revenue was over $9 million, while income from ongoing operations was just over $2 million. That means they lost over $7 million in the systems business. So, if they didn't have all that technology to license, this company would be losing a lot of money. And that means, if they fail to obtain more of those licenses, MIPS is at risk of not making a profit.''

He ran his finger up the quarterly chart. ''So where is all the money going? There. SG&A [selling, general, and administrative] is running at about 50 percent of product revenue. That's fairly high—normally in a technology company it'd be about 35 to 40 percent. . . . Oh, and R&D [research and development] is running at about 30 percent of product revenues, whereas normally in a technology company it would be more like 15 or 20 percent at this point.

''This company is clearly far from making money on operations. They have to spend all that money on R&D and on SG&A if they're going to be successful. So what I'm seeing is that here is a company that has a business model with some degree of risk in it, that the technology revenue is a high one-time component. I also see that they had some pretty substantial losses from discontinued operations [the Synthesis subsidiary] and that there was also a really big write-off in the second quarter where they obviously were trying to clean up their financials because they were anticipating a public offering. And finally, I see that they are not terribly profitable on a net income business, but that it was only through the termination of that business that they managed to produce a set of financials that were appealing, attractive, and suitable for a public offering.

''So what does all that tell me? That from an operating point of view this is not a company that has a sterling history of successful operations and profitability. That they have had unsuccessful activities and have dealt with that issue and basically are bringing public the successful parts and leaving behind the unsuccessful parts. Which is fine. As an investor you certainly don't want to buy problems. So, if they managed to get rid of them, that's good. But it also says that this company until very recently was trying to make a go in an activity that ultimately was not successful.''

Herwick pondered for a moment. ''I think the thing that is the most concern to me now as I read this is to understand how product revenue growth can be made to pick up and to see if there is any predictability to the technology revenue. And to do that [he turns to pages 13 and 14] I want to go to the MD&A [management's discussion and analysis of financial condition and results of operation] and the section on technology revenues because that's going to give me detailed information on where MIPS gets the licensing money from. [He reads] 'To date, substantially all technology revenue has been derived from nonrecurring up-front payments.' That's the key sentence. 'In some cases, the technology licenses include prepaid amounts relating to either the initial technology license fee or to prepaid royalties.'

"Okay, 'prepaid royalties' tells you that not only are these revenues nonrecurring, but in fact include some advance royalties paid by some of these licensees. That means MIPS won't see any more royalties from these guys until after it passes some sort of minimum shipment level. So MIPS is clearly borrowing from the future to produce revenue in the short run. And that produces a level of profitability which allows them to go public."

Herwick is pleased, like a detective who's uncovered a vital clue. But this kernel of bad news is not enough to dissuade him from the offering, because the same paragraph also discloses some good news: that MIPS has $15.4 million in deferred revenue it will be able to recognize in the future, that the amount is growing, and that at least $5 million of that will be recognized in 1990.

"All of this tells me that I should be very interested now in MIPS's ability to get new licensees—how many opportunities there might be and how much those future licensees will pay. It means I will want to better understand the timing and the magnitude of these royalty payments, as they will have to replace the current one-time license income as a source of revenue and profit. The MIPS people are going to have to answer all of these questions in their road show."

Still, Herwick is impressed so far with MIPS's ability to anticipate most of his questions. "They understood they had to give visibility and plausibility to these future strains of license income and royalty income because clearly product sales aren't enough. So, the next question is: Will product revenue grow rapidly enough to diminish the losses?

"For that, I've got to look [turns to previous page] at the product revenue section. No, they're not telling me very much. It's mostly ancient history. Okay, so let's look at the product section [pages 23 to

26]. It says they've got new products. Well, I happen to know there is a new generation of product coming. They'll no doubt talk about it on the road show. See, it's very difficult in a prospectus to talk about future, unannounced products. The SEC doesn't like that. But, typically, you have more latitude in the road show to talk about future goals, in a quantitative way. You can't give specific revenue and profit expectations, but you can talk about operating goals in terms of growth and percentage contributions from different revenue sources and about new products.''

Herwick paused in his reading. ''You see, one of the major functions of the road show is to anticipate—and answer effectively—the obvious questions an analyst would have reading a prospectus.'' He shook his head in dismay, ''Of course, some people read the prospectus only after they go to the road show.''

He glanced again at the products section, especially at the listing for the new R6000 Enterprise Server. ''I think everybody accepts the fact that the company's technology is very good. Most people involved in technology would recognize that 55 mips is a lot of performance. They would also recognize that the price range is kind of a minicomputer price range, but that the performance is much greater than that of a typical minicomputer—so that it is a very attractive alternative.

''Even the average investor could look at this chart and say, 'Gee, this company has a broad product range, and they really get a high price for their products. Somebody out there is going to pay several hundred thousand dollars for one of these things. They must be good.' ''

With that, Herwick closed the prospectus, then opened it again on the first page. In fifteen minutes, looking at six pages, he had completed his first analysis; he had determined what he believed are the critical issues about MIPS and how they might affect the value of the new stock offering.

''Now I'm going to go through this document more carefully. I now have a sense of the thing and I'm ready to go through it more systematically, especially the sections that are carefully worded to describe any past experiences or future risks. At this point I can say that I know I should be interested in this company because it's so successful. But I also can see that there are a lot of issues that I need to address regarding revenue streams in the future and profitability and so forth. Now I want to see if I can find any information that will help me develop the questions I want to ask at the road show.''

He turned to the prospectus summary. "Probably the most interesting thing here [page 3] is the list of customers. And if there's one thing every investor understands, it's that, hey, this company has a pretty impressive set of customers. Page 4 is so summarized it's not of much use; it's all boilerplate. Page 5 is a summary description of what's going to come later, so I'll kind of look at it.

"Now, page 6. Here we go: risk factors. 'Adoption of the Company's RISC Architecture'—now that's one that doesn't appear in every prospectus, so I'm going to look at this one. Yes, it is indeed critical to the company's success that it's adopted by a wide number. 'Application Software Capability'—well, that's important, but there's nothing unusual here. 'Reliance on Third Parties'—that's important, so let me read this. Okay, the first three [suppliers] are well-respected semiconductor manufacturers, the other two so-so. That tells me that MIPS really does have strong support from semiconductor manufacturers. That's very reassuring."

He skipped through the next three risk factors. "Okay, now 'Competition'—nope, no names of competitors here. So this section is just boilerplate. 'Single-source Components'—wow, that I'm definitely going to read. Hey, this is interesting reading. They acknowledge that they have not yet begun to develop an alternative source. So now I know they're in Bipolar. That makes me curious about how good this supplier is, where it is, what its ability is to produce these chips. I know that making an ECL chip with as many elements on it as this one has is very challenging. It's tough to produce a part that big and that dense. And I also know that Bipolar Integrated Technology has had trouble in the past producing significant quantities of parts.

"Okay, so this tells me that maybe I should discount [the value of MIPS's stock] just a little bit for this one problem. Okay [he continues reading the risk section], 'Management of Growth' is boilerplate. 'Shares Eligible for Future Sale'—600,000, that's a hefty number. [He reads on to the additional 12.7 million shares eligible for staggered sale in the 240 days after the IPO.] So, there's going to be quite a supply of stock coming out. That, as an institutional investor, would give me a little pause, slow me down a bit."

It had taken Bob Herwick just four minutes to slice his way through a week of carefully edited writing by Ludvigson and crew. In the process Herwick had found the nuggets of vital information hidden within the slag of verbiage.

He next reached the seven pages of charts and footnotes and again focused on the MD&A section. This time he read it line by line. "Oh, look! One more time we're reminded that technology revenue is nonrecurring. You can tell the lawyers were very careful on that. They understood what the issue was.

"Now I'm reading through the ancient history of 1987 on the top of page 14. I'm seeing that the revenue increase from products is due to computer system sales. So that tells me the mix is changing in the way I like. Good. That means they have successfully migrated to a systems strategy because it is inherently more profitable. It generates more revenue and profit in absolute dollars. I'm more comfortable now. It looks like they had a tough time when they were trying to be in the manufacturing business. Reading this section you can see the evolution of the company to a more profitable strategy.

"Oh, here they mention there might be gross margin percentage decline with the introduction of their desktop products. That's just to remind us that this is a highly competitive business, so that we don't get too ambitious in our projections."

Herwick continued page by page, sentence by sentence, commenting on key phrases, becoming amused at the third or fourth appearance of a warning phrase, being pleasantly surprised at some unexpected discovery: "There! Screaming at you is the fact that . . ." and "That certainly raises a little red flag. I've got to do a little eyeballing on these trends."

He looked up from the prospectus: "This company clearly is laying out a very plausible scenario for improving profitability. It's a scenario that is very understandable, acceptable. They have clearly cleaned the place up; they've gone through and any operation that wasn't doing well they said, 'Let's deal with it now, not after we've gone public.' That's attractive to me. It means I'm buying an ongoing entity where, while there may be risks, these guys have recognized them and developed a plausible scenario to overcome them."

He moved on into the long business section. He recognized some of the phrasing: "People who write prospectuses happily plagiarize because they're under time pressure."

Service: "Tandem is a good service organization, but maybe a funny choice for a company like MIPS that's primarily in the workstation business."

Resellers: "That's expedient in the short run, but long term that's a tough way to build a business. You don't become a multibillion dollar company selling through resellers.''

MIPS's business model: ''I'm seeing a company that's licensing its technology to a lot of folks, that's selling its products through a lot of folks, and that says that its technology is going into a lot of places where one set of licensees and resellers is going to compete with another set. That means a lot of competition and conflict.''

Customers: ''Boy, that really is an impressive list.''

Manufacturing: ''Once again I'm reminded of the single source thing with BIT. Their lawyers are really supersensitive on the subject. They probably should be.''

He moved on into the section, beginning on page 33, on MIPS's relationships with Kubota and DEC. ''Well,'' he said, ''Kubota certainly has its hands around them. How about DEC? Wow! DEC paid $15 million. There aren't too many people around willing to plunk down $15 million on the future.''

Employees: ''Typically a company will have $150,000 to $200,000 in revenue per employee. At MIPS it's about $175,000, so that looks okay. But remember, an awful lot of that revenue is from technology licenses. So the productivity of the employees in terms of direct product sales is really not that high.''

He moved on to the management section and appraised each executive and board member in turn. The process was cold-blooded.

The executive team:

Miller: ''Joined in 1987, so he's not a founder. Senior management positions at Data General. Well, DG of late hasn't been doing too well, so that's not the greatest place to be from. But he was senior vice-president, so this is a solid guy with lots of experience. So we overlook the DG and look at his personal record.''

Boesenberg: ''Apple. Not the most obvious fit with MIPS in terms of experience. But then I see he was at DG before. Miller must have had a good opinion of him there and brought him into MIPS.''

Jobe: ''He's been around a bit, but I happen to know him personally from his VC days and he's a pretty solid guy. The Plexus connection only says that he went into a start-up and it didn't work and he moved on. Many people in Silicon Valley have done that.''

Vigil: ''HP. That's usually good. Elxsi. Well, everybody's entitled to make a mistake. When you come out of HP you're a little naive. A lot of HP people go into the wrong start-up, but they're basically good people and they eventually figure things out. This guy was with Burroughs, so he's solid, experienced people." [Herwick dismissed Vigil's lack of a college degree as "ancient history."]

DiNucci: "I knew him at DEC. He was well regarded. A real driver in their success in the workstation area. He can help MIPS understand DEC."

Hime: "Knew him from Sun. John's been around a bit. Maybe he's been a few too many places. Like he was at Frame for a little over a year. That's a little surprising."

Ludvigson: "Strong accounting background. More than enough capacity for his job."

Rohrs: "HP again. That's good in manufacturing because HP is touchy-feely with people."

Stritter: "Good technical credentials. Positioned in a way that means he can contribute without doing any harm."

Hennessy: "Again, safely positioned."

Sweeney: "Everybody needs a lawyer."

The directors:

Davidow: "Highly regarded. When he was at Intel a strong force."

Fuller: "There because of the DEC relationship."

Lorentz: "Same deal with Honeywell Bull."

Treybig: "Creative. Will ask a lot of fundamental questions. So there's a good guy to have."

Herwick's conclusion: "All in all this is a team with above-average experience. Also above-average age. A good sign."

He next moved carefully through the extended descriptions of the Kubota, DEC, and Synthesis transactions. Nearly two hours had now passed since he first opened the prospectus. Now, as he headed into the final financial tables, Bob Herwick felt he had as good a sense of MIPS as is possible for any outsider. All that was left was to check the tables for any hidden land mines or pearls.

He found a few: "Let's see. DEC's deferred revenue is recognized over a twenty-four-month period and that means it's—WHOOPS!—come September 1990, lo and behold, it's over. DEC drops out. So that big revenue stream drops off. That's good to know. . . .

"Oh, now I feel a little better about something. Prepayment royalties are to be recognized on a pro rata basis and that there's some additional royalty from product sales. That gives me a little confidence about the company's future revenues. . . .

"I've got to check out what the tax rate's going to be in the future. . . ."

Herwick closed the prospectus and set it down. Was MIPS stock worth it? He had long since reached a decision.

"Yeah, it's fair, but at that price they certainly aren't giving it away. Still, for an investor taking a long-term perspective, this is an important company. It has a complex business model, but it's also got a strong team. And, along with Sun Microsystems it is one of the two opportunities to invest in RISC technology. So there's a scarcity value in investing in MIPS.

"But investors will need to have the confidence that MIPS can and will make a transition from its heavy dependence on one-time licensing income to the steadier source of product revenues. That will be the key to the future of the firm."

And so, like every other major industry analyst, Bob Herwick recommended MIPS stock to his readers. The prospectus, Dave Ludvigson's hard-fought document, now stood riddled with shot above and below the waterline, demasted, and listing to one side. But it was still afloat. Now he, Bob Miller, and Chuck Boesenberg would have to sail it around the world.

CHAPTER 11

The Joker

IN ANY SELF-CONTAINED, circumscribed industry, be it automobiles or computers, there is a continual migration of people from company to company and from competitor to competitor.

Sometimes, when the gypsy employee is a talented scientist, this job-hopping can lead to a nasty and protracted lawsuit over intellectual property. But more often it leads to a certain grumbling on one side and smug satisfaction on the other.

MIPS was not immune to all this. Throughout the company, one could find engineers, line workers, and administrative people who had worked for each of the company's competitors. Even at the executive level, Texan John Hime, vice-president of marketing for the systems products group, had, from 1984 to 1988, been director of marketing at archrival Sun Microsystems.

But most interesting of all was Hime's counterpart, Joe DiNucci, MIPS's vice-president of marketing for the entry systems group. For DiNucci had not only worked for MIPS's biggest customer, Digital Equipment, but while there had engineered the deal with MIPS, the contract that had turned the little company around. As a result, he, perhaps more than anyone inside the company or out, had MIPS in perspective.

And DiNucci was a singular Silicon Valley character, something of a local legend. A few months hence, author Malcolm Kushner would use a DiNucci anecdote to kick off his book about the use of humor in business, *The Light Touch*:

"Joe DiNucci had just been named U.S. workstation sales manager for Digital Equipment Corp. A vice president arranged a dinner so that

DiNucci could meet Digital's senior research managers. During the dinner an engineering manager known for his blunt opinions said that Digital would produce the world's best workstations in three years.

"DiNucci was not impressed. He said, 'If we don't do it in two years, it will be too late.'

"The tough-talking manager replied, 'You know, you're really full of [expletive deleted].'

"A dead silence reigned. No one knew what to say. So DiNucci broke the ice. 'You know, that's an amazing insight,' he said. 'Most people take months to reach that conclusion. You came to it in forty-five minutes.'

"The engineering manager laughed and the dialogue opened up again. By the end of the evening the manager was completely won over. . . . Just two years later, Digital's status had changed dramatically. A plethora of new workstation products had captured the attention of the entire computer industry. . . ."

Joe DiNucci is the kind of guy who makes people smile, shake their heads, and say, "The guy is crazy." He is fast-talking, profane, and warmly engaging. And he loves the big effect. That's why he drives a Ferrari Mondiale and a 1964 Mustang convertible and talks about building a 289 Cobra. That's why, a few months before, the *Mercury-News* carried the story of the DiNuccis' twenty-fifth wedding anniversary. It seemed that Joe celebrated the event by handing out to the celebration guests an annual report on the first quarter century of marriage. It included such chapters as "Children: Pros/Cons," benchmarks of twenty-five years of marriage (36,000 checks, 31 cars, 4 beds, 1,300 movies), and how to make marriage work ("serial monogamy with the same partner").

The transcript of an interview with this pugnacious, bald, and bearded character is a series of one-sentence questions followed by three-page answers. Buried within this lengthy, entertaining, and relentlessly upbeat verbiage are the details of DiNucci's life and philosophy, complete with an extraordinary memory for dates.

Birth: "I'm from Pittsburgh, Pennsylvania. Was born in the perfect year to be born, 1942, December 3rd, because that way as you grew up they invented rock and roll for you—and you still got out of college before drugs started."

Antecedents: "First generation American, my parents were both one of thirteen children. Ellis Island stuff. My father's Italian, my mother's

Alsatian, German-French. My dad was the first in his lineage to attend college. He became a mechanical designer. He and my mom met in Pittsburgh. And my mom was a hair dresser and a hair stylist and the funny thing is they got married in 1931 and my dad was real proud that he didn't work blue collar, he worked at a drafting board designing machinery. And two months after they got married he got laid off because of the Depression and didn't work again for four years, except laboring. Meanwhile, my mother never lost a day's work because the rich people still had money and still got their hair done. . . .

"My grandfather was a real Eric Hoffer-type of character. His trade was stonecutting. He had thirteen kids and a mortgage. In 1920 he bought a house and had a $10,000 mortgage. He was like me: If he had $8.00 he spent $12.50. Always out there extended. . . . He was a big strapping, hulking guy. He had three jobs at one point: stonecutting, driving a streetcar, and working at the Ford factory. He was a salesman too—insulation, bricks, weather stripping, just trying to make a dollar. But he was really a master stonecutter—his facades are still up all over Pittsburgh. He did the face of the Frick building and the old U.S. Steel building. . . ."

Education: "And so I graduate [high school] in 1960. Went to Carnegie Tech to be a mechanical engineer. Naturally, that was what my dad was. I hated it. I got out of college with a reasonable average because I used to ace courses in psychology, economics, ROTC, and then stagger through thermodynamics and calculus."

Marriage: "I met my wife in 1961. Here's a picture of us the month I met her and this is us almost thirty years later. March 1961 and she was going into nurse's training and I was a freshman. And she and I have been together ever since."

Career: "I got out of college in 1964 and went to work at Jones and Laughlin Steel, which was a big, integrated, seven-mile long steel mill on the Ohio River, 50 miles south of Pittsburgh. Iron ore and coal in one end and nails out the other end. I was an engineering trainee. Thirteen thousand hourly workers. The biggest [steelworkers union] local in the U.S. Now that mill is stone cold dead. There's been nothing there for twenty years.

". . . I worked in the steel mills for three years and I got off on the macho part. It's part of Pittsburgh's culture. It's neat to be in the middle of it. But I was a professional. I had a degree. I was making $603 a month, $7,200 a year, which we put in the bank because my wife was a graduate nurse and she made $80 a week working in the operating room, which we lived on. I bought a new Corvair.

"I was enchanted with the sales guys who came in and sold us equipment. I liked their lifestyle because they got to be in a different place every day. Meanwhile, I'm sitting in this dingy engineering department in this rotten steel mill with these old fart guys that my dad had worked with thirty years before—but he had gone off to bigger and better things and they had stayed there. And I thought, this is not cool, this is not where I want to spend my life.

"[I wanted to get into sales, but couldn't, because] it was real structured, you couldn't get in there unless you were born there. So screw that. I quit and got a job selling process control equipment. . . . I called over the Ohio Valley and I really loved it. It was great. I got a big increase in salary and a company car and an expense account and started dressing like a salesman and I went to graduate school at night for four years—Duquesne University—and got an M.B.A.

"An M.B.A. was kind of unusual in those days. I had written to my management and asked whether they recommended I get a degree in engineering or business and they said, 'Oh. Engineering.' And I thought, why? I hadn't used a Jack's crap of what I'd learned at Carnegie. So went and got the M.B.A. . . .

"This headhunter told me that 'There's an opportunity at a company called Digital Equipment Corporation. It's a fairly new company, and you don't have what they're looking for from a technical standpoint, but they might be interested in you because you're a good salesman. And you know everybody in the Ohio Valley, from Firestone to Goodyear to the steel companies, and they're trying to get in there.'

"So I went to the library and read all I could, learned all I could about Digital. They'd just introduced the PDP11—this is 1971—and they were a $100 million a year company, about the size MIPS is now, only they're already public and have like 5,000 employees. . . .

"So I tried to get a job, but they wouldn't even interview me because I didn't have a computer science background, never even taken a computer course. I didn't know baud from byte. The local guy wouldn't even talk to me. The headhunter said, 'That's too bad because the regional manager, three levels up from this guy, is in town interviewing the final two candidates for a sales position. Too bad you can't get past the first level guy.'

"So I call the regional manager, his name is Jerry Moore, and he's staying at the Holiday Inn out at the airport, and I said, 'I'm Joe DiNucci and I'd like to interview for the job.' He said, 'Well, call our local guy.' I said, 'No, he won't talk to me.' He said, 'Well, send your resume to me in Chicago and I'll get back to you.'

"Okay, I said, then got off the phone and realized I'd just gotten screwed. So I call him back. He said, 'Look, I really don't have time to talk to you.' I said, 'I know, you already told me that. But I'll tell you what: Do you have a rental car? Your plane's at noon. I'll be in the lobby at eleven and I'll drive you to the airport. No obligation.'

"I had the job right then and there. Salesmanship. Luckily his plane was an hour late and so we just sat there in the Cleveland Airport. He told me I had nothing DEC was looking for. And I told him that unlike the other guys, who were looking for salary increase, I was looking for a career. I told him, 'I'm not really your common, average guy. You invest a little in me learning about computers and I will open doors up and down the Ohio Valley and we will get along great for a long time.' I sold his ass. I got the job and spent eighteen years at DEC. . . .

"When I started, my stock in the company was worth about $50 a share. Factoring in splits and everything, it eventually was worth $600 a share. It bought me a lot of sports cars. It bought us a house in Carmel and sent my boys to college. It bought me a lot of good times. I loved roaring around Silicon Valley in my Ferrari. So, when people would talk to me about IPOs and going public and all the money that could be made, I'd point out to them that were other ways, like staying with a good company."

The MIPS-DEC deal: "MIPS is delivering stuff, the R2000 chips, sample quantities of R3000 are being talked about, and the stuff is real and the compilers are great. So we started putting together a little project in Palo Alto that said there's a new [DEC] VAX station coming. If we redesigned one board, powered by the R2000 MIPS thing, we could very easily, with a minimum investment, have a MIPS RISC-powered product in less than a year and we could meet our goal. It would be really cool. Now, it's going to piss off all the power inside DEC who think they're inventing their own RISC thing, but jeez, isn't that a cool idea?

"Then, on March 27, 1988, I went to—completely unrelated, I thought—a two-day workshop held by Robert Bly and Michael Mead on mythology. My wife had heard Bly read poetry in Santa Cruz and she said, 'I hate to tell you this, but if he had looked down in the audience

and said "Follow me off the cliff," I would have gone with him. He's
having a seminar in March, why don't you go?'

"Well, it was wonderful. It got all into getting rid of naivete. I used
to say things like, 'We don't have any adversaries in this project; we
only have people that don't have our data yet.' Bullshit. You got real
adversaries. You got people who have all your data and more, know
you're right, know you have the truth, but they've got a different agenda,
and they will sabotage you. And if you misunderstand that or ignore it,
you're a fool. I was like [the inverse] of Bob Miller in those days.
Utterly naive. Miller's a tough guy. Miller sees around corners. He sees
subterfuge that you haven't even thought of yet. That doesn't mean
that's the way he thinks; he is just anything but naive.

"In that workshop I picked my 'break-out.' It was the Ares myth. The
warrior. You have a purpose and nothing dissuades you. And when I
came to the office the next day after that weekend, I said [to my team],
we've been kicking around this MIPS-powered initiative now for about
six weeks and everybody here in Palo Alto just thinks it's super-neat and
super-cool and there's no chance in hell to sell it to DEC [corporate].
Well, do we believe this is the right thing for DEC? Yes, it is. Okay,
then we are going to take it to the mountain. And they said, 'You realize
this is career altering?' I said, 'Yes.' 'Are you ready for the consequences?' 'Yes, are you with me or not? Let's go.'

"I told my secretary, 'Here's a list of eleven DEC vice-presidents and
then Ken Olson. Over the next three weeks I'll make three consecutive
trips back to main [headquarters] and I'll see each person on this list. I
don't care what the order is. Start booking them.' And we got on the
red-eye that night.

"We get off the plane at Logan Airport at 6:00 or 7:00 A.M. and who
are we set to see first? Jack Shield [DEC executive vice-president], the
meanest Machiavellian son of a bitch, hard-ass there is, my boss's
boss's guy. The only man in DEC I was afraid of.

"I thought, oh my god, this is terrible. I'm not ready. We had this
little three-page talking paper about why we should do this. But we said,
okay, we're the warriors, we're going to go for it. Boom, we go right
in to see Shields. And he loves the idea. Absolutely loves it. He says,
this is great, where are you going to next? We said we had eleven other
VPs to go and he says, aw, forget that. You want to go see Olson . . .
right away, in the next twenty-four hours. We walked out of his office
and my Ninja were waiting for me.

". . . We went to see the Old Man [Olson] in the morning and he loved it. In eight minutes he said, this is a brilliant idea, this is absolutely the best idea I've heard in years. . . . He said, 'I smell "skunk works" engineering here. I smell that this has been going for a while.' I said, 'Guilty.' He said, 'I like that.' . . .

"That started about a five-week civil war inside of DEC that was fun to be part of. It became a movement and it became a big thing. But it never became a complete juggernaut. To this day there are people in DEC who spend their days figuring out how they can sabotage the MIPS product line. Which is human nature. They've got twenty years of success built around the VAX and they equate MIPS with non-VAX, which isn't true."

Joining MIPS: "Back before we put that proposal on the table to DEC I came down here [from the DEC office in Palo Alto] because I wanted to meet some of the people. I had met Dr. Hennessy and I was quite impressed with him. How could you not be? I had met Skip Stritter, too, but I'd never met Miller. So I come down for the first meeting with Miller and he's in his full-on iceberg mode. He doesn't show me jack-diddley. No expression. No feedback. Plus he's got on this gaudy-looking shirt with white French cuffs and a blue body. I remember saying to the guy I was with, 'This isn't going to work. It doesn't feel right.'

". . . When I come back the second time, they had talked it over and decided this was a serious opportunity and Miller was ready and I was absolutely enchanted. I just thought this guy is a genius. He said things, he had the insights. Then it all clicked and everything else I had seen and the quality of the other people and the strategy and all that was then more obvious. . . .

"So we reached the point where we were ready to go and pitch it to DEC, but I had to have a 'come-to-Jesus' with Miller. We were out of time so we had to do it by phone. I called him up and said, 'Bob, your people have been wonderfully responsive so far, and I need to tell you that I'm going to go ahead and back this proposal and put it on the table and I think we can sell it. I'm just concerned that in the enthusiasm to back us there may have been some commitments overstated. This is the time to move the throttle down 15 percent and make sure that everything that's committed is absolutely rock solid. Performance commitments, time-to-market commitments, and all. . . . I want you to say to me, "I absolutely guarantee this is going to happen." '

"A long pause and he says, 'I really like your style.'

" 'It's the only way I know how to do it. I don't have the patience for contracts and all that. It usually comes down to man to man and you either believe somebody or you don't. So tell me.'

"And he says, 'I will tell you that everything that's on the table is going to happen. There's nothing that's overstated. It's all the truth. I appreciate your support and your bluntness and let's go.'

"I said, 'You got a deal.'

". . . I was proud of what I did at DEC, but I was also getting tired of using so much of my energy inside the company. Plus, I was increasingly enchanted with the environment at MIPS. I had decided I was going to leave DEC in 1989. And then a 'wake-up call' happened one morning in February when I opened the paper and saw that Chuck Boesenberg was going from Apple to MIPS. I knew Boesenberg by reputation and I thought, son of a gun, this is really getting serious. These guys are putting some real power into that team.

"Meanwhile, [DEC] announced the [RISC-based DECstation] product on January 10, 1989, at the San Jose Convention Center in front of a couple thousand people and it was the performance of a lifetime. It was like going back to your hometown to quarterback the Super Bowl team and throwing an eighty-yard bomb to win the game. The corporate announcement was back East, and as they say, success has a thousand fathers. I knew where it began. A lot of good people knew where it had started. But by announcement time a number of people had kind of glommed onto this and a certain DEC VP had the bad taste to call me up about a week before the announcement to say, 'I'll bet you're real excited about this announcement, *too*.' He was going to do the announcement back there, a job I should have been asked to do.

"That was the last nail in the coffin. It just had to be that way; it was karma. I was supposed to be here at MIPS. If DEC had given me the VP strip in December, if they'd invited me to the announcement, if, if, if, if the stock hadn't gone from 198 to 85, maybe I'd still be there.

"I talked to my wife in March. I told her that I really wanted to go work for MIPS. That I was absolutely enchanted by Miller, that I thought he was an absolutely unique character, that I could learn from him. We decided. I called up Miller and told him, 'I'm going to leave DEC in '89. Is there any reason we should talk?' And he said, 'Anytime, anyplace. What do you want to do?' I came over, I put a little proposal on the table, and he liked it. We spent ninety minutes negotiating the job and about ninety seconds negotiating the deal, and it was done.''

The IPO: ''I have a house in Saratoga and a house in Carmel. Yes, DEC was good to me—and I was good to DEC. I have a lot of assets, but I have a lot of debt. The money isn't the biggest deal, but it's very important. I had a plan four years ago that by age 50 I wanted independence. It didn't mean I didn't want to work, but I wanted to be able to do whatever I bloody well pleased and if I had just had it up to here with Silicon Valley and frequent fliers and all that and if I wanted to have a custom lingerie shop in Carmel, I could bloody well do it. I wanted to help my wife with the Reach center for stroke victims she'd set up in Los Altos. I figured out how much that was going to take and frankly, in 1985, 1986, and 1987 I believed, miracle of miracles, that I could achieve that by staying at DEC. Then the stock crashed.

''Now, I just turned 47 and it looks like I may be able to make it from my MIPS stock.

''Not that I intend to take a walk then, not if we're having fun.

''And it isn't just money. If it was that my wife and I would have gone into selling real estate in Santa Clara County. No, the kids are grown and I'm not buying any cars for a while. I just think that the world of graphics, workstations, distributed computing, and open systems is very exciting. And I'm absolutely intrigued by the kind of company Miller's crafting. It's completely appropriate to the next decade. And on top of that, we may well have the last new computer architecture of the twentieth century.

''We've already had the model tested a couple times, when Miller's had to crack the whip. Companies many, many times our size thought they had us and tried to put the squeeze on Miller, like, 'Don't you have an IPO coming up?' But they picked the wrong guy. It's so cool thinking that they walked into that meeting knowing they were going to blindside him and then to have Miller come up with a response so spontaneous and accurate that he just extracted their hearts. So cool.

''Listen, this is not an easy-going, laid-back environment we live in here. Miller flies this place like an F-14 with the canopy off. But he does wear a seatbelt. He's got a full tank of gas and he understands the value of velocity, altitude, and weaponry. You can talk about the billion dollar management team and the 'aging gunfighters,' and there's some truth to the idea that collective experience has helped us. But the challenges we have to overcome are new to all of us, including Bob. Nobody's ever had the kind of lateral arabesque to execute that Miller's got to do between NEC and Siemans and Sun.

"He told each of us when we came on board, 'I didn't just hire my twelfth place kicker. I'm not going for depth right now, I'm going for breadth. We're still filling out the bench.' And if you don't ever offer anything, if you don't ever stick your neck out and put something on the table, even if you're not sure how he's going to respond, then you're useless and he lets you know that too.

"I like that. I want to stay around to see what happens."

CHAPTER 12

Hitting the Road

ON THE NIGHT OF SUNDAY, DECEMBER 3, 1989, in the midst of a three-hour flight from New York to London on the Concorde, Bob Miller pulled out a blue-covered, wide-ruled, spiral-bound notebook and began his diary of the MIPS IPO road show.

On the first page he drew up the columns and rows of a log: dates down the left side, then date, aircraft/airline, hotel, city, mileage, and number of presentations across the top. From November 29 through December 2 he listed New York City, which he'd used as a base with Barbara to visit relatives and to conduct some business at Morgan Stanley.

Today's listing was British Airlines Concorde, Berkeley Hotel, London, 3,600 miles, no presentations. Tomorrow, he knew, would be a living hell: a quick charter flight to Edinburgh and the Caledonian Hotel, followed by five presentations. And all on just a couple hours sleep.

That gave Miller another idea. Turning the page, he started a second table. Again, dates were listed down the left side, but this time across the top he wrote wake-up time, total sleep, from/to, in-route time, and reception/presentation time. That would give a far more accurate measure of the personal toll of the road show.

Traveling was nothing new to Miller; it was part of being an electronics executive in the modern world. But, as CEO of MIPS, with its far-flung strategic partnerships to be prospected, negotiated, closed, and then tended, the amount of time out of the United States had been extraordinary.

A week before, *Business Week*, in a special report on RISC chips, had run a sidebar about MIPS focusing on a September run to Europe Miller had made in search of deals. The accompanying photograph showed Miller, in trenchcoat, grinning but obviously exhausted, his black hair plastered across the top of his heavy forehead, standing in front of a foggy Amsterdam canal.

The lead to the story read: "On a week-long swing through Europe last September, Robert C. Miller landed in a new city every five waking hours. By the end of the month, the bleary-eyed president of MIPS Computer Systems, Inc. had logged 60,000 miles. But he had deals to sell $85 million worth of computers—more than twice MIPS's 1988 revenues—to West Germany's Nixdorf Computer and France's Groupe Bull."

After all the good news, the article noted how far MIPS had come: "Not bad for a company that was on the ropes just two years ago. When Miller arrived from Data General Corp., MIPS had run through its $23 million in venture capital and was floundering, with a muddled strategy to build chips, circuit boards, and finished computers."

It closed with a flourish: " 'There are two types of people in the world,' Miller declares, 'Gunslingers and targets.' These days, he's keeping his six-shooters drawn."

A nice piece of publicity—even if it did come a page later and was of half the size of a sidebar on Miller's old boss Ed deCastro's attempt to get Data General back in the race.

There'd been a lot of publicity for MIPS lately. This piece in *Business Week*, a big profile in Dick Shaffer's *Technologic Computer Letter*, a cover profile in May in the Business Monday section of the *San Jose Mercury-News*, numerous articles in trade magazines—enough to fill a notebook on the desk of public relations director Bev Jerman. The pieces were all laudatory, all toasting Miller and his "over-the-hill gang" of veteran senior executives for turning the company around, many suggesting that MIPS was the hot new Silicon Valley company.

This was the kind of publicity companies dream of, but it was too much of a good thing. Now the company had to duck opportunities for print, to act like it was anonymous and unimportant.

That was one of the nuttiest things about going public—the so-called "quiet period." For three months before and three months after the IPO, the company was not supposed to do any promotion, advertising, or product introducing that was not consistent with the company's normal operating style; it was not supposed to do anything that could be seen as hyping the stock.

But what was normal business behavior in a four-year-old company that just two years ago was nearly bankrupt and was now regularly landing enormous and unprecedented new deals? MIPS wasn't old enough or stable enough yet to have determined normalcy. And meanwhile, the press, seeing the first big tech stock offering since the crash, was calling day and night trying to get a story. Talk to reporters and the company risked having the SEC delay, or even suspend, the IPO. Don't talk to reporters and they would write the story anyway, often quoting competitors, and then the SEC would blame the company anyway. The SEC had already gotten "ticked off" over an article about the MIPS IPO in the *Wall Street Journal*. "It really got their noses bent out of joint."

And now *USA Today*. That newspaper, which he rarely read, was in Bob Miller's mind a lot these days. In late September and early October the paper's Silicon Valley correspondent, Kathy Rebello, had conducted a number of interviews in preparation for a profile of the company. All well and good; nothing like a major profile in a national publication, especially just weeks before filing with the SEC. The timing would be perfect. The paper's photographer was scheduled to come by on October 17.

Unfortunately, the photographer had more important things to do that day, like cover collapsed homes in Los Gatos and earthquake fault fissures in the Santa Cruz Mountains. So did Rebello. The story had been bumped indefinitely.

Now, when the timing was perfectly wrong, *USA Today* seemed to be gearing up to run the piece. Rebello had called for updates and would not be deterred. Miller had visions of the SEC examiner opening his *USA Today* one morning, turning to the Money section, and going apoplectic.

But what could he do? "As far as I know, the First Amendment is still operative in the United States. So we can't stop the press from writing articles. We can't even cool them off. That's our position with the SEC. If they want to delay the IPO, then there'll only be more articles.

"The SEC has kind of decided, 'We're not going to take an official position until we see what the story says.' And *USA Today* says, 'We'll run it when we feel like running it.'

"I can't control that. At the time it was done it seemed the reasonable thing to do in terms of continued PR exposure for the company. Now all we can do is ride it out. You can't overreact in either direction."

This was one of those unexpected obstacles in going public about which Miller had warned his staff months before.

As the silver splinter of the Concorde rocketed high over the North Atlantic, Miller reviewed his road show presentation. Then he intended to catch some sleep. He figured the road show, with all its demands, would be survivable, if only because it included two night flights on which Miller and his team could sleep.

If there was anything good to be said about the punishing tour ahead, it was that it took Miller, Ludvigson, and Boesenberg away from the zoo back at the office. The hysteria to get in on the MIPS IPO was building throughout the world's financial community, especially so in Silicon Valley.

"I had six calls over the weekend from friends of mine wanting to know how to get some stock," Miller had said a week before. "All of us are getting calls like that. Sher Parker [Miller's secretary] figures she gets about nine calls an hour wanting to buy stock. I just refer them to Morgan Stanley and Cowen. But I tell you, every one of them has some angle. One tried to justify why his firm should be in the syndicate by saying they'd once used one of Morgan Stanley's charts in a presentation. So therefore they should be included! Can you believe it?

"Sometimes you can make what seems to be a very subtle decision that turns out to save you a lot of grief. Ours was that there'd be no directed stock, because I didn't want to explain why one guy got it and another guy didn't."

It was still remarkable to Miller how quickly it had come to this. Little more than two years before he had been senior vice-president of the information systems group at Data General in Westborough, Massachusetts. It was a prestigious position in a legendary computer company. He had been there when Tracy Kidder had immortalized one of the product teams in the book *The Soul of a New Machine*. For six years it had been like making history.

Nevertheless, Miller had not liked working at Data General, especially in the last few years. It didn't operate in the way he would have run a firm. Looking back, sometimes he would grow bitter: "They don't know what straight is. They wouldn't know how to find it."

Part of the bitterness came from Miller's appreciation of what he had left to join Data General—fifteen years at IBM, working his way up from the engineering ranks into senior management. IBM had taken a young man from Long Island, with a B.S. in mechanical engineering from Bucknell University and an M.S. in thermal dynamics from Stanford, and turned him into a business leader. It was at Big Blue that Miller earned his stripes as a technologist as well, being awarded six U.S. patents and authoring a number of technical articles relating to computer architecture. At one point he was director of the company's Kingston Laboratory, putting out the 4300, IBM's first 16-bit computer.

Leaving IBM had been the hardest decision of Miller's career. And that only made his unhappiness at Data General more painful. He had made millions of dollars from the jump, but that was less important to Miller than the right job.

At least there were some interesting job offers to mitigate the misery somewhat. Miller knew that at any time he could walk into a top spot in a multinational. But even that wasn't enough. He wanted his own company.

"I don't do things for the monetary play. I had an offer to be the number three guy at a Fortune 5 company. It would have been a million dollars a year salary, compared to $150,000 here at MIPS. But I'm not into the power at all. I'm really not. I didn't want to inherit a GE. I didn't want to inherit an IBM. Somebody else built those companies. I wanted to be a Morita [of Sony]. I wanted to start out with a rice cooker, find out that was the wrong thing to do, and be smart enough to change and keep changing when I saw what the market wanted."

That's why in early 1987 Miller agreed to meet on a Sunday evening with two venture capitalists and the founder of a troubled Silicon Valley start-up firm called MIPS. Steve Croix and Grant Heidrich from the Mayfield Fund and MIPS co-founder Edward P. "Skip" Stritter had, two months before, forced out the previous president of MIPS and replaced him with an interim CEO. Now, as the firm was sinking into oblivion, they were racing around the country trying to find a white knight. Miller had come highly recommended, but the odds were against his even seriously considering the offer, much less taking it.

Recalled Barbara Miller, "Bob said, 'We'll go out to dinner,' and I said, 'No, these guys have been traveling. They probably hate eating out. I'll make them a chicken dinner instead.' "

So, the beleaguered recruiting team, their target, and his wife had their first meeting over chicken around a crowded kitchen table.

At first, they put the press on Miller, teasing him with the prospect of his own company, of founder's stock, of the thrill of directing a turn-around. But Miller wasn't jumping, and soon the team, recognizing that Bob made all decisions jointly with his wife, set to work on Barbara.

Barbara was no easy mark for either flattery or interrogation. Her 1967 Miss New York Subways card had read, "Auburn-tressed Barbara works in the Manhattan Section of the FBI. She also participates fully in FBI recreation and social activities. In her free time, Barbara volunteers-in-aid to the Sacred Heart Home for the Aged and the Cardinal Spellman Serviceman's Club. With three other sisters at home, Barbara enjoys a lively and affectionate family life. She looks forward to her own someday." And, with a master's degree in international finance from Sofia University in Tokyo and a stint on Wall Street, Barbara was also invulnerable "to any bullshit" the MIPS team tried.

After the MIPS group left, the Millers debriefed. Recalls Barbara, "I told Bob, 'I really like them. They seem to be a really good bunch of guys.' And you know what's interesting? I've never changed my opinion about them."

So Bob Miller came out West to meet with the venture capitalists behind MIPS, Gib Myers and Grant Heidrich of Mayfield and Bill Davidow, newly arrived at Mohr-Davidow Ventures. Grant and Gib had worked with MIPS from its founding. Davidow was a Silicon Valley veteran, most recently a senior vice-president of Intel and one of the co-holders of the "fail-safe" computer patent behind Tandem Computers. Davidow already had some ideas about a new type of corporate organization that might sort out MIPS's current confusion.

For Miller, this meeting with the venture capitalists was nearly as important as the company itself. Miller had his own prejudices about venture capital, most of them from dealings with East Coast venture capitalist giant Fred Adler: "Fred many times would ask me to go look at some of his companies and give him an opinion. Or he would try to sucker me into buying one of his dogs when the thing was already in intensive care and they were ready to pull the tubes out . . . diseased skeletons where people were really being exploited. It was bizarre. So I had a very stilted view of venture capital.

"So I came out and I met Gib and I met Grant and I met Bill Davidow. . . . Well, I didn't know if I was getting suckered or these guys were too good to be true, but they were such an extreme from the Fred Adler style of venture capital.''

Miller was intrigued and willing to push the MIPS deal to near the top of his list. A day and a half later, after visiting the company and having extended meetings with company executives and board members, Miller decided to cancel another interview—with entrepreneur-investor Max Palevsky—choosing instead to have a Saturday night dinner with MIPS's top management.

Miller came away from that day at the company and that dinner nearly convinced to take the job. He was convinced he could turn the company around and find the right management team to do so, but only if he had the support of the man Miller identified as the key figure in the firm: manufacturing and engineering vice-president Jake Vigil, a huge, taciturn man with dark skin, a bad eye, and the solitary manner of a grizzly bear.

"When I went into MIPS and spent the day there, I interviewed one-to-one everyone in senior management. And the only guy I couldn't read was Jake. I just couldn't get a read on him, the needle wouldn't move.

"Finally I said, 'Jake, would you meet me for breakfast tomorrow morning?' [Barbara and I] were in San Francisco at the Stanford Court Hotel, so I said to him, 'Look, the most convenient thing for me is if you could come into San Francisco.' He said, 'Oh, I'll do that.'

"So Jake came in and we had breakfast. And I looked at him and I said, 'Jake, let me ask you a question. This is going to come straight— you'll find one thing about me, I don't pull any punches—is there anything in this world that ever makes you smile?'

"And that's when Jake started talking. About his whole life. And I sat there listening, and I finally said, 'Okay, at least now I understand.' ''

Miller informed the venture capitalists that he was taking the job.

For the ex-IBMer, arriving at a Silicon Valley start-up was a series of rude shocks. MIPS wasn't Big Blue, nor was it Data General. This was a little company in two buildings that was demoralized and nearly broke. It had slashed its employment rolls by nearly half to 150. It had burned up most of its $20 million in venture capital. Much of the furniture was surplus. After three years of effort, MIPS still didn't have a product strategy that worked.

The first order of business then was for Miller to go hat in hand and beg investors for more money. He learned quickly that not all Silicon

Valley venture capitalists were like Heidrich, Myers, and Davidow. One of his first visits was to Valley pioneer Don Valentine, head of Sequoia Capital, a $400 million venture fund. Sequoia had been involved in an early round with MIPS and was more than dubious about doing any more.

The meeting was, to put it mildly, stormy. "You can have confrontation, but it doesn't have to be personally demeaning confrontation," Miller would recall, comparing the experience to being asked to kiss the cardinal's ring. "Yeah, I think that's what he was looking for. And there was no way he was going to get it from me. Jake Vigil was with me at the meeting. And I think Skip was there. And Jake kind of said to me beforehand what Valentine was going to be looking for—and I said, 'Well, he isn't going to get it.' "

But that wasn't the end of it. Soon thereafter Miller was contacted by Sequoia with a question that "really pissed me off. . . . It was like 'Mr. Valentine wants to know if it bothers you that your vice-president of engineering doesn't have a degree?' You know, a real shit way of asking it.

"And I said, 'No. And let me tell you something: my sense with Jake Vigil is that if there's one guy you can always take to the bank, it's Jake Vigil. He's going to tell you when you're in trouble. He's going to tell you when you can make something. You can just take him to the bank.' And that's been my experience with Jake ever since."

Just as difficult for Miller, after the button-down world of IBM and East Coast business, was getting used to the unusual nature of office life in Northern California. For example, soon after his arrival, there was trouble on the manufacturing line. Many employees on the line were Vietnamese, primarily boat people. Most spoke only limited English and few had any technical training. So, like immigrant groups before them, they tended to cluster with their compatriots in companies where they had some foothold. MIPS, for some reason now forgotten, was one of those firms. And, as was common practice in such situations, there was one individual who served as the ad hoc spokesperson for the group.

At MIPS that person was Tu Chau. In the early days of MIPS, when the company needed to hire new assembly people, it had merely to ask Chau and he would appear the next day with the required number of Vietnamese men and women. As the new employees were inevitably hard-working, disciplined, and legal residents, the arrangement worked neatly.

But it couldn't last forever. With the arrival of Bob Miller, the infusion of new capital, and the changing business strategy, the company began to expand. And, in one of the first steps of this expansion, Jake Vigil hired a lieutenant to take over supervision of manufacturing—an experienced professional named Judy Sims.

The explosion on the assembly line was nearly instantaneous. Suddenly Tu Chau, who had been the quintessence of the reliable, low-key supervisor, seemed to undergo a personality inversion. He became belligerent and was under so much emotional stress that his health started to collapse. Then he started making accusations, first at Vigil and ultimately at Miller.

"I talked to Tu Chau after he wrote me a letter essentially accusing us of discriminating against Vietnamese. So I called him in. But before that I got a hold of Sweeney and said, 'Let's check out this guy's background. I get the sense that we're not dealing with some guy who was working a rice farm before he came over to the United States.'

"And Joe did some checking, including talking with Tu Chau himself, and found out that Chau had been a colonel in the secret police in South Vietnam.

"We finally realized that Chau clearly saw himself as the spiritual leader of his ethnic group at the company, and he was now suffering an incredible loss of face.

"He was [basically] a politician. And what's the most powerful thing a politician can bring to anything? Jobs. And so he was a jobs broker: He'd tell other Vietnamese, 'I'll get you a job in MIPS.' Prior to [Sims's arrival] Chau could, if he wanted to hire somebody, simply hire that person. And none of the Vietnamese were breaking the code of silence, and that in turn was giving Tu Chau more and more power in the community.

"Now all of a sudden, some of his candidates weren't getting jobs. And, on top of that, to have a woman come in and doing the rejecting. It was too much."

Chau soon quit MIPS. But for months afterwards, even away from the firm, he still acted as the spokesperson for the MIPS Vietnamese employees, advising them, sending over job applicants, asserting his waning power.

Dealing with a Southeast Asian contingent within his firm was only part of Miller's initiation into Silicon Valley life. Equally disconcerting was the odd mixture of hard work and casual manner that pervaded the community.

"One day some employees came to me and asked,'Do you mind if we all wear costumes to work on Halloween?' " He laughed in remembrance, "You definitely don't see that kind of thing at IBM.

"But I was definitely concerned at the time about morale in the firm being so low. It was just terrible. What I used to say to people is that a start-up should be fun, it shouldn't be painful. It's supposed to be exciting. But if you went around MIPS at that time you'd have heard comments like, 'We're just this small little company and not only do we have all these problems, but we behave like a large company. People are just not relaxed.'

"So I said 'Okay,' not thinking who the customers were who might be coming on Halloween."

The customer was Sumitomo Electric Industries, Ltd., a crucial potential strategic partner. And it wasn't just Sumitomo, but Kosaka, Sumitomo's president, and his retinue.

"So, that morning, our receptionist shows up in one of those real high-quality gorilla outfits. I mean really high quality—you had to look twice to see it wasn't an actual gorilla behind the counter.

"And these Sumitomo guys come walking in for the meeting, Kosaka and the crowd, and they're like WOW!" Miller imitates stunned paralysis. "You know how the Japanese are so big on studying the environment they're going into. Well, these guys just stood there looking like everything they've been told in the Japanese handbook about Silicon Valley had just gone out the window.

"So, we finally get them into a conference room. I was sitting with my back to the door. And all of a sudden I see Kosaka's eyes get as big as silver dollars. So I turn and look behind me and there's Red Bob in a full wet suit with flippers on, and he's going by walking backwards."

It was a measure of how far Miller had come that, at an employee gathering in mid-1989, in a play on the press stories about MIPS's "over-the-hill gang" of veteran executives, Miller and his management team showed up in cowboy regalia riding broomstick horses.

These were some of the lesser known, more human requirements that came with being a CEO, a job that in the cold listing of the prospectus was announced as paying $311,863 per year, plus an option for 200,000 shares of stock at $2.03 per share.

Also not mentioned in any description of the CEO's job duties was the personal participation in the tragedies that inevitably befell any grouping of human beings. No amount of pay was sufficient for this responsibility.

A case in point was the man in the wet suit, Robert "Red Bob" Knox, a tall, rangy young man who earned that nickname for his long red hair and beard. Red Bob was one of those individuals whose specialized expertise and dedication make them fixtures in any business, so that they seem as permanent and as irreplaceable as the very walls themselves.

Red Bob was the computer guy, the man who set up MIPS's internal computer network. He hooked up everyone's equipment and told everyone how to use it. He seemed to know everything there was to know about personal computers and data networking. "If anything happened to your equipment," recalled public relations director Bev Jerman, "you didn't touch anything, but immediately called Red Bob. And he'd make things right."

One Saturday morning Bob Miller got a call at home from Jake Vigil. The police had telephoned MIPS. Red Bob had drowned in a scuba diving accident off the coast of Santa Cruz—in the wet suit he'd worn that Halloween day at MIPS. The only phone number the police found in Red Bob's wallet on the beach was that of MIPS. To Miller and Vigil fell the task of notifying Red Bob's parents.

Monday morning all of MIPS was in shock. After the dark days, when the company was at last beginning to turn around, now to lose Red Bob, a man almost synonymous with the company. It was decided, almost without saying, that Red Bob would be fully vested his 10,000 shares in MIPS, to be awarded to his family. And, as a gathering of employees watched one afternoon, a small tree was planted in Red Bob's memory on the lawn near the front doors of MIPS headquarters. And a few months later MIPS employees arrived one morning to discover to their pleasure that Red Bob's tree bore bright red blossoms.

Bob Miller could see Red Bob's tree from his office window. It was now half again as tall as when it was planted. And somewhere out there, an elderly couple were holding 4,000 post-split shares of MIPS stock—

Red Bob's legacy, his reward for having worked toward a day he wouldn't live to see.

But of course, that legacy would be valueless if MIPS failed in its attempt to go public.

Just one more burden on the chief executive. As the Concorde slipped through the Arctic night, Bob Miller took one more pass through his road show speech.

CHAPTER 13

Road Show

FROM BOB MILLER'S DIARY:

12/4: 2½ hours sleep. Presentation to Morgan Stanley Sales-Europe at 8:30 A.M., then one-on-one with Touche Remnant at 10. Interesting, semi-tough questions . . . primarily around technology licensing issues. Robert Fleming [of U.K. Investment Co.] one-on-one at 11 A.M.: nice guy, had good knowledge. Presentation went well.

Then went with Morgan Stanley's people to Butcher's Hall for first group presentation. About 20 individuals, all potential investors. Stephen Lowe [from Mercury Asset Management of London] sat on my right at lunch, was very knowledgeable. Interesting: many investors said the MIPS IPO was the first high tech IPO they had looked at in years.

Left for Edinburgh at 3 P.M. on a charter. Question by pilots to us before take-off: "Just in case of fog is it okay to land at Glasgow?" Thick fog on take-off—10 seat jet with 2 engines, one flight attendant. Light fog on landing—in the blocks at 4:30 P.M. Met by two Rolls-Royces. To Caledonia Hotel. Reception 5:30 P.M., presentation at 6. Five potential investors—very young, very cynical. Concluded at 7:30 P.M. Dinner in Edinburgh: candlelight, would have been very romantic except I was with six guys. In room at 10, called office. To sleep at 11:30.

12/5: Up at 6:30. Slept like the dead. Totally caught up in this now. Out of the hotel at 7. Steven Strandberg [of the Morgan Stanley team] got word that Touche Remnant and Stephen Lowe each signed up for 150,000 shares. Ludvigson and Steve bet that we'll get more than 10,000 out of Edinburgh.

Wheels up at 8 A.M. In the blocks in Zurich at 10:45. At hotel by noon; start presentation at 12:30. Good audience; excellent response from the Swiss. My presentation is smoothing out.

Out by 2 P.M. Wheels up at 2:30. Into Geneva at 4:00. Bill Berger, Cowen salesman, gives us a one-hour walking tour—brisk—of Geneva. Really beautiful; it's Christmas season. The Boes breaks out his Humphrey cap [a British driving cap] for the first time. Unfortunately I don't have my camera.

Geneva turn-out is good. A fellow from Lloyd's Bank says he intends to buy. But, for the first time, I saw two people in the audience sleeping.

Well out of Geneva at 8 P.M. In Paris by 9, at George V hotel by 9:30. ICR, the Morgan Stanley Associate, has been doing a great job on logistics.

We get to the rooms—mine is 50 yards long. I can't believe it! Then the porter brings up two bags. Only they aren't mine. And he only speaks French. I don't know how to explain. He disappears. First time on the trip I've had any anxiety. Then 15 minutes later a new porter shows up with my bags.

We go to dinner at a 5-star French restaurant. Food is out of sight. I have duck and escargots. Wines are great. Morgan Stanley picks up the tab; KR has to use multiple credit cards.

Paris is as beautiful as ever. In room at 1 A.M. Call office. Sher tells me that I have a message from Hoomin Toong [a former MIT professor, author, and MIPS employee who is taking care of Jonathan, Bob Miller's teenage son from his first marriage]: Jonathan still has a sore throat. I told Hoo to take him to see Rich Lenon [a friend of the Millers].

Talked to Jake—everything okay. Talked to CB—we're still having problems with Gain [Communications Inc.] and Sumitomo workstation orders. Boesenberg says Gain had many DOAs on last shipment—ugh! Told her to talk to Garth [Neil of MIPS] and keep in touch by fax. Called Babs at her sister's. Everything okay . . . says she misses home. So do I. Oh well.

Finally get to sleep at 2:30 A.M. At 3:00 Hoo calls. He says he's got Jonathan an appointment with Lenon, but worries that Lenon says he hasn't treated anyone Jonathan's age for 20 years. I told Hoo that Lenon was the best. Finally to bed.

12/6: Woke up at 10 A.M. Good sleep. Coffee and a half-croissant. Pack and out. Ian says Robert Fleming placed an order for 150,000 shares. Head for one-on-one at Parabas. Chuck and I get into limo. Ludvigson, Strandberg, and Ian get in the other. Chuck and I are so busy talking we don't notice the driver isn't moving. When we ask he says he's waiting for KR. We inform him that KR isn't going to Parabas. Then the driver says he doesn't know how to get there. We say, "Follow the other limo." He says, "But it left ten minutes ago."

Boesenberg and I look at each other: We've got Inspector Clouseau for our driver.

We finally get the address and get the driver going. We arrive in time to see Ludvigson, Strandberg, and Ian still standing out front. We tell the driver to pull over. He says "Okay," then proceeds to drive us around to the side door.

At this point the history of the road show and of MIPS itself nearly changed. As the limousine pulled in front of the hotel, Miller opened his door and began to step out. "My next image was of something flying by and sparks coming off everything."

From the limousine behind Boesenberg saw Miller begin to climb out, and then, seemingly from nowhere, a Peugeot roared past and clipped the door with a crash, sparks and pieces of torn metal dragging on the ground.

"Oh, my God," he remembers thinking, "They just killed our president."

The Peugeot, its passenger-side quarter panels nearly torn off, careened to a stop against a distant curb. Miller, stunned, carefully climbed out of the limo and checked the damage. Like any Silicon Valley president approaching an IPO, he had often warily joked about the chief executive of Eagle Computer who, on that firm's Going Public Day, had gone out drinking and celebrating with his yacht salesman and then died when his Ferrari went off the freeway into a Los Gatos reservoir. Miller, by a fraction of a second, had just missed an equally absurd exit.

In something of a testimonial to Mercedes, the limo's door had only suffered a dent "the size of a half-grapefruit," Miller recalled. "Meanwhile, the Peugeot was wiped out. Its whole side was gone. Our driver looked pissed. But it was the guy in the Peugeot I felt sorry for."

Shock and all, there was still no time to waste. Investors were waiting inside the hotel. Miller turned to Strandberg, pointed at the wrecked

Peugeot, and said, "I think Morgan Stanley just bought a Peugeot."
Then he and the rest of the road show team raced inside.

After all that, the presentation goes well. The audience had done its
homework. On to the reception. Great audience of about twenty. Very
responsive. Strandberg feels this is my best presentation to date—
something about close brushes with death that are exciting. I decide not
to try duplicating the experience when [the road show makes its most
important presentation] in New York City. I'll have to get up for that
some other way. . . .

The team walked out of the Bristol to find a new limousine waiting for
them, but with the old driver. "Boy, that guy was absolutely pissed at
me," Miller would recall. "He looked at me like, 'You stupid Americans. Do you know the pain you cause me in my life?' "

. . . Morgan Stanley has a suite at the Bristol. We change after, then hit
the Paris streets. I go to La Nan Bleu and get Xmas presents. Then we
walk to the Arc de Triomphe down the Champs Élysée. Go to the top of
the Arc, but still get back to the Bristol with three minutes to spare and
head for airport.

   In line at the JAL terminal, we discover John Sculley [Apple Computer CEO] is in line in front of us. Chuck's old boss. It definitely is a
small world. . . .

During the flight Boesenberg and Miller gave Sculley a version of
the road show, complete with hard-copy prints of the slides. "He was
very impressed—I think," said Miller later. "He's a hard guy to get a
read on."

. . . En route get faxes—this is definitely a world of improved
communications—major deal summaries: Hyundai, Microsoft, Digital,
ABI proposal. Also, Strandberg, Ian, Ludvigson, and I are really beginning to posture on when to close the [stock offering] deal. Dave, Ian,
and I favor after New York. Morgan Stanley wants to do whole U.S.
road show.

   Sleep 1 hour on plane, then work. Twelve hour flight, I'm going to
need another 2 hours sleep . . .

*   *   *

At this point, Miller's diary changes. From pencil to pen. The forward slant of his writing shifts to a backward slant and the words become increasingly illegible. Some dates are missing, so all subsequent listings are approximates.

12/5 [over International Date Line]: Arrive Tokyo at 3 P.M. local time. Airport really empty—unbelievable. Get into Tokyo in 1½ hours—also unbelievable. At the New Otani Hotel by 5:30. Get into a dispute with the bellboy—no way to change the Japanese process—he *has* to carry my bags.

Get to room. Shower/shave/dress. Buy Mont Blanc pens [for a side-trip: a contract signing with a customer, listed only by the code name "Thor"]. Call U.S., everything okay. Dinner with Morgan Stanley guys, then back to room. Confirm 7 A.M. meetings, then call Barbara. Everything is okay.

To sleep by 11 P.M.

12/6: Up at 5 A.M. Call office. On phone for 1½ hours between Thor, Hermes [code name for a U.S. company], and J——. Then down to meeting with Tom Laux [MIPS sales manager in Japan], Yasu [of J——], Ludvigson, and Boesenberg. I tell Yasu that if they don't take more than 1000 of our boards I don't want them as a customer—sometimes a president can be a PRESIDENT.

Off to Thor. Meeting with E—— is great. I give him pen after I sign the deal. He's delighted. No question they think the deal with us is important. (E——'s office overlooks Tokyo from the top of the "Thor" building). K—— (company president) made a cameo appearance.

Ian tells Dave that [stock orders] are now up to 24 million. . . .

We head to reception at Palace Hotel. Jack Wadsworth, who runs Morgan Stanley Japan is the host. A really neat guy; he took Apple public. Shows me photos of the Apple closing dinner—Jobs and company look like they went out of their way to look like slugs. . . .

We have a great meeting. About 50 investors. Carter McClelland [managing director of Morgan Stanley's technology group] shows up. Good old Carter, really being coy with me over the demand for the stock. But Ludvigson tells me Carter is excited when he talks to him. I invite Carter to go to Seoul with me—he politely declines.

After reception go to Morgan Stanley's Tokyo office. It's very clear Wadsworth runs a tight ship.

I call office to get DiNucci. He's left a voice mail on the restaurant where I can reach him. I call; they ask what he looks like. I say he's the handsome short bald guy with a beard. Five seconds later he's on the phone. Joe confirms Chung at Hyundai is not going to negotiate manufacturing commitments. [Later, Miller would explain: "What Hyundai wanted us to do was give them a volume commitment that we would buy so much product from them. Which I wouldn't do."]

Okay, I say, then I'll go to Korea.

We head for the Narita Airport. Everyone else is going home at 6 P.M. I'm going to Seoul an hour later—where's the justice?

Anyway, it's off to Seoul. I sit next to a Standard & Poor's ratings guy on his way to "S" for a fun weekend.

Arrive Seoul 10 P.M. local time. K.S. Lee [MIPS's country sales manager for Korea] meets me. I'm tired and irritable. Of course, he tells me about the Hyundai [situation]. I really get pissed. Seoul traffic is a nightmare: 11 at night and it's bumper to bumper. Get to Hilton at 11:30. I tell KS no manufacturing commitment for Hyundai: he looks dejected. I call Barbara. Talk to Annie. Everyone's okay. Go to sleep at 12:30 A.M.

12/7: Wake up at 4:30 A.M. Call office at 5:30 to check bookings. Hear the latest comments from the SEC. Ludvigson, Latta, Segre, and Bennion are already working on answering them. They didn't sound major to me.

I'm told we didn't get the [replies to] confidentiality [comments] back to the SEC because of a snowstorm in D.C. on Friday. Well, so far now we've been through a Black Friday [the market's drop of 150 points in October], an earthquake and now a blizzard. Who ever said we live in a stable world?

Talk to DiNucci about conversation with KS. He confirms *no* manufacturing commitment.

Meet with [Hyundai] at 8 A.M. I like Chung a lot. Meeting goes great. We discuss philosophy: he agrees with right of first refusal concept without commitments on manufacturing. We've broken the deadlock. Everyone delighted. Meeting ends at 9:30. I go to room and call DiNucci. He's delighted too.

Off to airport. On plane at 10:45. Same crew. I sit next to a lady from W. Virginia who at 28 divorced an alcoholic husband and took 2 young children to Tokyo. Found a job, got remarried and is on plane with husband, Ron, who worked in Silicon Valley but is on assignment as president of his company's Japan operation. I admire the lady's sense of adventure. Reminds me of Barbara. God I miss her!

Get to Tokyo and call New York, Park Lane Hotel, and get Barbara. She's just gotten in after a night out with her girlfriends. United lounge at Narita [Airport] is as crowded as ever. Can't wait to get on plane.

In air at 6 P.M., headed for JFK. I'm dead tired. Have light dinner and sleep seven hours. Arrive at JFK at 4:30 P.M. Limo waiting. Into city to see Barbara. I can't wait . . .

After nine days, nearly 50,000 miles in the air, and an average of four hours sleep a night, the MIPS international road show had at last come to an end.

Bob and Barbara Miller spent the weekend Christmas shopping in New York City. Sunday night they attended the musical *The Fantastiks*, which they had wanted to see for years. Miller fell asleep during the first act.

At 6:30 Monday morning Bob Miller was on the shuttle to Boston. He arrived to find the city "dreary, cold, and snowy." Tuesday morning the team was back in New York for presentations there. Miller awoke to a message from Frank Quattrone of Morgan Stanley informing him that articles on the MIPS IPO had appeared in the *New York Times* and *Barron's* and that he "was worried that the SEC would jump us again."

Miller made a quick call to attorney Larry Sonsini: "Sure enough, [the SEC was] up in arms about it . . . and have refused to give us the confidentiality comments as promised because of this 'gun jumping' issue."

The domestic road show had begun.

CHAPTER 14

Heading Home

AFTER THE HYSTERIA of the international tour, the domestic road show was simply frenzy. The *New York Times* and *Barron's* articles on Tuesday morning landed like a pair of incoming artillery rounds.

Bob Miller recalled: "[Cowen partner] Barry Rosenberg looked at us and said, 'I've never seen a group so depressed over a good story.' And we're in the car and somebody says to Dave [Ludvigson], 'Well, these things are unavoidable.' And Dave replies, 'This one could have been avoided.'

"Let me tell you, Dave was fantastic during this whole thing. The Morgan Stanley people I think would tell you he was the best CFO they'd ever seen. Solid as a rock. What impressed me the most was that he saw the goal right in front of him and nothing was going to stop him from getting to that goal. And now these things not in his control were happening and he was like 'I delivered the financials; I got the audited stuff, I got the SEC filings in—and this crap is screwing everything up.' "

Back at MIPS headquarters the public relations department found itself in the unpleasant position of trying to undermine its own efforts.

MIPS had two public relations operations. The firm had worked with an outside agency, Waterside Associates, almost since its founding. Waterside's president, Jackie Ray, knew more of the history of the company than any of the firm's executives. The MIPS in-house public relations department consisted of a director, Bev Jerman, and her assistant, Joanne Hasagawa.

For more than a year Jerman had developed and implemented a publicity strategy to get MIPS on the map. By mid-1989, thanks to a flood

158

of press releases, interviews, and trade show exhibits, her strategy had begun to bear fruit. There had been the cover story in the Business Monday section of the *Mercury-News* at the end of May and another (in PR parlance) "hit" in Dick Shaffer's newsletter. The next big step, the cross-over into the mainstream national press, was to occur with the planned article in *USA Today*.

Then the earthquake hit and Bev Jerman's grand strategy began, by its own success, to sour.

The SEC has well-established rules regarding the quiet period, which stretches three months before and three months after a planned Going Public Day. During this period companies are not to indulge in extraordinary publicity efforts, but may continue at about the same level as during the previous year. The purpose of the rule is obvious: The SEC doesn't want companies to save up big announcements until the weeks just before or after the IPO in hopes of boosting the stock to an inflated price and then cashing in.

Its purpose may be clear, but the question of how to abide by the quiet period rule often sows confusion in the company about to go public. This is particularly true of a fast-growing, young company for whom the precedent of the past year may be an inadequate reference for the present.

That was Bev Jerman's lament as she tried to fend off press requests at the beginning of December and watched helplessly as story after story appeared. "I don't know what the SEC wants," she said. "We're a fast-growing company. This is nothing like a year ago. We're introducing new products. We're signing up new strategic partners almost every week. Are we supposed to *not* announce those things?

"And what are we supposed to do about stories that appear in the press? Our going public is a big story and everyone wants to write about it. We ask them to wait until after the IPO and they write the story anyway. We refuse to do interviews and they just dig up quotes from old stories and use them. And then the SEC blames us for the story when it appears!"

The *New York Times* and *Barron's* articles were just the latest and biggest of the articles that had appeared about MIPS during the quiet period. Still waiting out there and worrying Jerman the most was the *USA Today* article, which had been prepared before the quiet period. Whereas the other articles had been more the product of newspaper morgue research and quotes from industry watchers, the *USA Today* piece would be full of original quotes. As such, it more than any other article posed the real threat of sinking the IPO.

Jerman pulled every trick she knew, if not to kill, then at least to postpone, the article. She even tried contacting friends of the reporter, Kathy Rebello, in hopes they could explain to her the dangers that now accompanied this long-delayed article. But Rebello was implacable. An experienced reporter, she knew that she had a big story in her hands. Furthermore, she was growing increasingly irritated by MIPS's stalling tactics; its sudden refusal, after being so open, to provide information and quotes. *USA Today*'s readers deserved to know about MIPS, she believed, and not after the IPO.

Summoning her courage, Jerman at last called Rebello with a proposal: If *USA Today* would hold the MIPS profile until the day of the IPO, it would be given an exclusive interview about the event with Bob Miller. No deal, Rebello reportedly replied. The story was slated to appear the second week of December. Jerman and Hasagawa didn't know this, of course, but could only field calls from the press and wait for that one dreadful morning.

Meanwhile, the road show team continued its domestic tour, living on faxes and phone calls to headquarters. The presentation grew more monotonous, the faces in the audience more anonymous. Two weeks of practice had also made it more polished. The televised presentation, which consisted of Miller and company standing before cameras and monitors bearing faces from the cities in the Midwest and Northeast, was a mild diversion from a seemingly endless succession of hotel banquet rooms and the glow of an overhead projector.

What amusement the weary team found now came only from little moments of novelty and coincidence. For example, there was Boesenberg's Humphrey driving cap, which had made its first appearance in Paris. By the time the team reached Chicago, according to Miller, "it seemed like everybody on the street was wearing one." So Miller, keeping the joke alive, bought one for himself. Finally, in San Diego Ludvigson stepped into a phone booth to make a phone call and found just such a cap hanging there forgotten, and came out wearing it. This was taken by one and all as a good omen that the trip had been a success.

The final stop was San Francisco, just thirty miles from home. The show took place in the Embassy Room of the Mandarin Hotel in the city's financial district, a hotel surrounded by banking and investment—Mitsui Manufacturing Group, Citicorp Savings, Sumitomo Bank—and, appropriately, about a hundred feet away from the Pacific Stock Exchange.

Within the Mandarin Hotel, Bay Area Security was holding a luncheon in the "Boardroom" suite and, down the hall, Desk Scan-Tech Systems was having its Christmas party in the "Library" suite.

The Embassy Room was decorated for the holidays. The pale green room, with floor-to-ceiling beveled glass mirrors and floretted wood trim, was bedecked with pine cones and evergreen swags. Pine boughs hung from the chandelier, and a Christmas tree lit up a corner of the room. The only reminder of the hotel's ownership was a Coromandel screen which concealed the service door. It featured images of mandarins of another era.

The mandarins of this era sat at a score of tables crowded into the comparatively small room. Sober and besuited men and women, with name tags announcing employers like First Interstate Bank, Transnational Bank, and Commerce Bank of San Francisco, they lunched on a seafood selection of mussels, clams, shrimp, crab, and lobster. As they began the dessert of strawberry shortcake, Frank Quattrone of Morgan Stanley stepped to the podium and opened the presentation.

He began with some housekeeping, noting that the number of shares offered in the IPO was now down to 4.25 million because one of the "selling shareholder companies has decided not to sell" its half-million shares—good news in one sense, as it showed investors wanted to hang on to their MIPS stock rather than unloading.

Quattrone went on to note that "we expect to price the offering sometime next week subject to SEC comments.

"As many of you know, the MIPS initial public offering is about the most eagerly anticipated one that we've seen in quite some time. The reason is that MIPS is the clear leader in a new technology called RISC that is changing fundamentally the computer industry. . . .

"We believe that MIPS stands to be a primary beneficiary of this trend because the company has the leading RISC technology in the marketplace, it has a very innovative business model, and it has a world class management team aboard." He closed with a version of the phrase that had enjoyed more mileage than the road show: "MIPS is a $100 million company that we believe has got a multibillion dollar management team."

Quattrone then introduced Miller, Boesenberg, and Ludvigson. Because the presentation was so close to Sunnyvale, other curious MIPS people had also sneaked up for a peek, including two of the founders, John Hennessy and Skip Stritter, and two of the venture capitalists, Gib Myers and Grant Heidrich. They were also introduced.

Miller stepped up to the podium wearing a double-breasted pin-striped suit with the lapels a tad wide, suggesting that he'd bought it years before for such rare occasions. He began his talk like a stand-up comedian doing the weary routine: "Thank you very much, Frank. On behalf of all of us at MIPS, I can't tell you how happy we are to be here, back in San Francisco. MIPS, as you know, has been on a road show. It's been about fifteen days, and this is kind of like playing fourteen away games and finally getting a chance again to play at home. During that time we've made this presentation thirty-four times, traveled 28,000 miles, been on seven different airlines, eaten thirteen different chicken dinners—six of which were edible—and now we finally get to come back to San Francisco and tell you about our company and what it is that MIPS is all about."

Miller's presentation was as smooth as one might expect from a man who'd lived it for two weeks. The overhead slides came up at the right moment, the proper emphasis was placed on the proper words, there were no deviations from the script after the custom-fitted opening, like an engine rolling down the tracks:

"Probably the most important thing to know about MIPS is that MIPS owns the technology that at this time is revolutionizing the computer industry. And that technology, I'm sure you all have heard, is RISC. . . .

". . . In fact, the name MIPS, even though generically in the industry is known for 'million instructions per second,' when the company was founded by three people from Stanford, actually stood for 'microprocessor without interlocking pipeline stages.' So, when people talk about RISC, the thing they need to understand is the importance of pipelining, not necessarily that it's a small number of instructions . . .

". . . Another thing you should understand is that we set out a strategy over two and a half years ago that the key to the success of our company was to make its architecture pervasive, as pervasive in the nineties as the Intel [80286/80386] architecture was in the eighties. . . .

". . . Now what's very important to understand about a corporation's commitment to an architecture is that it's not like buying a PC through a purchasing agent; it is a fundamental strategic decision, because the microprocessor represents the important engine of change in improving the performance, the functionality, or the cost-effectiveness of future products. So, when the companies you've just seen [listed on the preceding slide] make a commitment to MIPS, they've made a strategic decision—usually at the senior executive and most often at the board level. . . .

"MIPS is also a company that has been able to achieve design links to corporations that are known to be the world's best system developers. . . . In two cases, Digital Equipment and NEC, internal programs were *terminated* to adopt the MIPS architecture. . . .

". . . The other thing that's important to understand about MIPS is that it has a very unique business model. . . . We didn't have hundreds of millions of dollars to invest in building leading edge plants. We didn't have thousands of salespeople and application engineers around the world that could reach the tens of thousands of engineers who could be customers for this technology. We didn't have the field service and support organization of four or five thousand people that could be in place around the world to report what we saw as the high unit volume potential in this type of architecture. And we didn't have the credibility: We couldn't exactly walk into DEC and tell them to bet the next ten years of their product line on us.

"But we went forth with a relatively innovative approach, that said strategic partnerships are important. We found people like NEC and Siemens who could invest hundreds of millions of dollars and have thousands of salesmen to give us marketing leverage in high-end process technology. We found Tandem to help us with the customer support problem. We found Kubota, who was willing to invest to build a manufacturing plant in Japan that would allow us to dual source our system products and relieve some of the pressure on our workers back home. And MIPS has been able to put together this consortium in a way that, unlike many of the high growth Silicon Valley companies—we don't have the same cash burn rates and can take advantage of what other people have proven themselves good at . . .''

Miller's final road show speech was over in fifteen minutes. He introduced Boesenberg, who spoke for a similar time on MIPS's marketing strategy. Then Quattrone introduced Ludvigson, who spent just five minutes giving MIPS's financial profile, most notably MIPS's impressive 60 percent gross margins and research investment of 15 percent of revenues. He also noted an industry leading average of $225,000 of annual revenue generated per company employee; and took pains to explain that the company's current 35 percent of income coming from licensing and other technology revenues could be expected to decline to 20 percent in future years—another way of saying that MIPS was not simply endorsing royalty checks but actually building products.

Then Miller took the podium to close the pitch: "What you've seen so far is a company that's a very young company, but one that has managed three product generations, who has managed a major transition out of the component business, who has built substantial channels of distribution in a very short time, and who has some of the leading computer companies as its customers. . . . So all of the key elements of the infrastructure and the support structure are in place to take this company through a major growth phase.

"The other important element of growth, one that I think the people in this room, more than any others we've probably talked to anywhere in the world, can appreciate, is that this management team has the experience and the ability to manage that growth. . . . This is not a company that is doing on-the-job training. . . ."

Now, to throw caution to the wind: "In fact, what you have with this corporation is a company that is positioned to be another Hewlett-Packard or Digital Equipment or IBM. It's a company that has the infrastructure; it's a company that has the market share leadership in what promises to be the next fundamental architecture in the computer industry. And it's a company that represents what I believe will be a model of doing business through partnerships in the 1990s. In fact, if IBM or Hewlett-Packard or DEC had been founded in the 1980s, instead of thirty or fifty years ago, it's my belief they'd look like MIPS [does today].

"Thank you very much," finished Miller, looking relieved. "We'd be happy to take questions now."

The first question dealt with the competition from Sun's SPARC model RISC architecture and Sun's claim to have a thousand applications developed for it.

Miller replied that Sun's product had been around longer, and MIPS was catching up in applications. Further, he noted "the fact that it's been over two and a half years since they announced SPARC and it's only been Sun that has adopted it in a meaningful way. . . . My belief is that [Sun has] a very fragmented strategy and I don't see its being a long-term player in SPARC as anything but a proprietary architecture for Sun." So much for MIPS's biggest competitor.

The next questioner asked if MIPS was concerned that NEC would be using MIPS's architecture to capture as much of the microprocessor market as possible. On the contrary, Miller replied to general laughter, "we encourage that because we'll just get more royalties from them. It's in their contract and they'd better get used to it."

The next few questions, about royalties, were answered by Ludvigson. Then a few on compilers and software were answered by Miller, including one about copyright or patent protection on MIPS's architecture, the keys to MIPS's kingdom. Miller's answer demonstrated, for the first time in the presentation, the value of the company's much-touted executive experience:

"How do we make sure after we're a great success that our competitors don't knock-off our compilers? While I could say that we have copyright protection and so forth and that we have other legal patents related to the chip which would make that somewhat legally difficult, I really believe, and this goes back to my own experience, that what we've accomplished with these compilers makes it very, very difficult [to copy them]. People would have to risk literally hundreds of man years to come up with something to replace them. . . . And I don't think that would be a practical thing to do."

From that moment Miller was in command. When someone asked when would MIPS realize that it couldn't make enough money in the chip business and focus on the systems business, Miller replied, again to laughter, "I think we realized that in 1987."

Finally, Lissa Morganthaler, a highly respected analyst with the *California Technology Stock Letter*, whose tough questions the road show team had dreaded, raised her hand. She lived up to her reputation. How, she asked, was MIPS, as it continued to "forward integrate," ultimately to keep from competing with its own customers?

Miller leaned into the microphone and replied, "We hired Chuck Boesenberg just to answer that question." The room laughed.

Boesenberg stepped up, "My family thanks you for that question [more laughter]. The key is that we're a RISC *technology* company. We provide RISC technology at all levels of integration: microprocessors, boards, and full systems. My ideal world is to have someone like Lockheed going out for bids on a project. They're a DEC customer, so DEC will be bidding their [MIPS RISC-based computer]. Meanwhile, Tandem's in there, too, also bidding with our architecture. There's a value-added reseller there, too, bidding a package that has their software on top of our system. But MIPS, as MIPS, is not there. One thing we won't do is come in through the side door and bid straight for that business. Rather, we'll have customers who are competing with other MIPS customers, adding value to the platforms that we're providing. That's how you manage conflict.''

''We won't compete with our licensees,'' Miller intoned, as if it were a sacred oath.

A couple more questions, and then Quattrone wrapped it up. Miller, Boesenberg, Ludvigson, and Stritter remained to answer private questions from a few lingering analysts. They did their best to look interested, to act as if this was the first time they'd heard the question, to come up with a suitably intelligent answer—and not to think about how that night they'd be sleeping in their own beds.

And then, to the sound of busboys clearing tables, MIPS's IPO road show was over. There were just six days left until the planned Going Public Day.

CHAPTER 15

The Home Front

SOMETIMES IT SEEMS as if the process of going public is like some sort of cruel initiation into the exclusive club of publicly owned corporations.

A company, especially in electronics, typically decides to hold an IPO to gain the capital needed to support its current explosive growth and to move up to the next level in its long-term development. In immediate terms, what that means is that the firm is growing so fast that it is seriously overextended in management, personnel, research and development, and manufacturing equipment and running short of cash and space.

Further, usually by the time a tech firm goes public, it and the market in which it competes have reached a sufficient magnitude and maturity to attract a host of giant competitors ready to swoop in and make the business their own.

Finally, by the time an electronics company is ready to go public with its stock, it is usually three to seven years old. Most of the founders are usually gone, having stormed out or been purged, and those who remain are, not surprisingly, exhausted from the years of hundred-hour work weeks, collapsed marriages, and the demands of riding through a young company's ups and downs. The employees are exhausted, too, having carried double or triple duties for months because hiring has not kept pace with expansion. In many such companies top executives can be seen on the loading dock helping to fill orders to meet shipping targets.

So now, take this young firm, torn and frayed from competitive battles, explosive growth, and overwork, and drive it through the going public gauntlet. Take top management, for whom there are already not enough hours in a day to run the firm, divide it in half, and put half of it through a grueling marathon of all-night meetings and then a debilitating round-the-world tour. Next, take entire departments of the company's middle management and devote them to filling out government paperwork or undermining everything they've done in the months before. And finally, distract every single person in the firm with the prospect of a big payday to occur sometime in the near future, but on an uncertain date.

Do all of this, and then demand that the company not only survive this process but actually continue on its already precipitous growth path or risk devastating financial punishment. And, of course, offer no guarantee that some external force—an indiscreet remark by the secretary of the treasury or a meeting of Middle Eastern oil ministers—won't render the whole ghastly, miserable experience utterly pointless, or worse, actually destructive to the firm's future.

And that is what going public is all about.

With the chairman and CEO, the executive vice-president of marketing, and the CFO being dragged around the world giving speeches, the task of keeping MIPS not only alive but thriving fell on the remaining executive team. In particular, responsibility went to the executive vice-president of field operations, William D. Jobe, and the senior vice-president of engineering and manufacturing, Jacob F. Vigil.

Aside from their sober names and comparable age, it would be difficult to find a more unmatched pair—the tiny, loquacious Texas cowboy salesman and the giant, taciturn Hispanic builder from Los Angeles.

Bill Jobe was so small and thin he looked like a chronic invalid, but his apparent emaciation had a typical modern source: Jobe had been an obsessive runner for fifteen years, proud to point out that he was one of the rare over-40-year-olds who has run an under-three-hour marathon.

And like a true electronics executive, he was obsessed with the quantification of his achievement. On any given day, as on this one in the first week of December 1989, he could list his running mileage in year-to-date (3,830 miles) or lifetime (40,470 miles). On these December runs he sported a new T-shirt that announced on the front "40,000" and on the back "Anything worth doing is worth doing to excess." On high-stress days it was not unusual for Jobe, 51, to leg out a brisk twenty miles. "If I ever need a charge, I just go run," Jobe would say proudly.

What was most stunning about the first encounter with Bill Jobe was his voice—a big, strong, Texas drawl that seemed to emanate from the

soul of a born salesman. Smooth, witty, impossibly friendly, and optimistic. The voice of a man who could not only sell you anything, but
make you thankful he did.

On this day, sitting in his office wearing jeans and a striped rugby
shirt, Jobe somehow managed to look exhausted and animated at the
same time.

"Yeah," he said, explaining his clothes, "it's been a crazy time. I
just got back from a twelve-day business trip in seven different cities and
got home at ten last night. I looked at my schedule and I didn't have any
business meetings, so I decided to wear jeans. I'd worn two suits alter-
nately during the trip, so I took those to the cleaners, along with one tie
I'd dripped lasagna on.

"I tell you, either schedule, the road show or the business trips, is
really tough. I don't envy the guys on the road show, not after they've
told the same story two or three times. In fact, I'm waiting for someone
to shoot at us, because that always happens when you do an IPO."

Jobe expected one such shot might come from the SEC. "Bureaucrats
can decide anything. And with the backlash from all the savings and
loan scandals, they'll be looking for ways to say, 'See? We *are* regu-
lating. We *are* serious about these things.' "

Jobe, a man almost obsessed with finding the positive in any situation, vented a not-unexpected salesman's frustration at Miller's philosophy of including every bit of bad news in the prospectus. "I had a
couple customers that we gave copies of the prospectus to come back
negative, saying things like, 'Hey, just how solid are these [strategic
partner] relationships? We've read the prospectus and it looks like
they're pretty shaky.' I mean, here we've gone overboard to assess all
the risks and to list them, to disclose them, and here we are now with
customers looking and saying, 'This is not so hot.' " Jobe shakes his
head, "Yeah, right, this failure of a company.

"I was looking at new [IPO] registrations in last Friday's *Wall
Street Journal*, and there's a computer company that's selling two million shares, with an additional two million shares of warrants. And I
look at this thing and say, 'Who are these guys?' I've never heard of
them. And I thought, this is crazy. Some unknown broker that I'd
never heard of, an investment banker, was bringing them out. So I
grab the *Wall Street Journal* the next week and in the earnings reports
there's the company—with revenues of $667,000 and *losses* of like a
half-million or million.

"Now tell me, how does the SEC let one like that get out? Our company has no debt. We're solid. Our balance sheet is sterling—in terms of ratios better than almost any computer company around. And we have cash."

This attitude and way of speaking are probably chromosomal. Jobe was born in 1938 in Corsicana, a small county seat fifty miles south of Dallas in central Texas. His grandfather had a wholesale grocery business in Sweetwater and "my dad was also always in sales. He sold a lot of different things. At the time I was born he was responsible for tires, batteries, and accessories for the whole state of Texas for the Service Oil Company. Then he got drafted, so he was gone a lot.

"During the war he was an instructor in ordnance in Baltimore, and after getting mustered out in '45 or '46, he ended up getting a Buick dealership. So now he wasn't on the road, so our life kind of changed. We moved to the outside of a small town called Coleman [south of Abilene in west central Texas]. We lived on a small farm and also had some farm property outside of town. Livestock. Before I was out of high school we had five hundred head of angora goats and some sheep.

"I went to Texas A&M University. It turned out to be one of the best moves that ever happened to me; but the reason I went there wasn't the same as most people connect with the place—football and girls—but because the students wore uniforms. Not that I particularly wanted to wear a uniform, but it meant that everybody had the same clothes, so it leveled people out. So you could be a farm boy from West Texas like me or you could come from a wealthy family in Dallas and it didn't matter because you all looked the same—and that meant you made a lot of friends and developed a lot of friendships.

"And I needed that, because frankly, we were in pretty tough shape. We'd had a seven year drought in West Texas and it had almost wiped my dad out. I paid for my first year by selling the '50 Ford that I'd bought and paid for myself while in high school. See, I'd always had a job someplace. I always worked. My first job was at age 7 selling newspapers for the *Coleman County Chronicle*. I like the commission structure: I sold each paper for a nickel, gave two cents back to the paper and kept the remaining three cents. I tell you, that was a great commission. I've never had a 60 percent commission since. After that I sold magazine subscriptions and used cars for my dad's company.

"So, I went to Texas A&M. Total expenses were $1,049 the first year and $400 of that was covered by selling my car. It was a great experience. I still keep a lot of the friendships and I'm a truly dedicated alumnus—I was just down to the A&M-Arkansas game recently—and over the course of my career I've personally arranged for the donation of over $1 million in new computer equipment to the school.''

Jobe decided on a degree in mechanical engineering, primarily because of a strong interest in automobiles, though he found himself taking many electrical engineering courses. Money remained a serious problem, unfortunately, and Jobe had to leave school for a year to earn tuition. He took night classes during his time off, but didn't graduate until he was 23 years old.

This hiatus turned out to be critical in Jobe's life, because he discovered that sales was his career. ''I was selling lithographic supplies for a company called Graphic Litho Supply and one month I was named salesman of the month. I sold more than anybody else, including full-time salesmen in places like Dallas. All I was doing was trucking around East Texas selling, but I made a late call one afternoon and sold almost an entire printing plant to the *Athens Banner Review*. That was just the right moment to make that one extra call.''

Offered a paid graduate assistantship in electronic engineering, Jobe stayed on at A&M for a year to pick up his master's.

Finally, in 1953 Bill Jobe picked up his sheepskin and, although he had worked all his life, went out searching for a real career. His first job was in the structural test lab of the aerospace group of LTV Corp. ''doing instrumentation and computer data acquisition-type work.'' He hated it. ''One day I was sitting at my desk and I said, 'What am I doing here? I was happier out selling. I'm going to go find a way to get a job selling technical products. Something that I'd be really good at.' ''

So he walked out of giant LTV to a tiny start-up called Sigma System, where he was the company's first official employee. With typical start-up company job title inflation, his first title was director of engineering. Two years later it was vice-president of engineering and marketing. ''That was my plan. I added the marketing role and then hired somebody to do the engineering and worked myself out of that job. That officially made me a marketing person and I've been one ever since.''

Jobe looks back on his early days at Sigma as his touchstone for engineering legitimacy. For one thing it was where he earned his one and only patent. But even in those memories the marketeer comes to the fore. Jobe still has an old Sigma strain gauge system he developed which was used in structural tests on the Boeing 727, 737, and 747 airplanes and to measure the pressure of the ice hitting off-shore oil platforms in Cook's Inlet, Alaska. Jobe likes to "look at it from time to time" not just because he developed it, but because of how he did so.

"The thing I'm proud of is that I got the order done under a demanding schedule. I think I worked 105 hours that week. I basically didn't sleep. We had a deadline because the ice [at Cook's Inlet] was getting a lot worse and we had to get the system up there and installed fast. I got the contract on Friday and delivered the first units one week later. And they were painted and the front panel was engraved and they worked.

"I did a lot of engineering," Jobe says with a rare full seriousness. "I think I'm still capable of picking up a tech manual and reading something and learning. I think technical sales requires that. You can't just be a smooth salesman. At a company like MIPS, where you're selling technology and high performance and RISC computers, you've got to know the product, and be able to express that."

By 1967 Jobe was sure enough of his abilities to start "a manufacturer's rep and a distributor kind of company," and in May of that year he founded Data Engineering of Dallas with a partner and $12,500 in cash. "We felt that small computers and peripherals were going to be a big deal." A year later, when Data General was founded, Jobe quickly fired off a letter of introduction, and his company became the first sales representative for soon-to-be high-flying Data General. That one hastily written letter made Bill Jobe a wealthy and powerful man.

Data General soon became the top line at the little company, and Jobe in turn helped make Data General a success. "I personally sold 10 percent of their worldwide production the first two years they were in business." Not surprisingly, before long the computer company came head-hunting. "Data General convinced me I really had a career with them. They kind of muscled me, I guess you could say, but they also made it worth my while. I got a lot of stock. I joined the company on a full-time basis on December 7, 1970, and stayed for eleven years."

To begin, Jobe remained in Texas, becoming Data General's southern regional manager. "I got that region going so well it was the absolute tops in the nation. Nobody beat us." Most of the sales came from selling to the prospering gas, oil, and chemical companies of the then booming Oil Patch.

Expanding into the southeast, Jobe shifted the strategy to focus on wholesale distributors and communications. His biggest coup was "closing" the Napa Parts chain, still one of Data General's biggest clients.

Now increasingly well-to-do, Jobe began to indulge in his private obsession, fast cars. For a decade he raced sports cars—Corvettes, Formula Bs, Opals, and Mazdas—and held records at a number of race tracks in Texas and Oklahoma. Later he raced at Watkins Glen and some other northern tracks, won the governor's trophy at the Arkansas Grand Prix, and was U.S. Corvette racing champion for two years.

At the same time he managed to put in eighty-hour weeks at the sales office. "By the end of 1973 I was running at 157 percent of goal. Meanwhile, the western region was at only 49 percent of goal, so they asked me to take it over. Well, it wasn't too exciting a prospect, except they sort of whispered in my ear that if I had national ambitions, this would be a good step along the way.

"So I came out here and ran Region 7, the northwest region of Data General, based in Palo Alto. I got to know the neighborhood—and started to love California."

A little too much, it seemed. Jobe's reward for taking the northwest region from 49 percent to 80 percent of goal in a single year was to be called back to Data General headquarters on Route 128 in Westborough, Massachusetts, to become a vice-president and national sales manager.

He hated the promotion. "I never got used to that snow. The first thing that happened, I went out of town on a one-week business trip and left my car parked at DG. When I came back, it was covered with snow and ice frozen around the wheels. Even after I dug the car out, I still couldn't get it to move. I had to get help from people in the plant—this is like midnight, you understand, and freezing—to help me push the car out. I didn't have a snow shovel or anything.

"And then there was the great blizzard of '78 while I was there. In fact, the first three years I was at headquarters we had the worst winters New England had seen in decades. All I could think of was 'Get me out of here!' "

Despite the climate, however, Jobe's boundless optimism again prevailed. And this time it was well placed. Data General was one of the hottest technology firms of the era, even, thanks to Tracy Kidder's *The Soul of a New Machine*, emblematic of the computer revolution.

And Data General's biggest cheerleader was Bill Jobe. "I was very happy. I was enthusiastic and I was driving it and I was interviewed by

magazines and things like that and I was given awards and I was building something. I loved DG. I had a huge DG logo painted that was about
30 by 40 inches and it hung on my wall with a spotlight on it. I was Mr.
DG. When you've sold the first machine and you've helped build the
company and your heart and soul is in it, you just feel so personally
proud. When we made the Fortune 500, I made for everybody in the DG
sales force a T-shirt with a 5 and then two DG logos for the zeros. And
when we hit the New York Stock Exchange, it seemed like we were
going to be a billion-dollar company. I was so motivated and so happy.

"Then, in 1979 things changed. And DG changed. And it has never
recovered." For Jobe, the mistake came when Data General decided to
manufacture its own chips for its computers instead of creating over-
lapping contracts with semiconductor vendors. As a result, without the
insurance of multiple sources, when yield rates fell on a crucial DG
input/output chip, there was no backup. Computers couldn't be built,
orders couldn't be met, and the company began to lose market trust.
"That's one of the reasons that Bob [Miller] and I, when we got together
and strategized MIPS, decided that we were going to get ourselves out
of the semiconductor business and have world-class manufacturers—
like the NECs, Sonys, and Siemens of the world—build our chips.

"So anyway, DG missed its target for the last quarter of the fiscal
year 1979. And that was enough. See, until then Data General had not
been a company, but a state of mind. And I was one of the captains of
the state of mind team. You might notice that things are fairly positive
at MIPS, too. Believe me, wherever I am things are positive because I
do not think negative thoughts. I wake up in the morning and I think
positive thoughts. Look, if somebody asks you how you're doing and
you say, 'Well, I'm doing sort of shitty today,' do you think they're
going to ask you again tomorrow? But if you say, 'Fantastic! I'm going
great!' they'll want to get in line with you; they'll want to work with
you."

Data General had stopped being a place of Jobe-like optimism and by
1982 he was gone, returning to Silicon Valley to become president of
now defunct Plexus Computers, then a manufacturer of multiuser UNIX
computers. As if to verify Jobe's claim that people flock to the man with
a positive attitude, a coterie of talented Data General salespeople followed Jobe and stay around him still. MIPS currently has on its rolls
members of Jobe's old DG Region 7 team, including Mike Powell,

Mike Lanigan, Dick Patkonsky, Mark Santura, Brad Hebert, and Bill White, MIPS's western regional manager, eastern regional manager, Denver district manager, customer service manager, Oakland salesman, and senior sales rep, respectively.

After Plexus, Jobe became a venture capitalist for the Cypress Fund in Menlo Park, just yards from the offices of MIPS directors Davidow, Myers, and Heidrich. It was Davidow who recruited Jobe to MIPS, a decision made easy by the presence of old Data General compatriot Miller, whose speech on the three phases of a salesman's career apparently was decisive.

Once at MIPS, Jobe, considering his three-year venture career a vacation, returned to the staggering pace of the early days at Data General. And the effort showed. In September 1989 alone, MIPS closed major deals with Nixdorf Computers and Groupe Bull in Europe and American Airlines and Control Data in the United States. "See," says Jobe, "for the last two years every deal for MIPS has had to be a new deal. And that means all of us, including Miller and me, have been involved. We've also stretched the legal department every way from Sunday. But that's what it takes. I've been through this before. It's only after a period of time, after contracts are established and customer relationships are established, that you can bring in an account manager to handle the account."

Not that Jobe isn't feeling the pace. "Back at DG, around '74, '75, I sort of got a handle on things. I still worked hard, but nothing like before—or now. I showed up in the morning about 8:30 or 9:00 and usually worked until 7:00, 7:30 at night. Sometimes I worked later and I flew on weekends sometimes. But I just didn't do that crazy breakneck thing any more. And now I'm back doing it again.

"[For example] I'm catching a flight on Christmas day at noon for Seoul, Korea. The sun will never set, but I'll arrive on the 26th. I have a dinner that night—which effectively means my Christmas dinner will be over business in Korea.

"I'm there for two days and then fly back here. But here it'll be only Wednesday morning the 27th, so I save another day—and that gives me three days left that week to finish up deals, ship things, and get things on the books before the year ends. Believe me, that's the way it is. A sense of urgency is everything in this business. If you're trying to build a company like this and really build it fast and really grow it, you can't rest and you can't say, 'I can't make that flight on Sunday.' We ask that of people we hire, as well.''

It becomes apparent talking to other people in the company that just as important as Jobe's attitude and salesmanship is his ability to attract and keep experienced salespeople in a highly competitive employment market. Both Davidow and Miller knew that to land Jobe was also to get his team.

"It comes down to friendships," Jobe says in explanation of his team's loyalty. "And you also have to treat people right. It's okay in sales management to drive people hard. It's okay to work their butts off and it's okay to give them some tough goals. But then you've got to be willing to go over and work with them and help them make those goals. You can't just sort of sit back here in an ivory tower and expect things to happen. You've got to be out there leading the troops. You've got to be willing to work as hard as they do. You can never say 'I'm too tired.'

"My people can call me any time after six in the morning and they can call me at night until midnight if there's a problem—so there's only a six-hour window in which I have to get sleep. I'm willing to go anyplace, anywhere, anytime and do anything that's legitimate to help build the business and build friendships and build mutual trust and respect. And when you can do that, you can ask people to come back and join you again in a new company.''

Jobe has his own loyalties. "Mr. DG" has never forgotten and still regularly meets with a group of ex-Data General people called the Gray Eagles "to drink and talk about girls—just like a bunch of old college guys." The Gray Eagles, which he founded, provide not only continuity for Jobe in an industry in which relationships are repeatedly splintered, but also a recruiting ground for additions to the Jobe sales team.

And if Data General was his apprenticeship in corporate business, car racing taught him something about competition. As he got older, Jobe noticed something about himself and other aging racers, such as Paul Newman, whom he encountered at Watkins Glen in 1973. "You go out and watch the young rabbits and they run like hell. They're gone. But the next time you see them they're sitting in the pits or on the side of the track. Meanwhile, the old guys have the sense to look at the red line on the tachometer and refuse to take the engine past 6,800 rpms. They don't get in a big hurry and try to do it all in the first ten minutes.

"Same thing is true in Silicon Valley. Sometimes companies go out and raise a lot of money and run like crazy early on. They look like starters, but they don't blossom, they don't mature. Other companies, like Sun or Apple, start out looking like they won't make it, but turn out to have great staying power.''

Bill Jobe, at an age when most Silicon Valleyites begin to drop back in the race, has proven he too has staying power. And with that have come the trappings of success. He drives a Ferrari 308 to the office each day. And he talks of using some of his $10 million gain from the MIPS IPO to buy a place in Aspen, and, he half jokes, perhaps that new $300,000 Ferrari F40. He also intends to give some of his stock away to his mother, his daughters, and his nieces and nephews, children of his brother, who is a part-time preacher and who runs the Baptist student union at Steven F. Austin State University.

But Jobe will also remember that a life of hundred-hour work weeks and complete identification with one's employer comes with some painful sacrifices as well. In the mid-1960s Bill Jobe married, and the marriage produced three girls. (The eldest daughter, Stacey Sanford, seems to have the Jobe blood. At age 23 she works at Harris-Lanier in Fort Worth, and ''last month was the leading sales rep in her division. And she managed that despite spending two weeks getting married and going on her honeymoon!'') Jobe's marriage came apart during his tenure in Massachusetts. ''Unfortunately, that's one of the things that also goes with this work. Too much travel and relocation kind of strained things. I was married for about nine years and so I've been single now for fifteen years. It's hard.

''It's also hard to sustain a relationship. It's a very difficult thing and I've had some relationships, with a couple of really tremendous women, that have just come apart . . . and frankly, it's the stress of the job more than anything else. One of the things that happens to you is you go out of town on a twelve-day business trip and you come home. You don't feel like going on a date or entertaining someone. What you really feel like doing is going home and getting some sleep.

''One woman I was dating for a while, she wanted to know when I was going to be home and she would pick me up at the airport and want to party, and so on, because 'I haven't seen you for twelve days and I'm so glad you're home and I've been waiting for you.' But I would be comatose and thinking, please God, give me a Scotch and put me to bed. And that's not a good combination for building long, sustained relationships.

''I never expected, by the way, to be single for fifteen years. I thought within three years I'd be married. That was my expectation. I was thinking 'at least I'm going to stay single for two years, I'm not going to rush into anything.' Now here I am fifteen years later and I'm still not rushing into anything.''

And even as he says this, Bill Jobe manages a smile.

There is a plaque on the wall of the MIPS cafeteria next to the entrance to a corridor connecting the two headquarters buildings. It reads ''Jake Vigil Memorial Tunnel,'' and it jokingly celebrates the year of work Vigil spent convincing contractors and the Sunnyvale City Council to let the two leased buildings be connected.

Vigil doesn't find the plaque especially amusing. Jake Vigil is rarely amused by anything, and then, at most, he exhibits only a slight turning upward of the corners of his mouth.

Jake Vigil, at age 53, is a bear of a man, with dark skin and black hair dusted with gray and a bad eye that embarrasses him. He is tough, taciturn, very bright, and extremely loyal. He speaks with a deep but reticent voice. He is rarely kidded, even by his peers, and he is rarely seen chatting in the hallway. And he is the man upon whom MIPS truly rests.

No one at MIPS has come farther than Jake Vigil. He is likely the highest-ranking Mexican-American executive in Silicon Valley.

Vigil was born in the Latino community of Los Angeles. His father was a one-time professional featherweight boxer who had been wounded in World War II. With the boxing career ended, Vigil Senior worked as a junk collector running a second-hand store and tried to make a living mostly as a gambler—small-time stuff like horses, pool, and poker. As a boy Jake drove in a truck with his father collecting ''paper and rags and batteries and mattresses. . . . That was convenient for him because then he had his own schedule and could gamble at will.''

Jake's parents had split up just before the war, which was why, despite having four kids, Vigil Senior had been drafted. As a result, the boy was nearly 10 before he met his father, in 1949. Jake would sneak out and catch the old Red Car line to see his dad. ''I used to go stay with him downtown. My mom became aware of it and let me go stay with him. I used to shine shoes, sell newspapers on the corner—that's how I'd make a few bucks.

''Eventually, my mom and dad got back together again and I started working for my dad. By the time I was 15, I was already driving his truck. In fact, all through high school and even in the last year of junior high, I used to drive to downtown Los Angeles, to skid row, and pick up guys to work for us. They'd cover the two sides of the street and bring the junk out, and I'd drive behind them in the truck collecting it.''

At school Vigil was a talented if indifferent student. ''I was a good student until the beginning of high school and then I got involved with people who liked to have fun. Everything was a big joke.''

He also ran into institutional racism. ''I knew I was good at two things: Math was easy for me, and I was always good in woodwork. See, when I went to school, if you came from the Mexican community as I did, they just sort of floated you through the last years of high school. You were told to take a lot of shop classes. And I think it was because the stereotyped Mexican kid wasn't seen as worth the work it took to do more than that.''

Upon finishing high school, Vigil contemplated going to a trade school and becoming a contractor. But the process intimidated him, and besides, ''I had to get away; I didn't want to live at home.'' So he enlisted in the air force.

During basic training at Lackland, Vigil did so well on aptitude tests that he was sent to Chanute Air Force Base in Illinois to attend pilots' school. The barrio boy, accustomed to being told he was a failure, was stunned. ''It was a shock, because being a pilot was something important.'' There were other shocks as well, including ''suddenly finding myself in a strange place with two hundred guys I didn't know. I learned to make friends fast.''

But the third shock was the worst. ''They sent me to this special place to sign up for pilot training and within ten minutes they'd taken a look at my eye and said, 'We made a mistake. We should have realized that you're physically not qualified.'

''I went through a real downer from that. I mean, in a matter of a couple of days I had gone from thinking I wasn't going to do anything with my life for four years to being a pilot—and then, all of a sudden I get hit with my eye again.'' He shakes his head sadly, ''I used to hate my eye when I was kid.''

However, by a happy coincidence, Lackland also had one of the major electronics training schools in the air force. ''It turned out to be very fortunate for me it happened that way.'' Vigil, it seemed, had an aptitude for electronics, and his early success in this new field gave him the most important educational victories in his life.

''I took the first test and I aced it. And all of sudden I was motivated. I was determined to ace every test after that. And I did, the first time since junior high school. I ended up staying there for a year and a half as an instructor. Then I went to the Philippines—Clark Field—put in a year and a half, and then got discharged as a staff sergeant. I did really well. My air force experience was very enriching for me.''

During this time Vigil also attended college at the University of the Philippines, though not long enough to graduate, and he returned to the states with a plan to earn enough money to complete his degree.

Meanwhile, ''across the street from my dad's store there was this market, and my dad had become good friends with the owners. Well, it seemed the owners' son-in-law was a manager at Burroughs Corp. in Pasadena and all the time I was in the service my dad and this son-in-law talked about me, and this guy, Nick, eventually became interested in seeing if I would come to work for them as a technician. So, when I got out of the service, Nick wanted me to interview for the job at Burroughs. But I wanted to go to college.

''To make a long story short, I ended up going to a trade school, Western Electronics Institute, one of a lot of places in L.A. at the time [1959] that leveraged off GI Bills offering A.A. degrees requiring nothing but courses in electronics and math—just the stuff I liked. So I did that and went to work as a technician for Burroughs in 1959 at $1.90 an hour, in manufacturing out on the test floor.''

Vigil was soon promoted to the engineering department, and within a couple years he had advanced into an engineering design job. In the next few years the kid who'd once been told to stick to wood shop earned ''something like nine patents.'' From there Vigil was moved into management.

''See, starting with the air force, I realized I could do more than I ever thought I could and I kept wanting to push it to see how far I could take it.''

Unfortunately, as Jake Vigil himself now admits, his new-found ambition began to run away from him. Married in 1960, he was divorced by 1965. ''I got really fucked up. My values became confused. I was so determined to find out how far I could take this thing that I used to live at work. I remember not even going home.

''It went on for a few years. Then one morning I woke up and my wife said, 'You've got to make a decision here.' And I said, 'See you later.' ''

Vigil stayed at Burroughs for twenty-five years, participating in the evolution of computer electronics from vacuum tubes to transistors to integrated circuits. During that time, as he progressed through the ranks, he moved from Pasadena to the nearby City of Industry, then to Santa Barbara, and finally to company headquarters in Detroit as a vice-president and group executive in charge of five thousand people.

During this time, Vigil learned how to make a career and family coexist. He married for a second time in 1973 and had two children.

Sometimes, as he sat in his executive office in Detroit, Jake Vigil would look around in amazement at how far he'd come—and how few people could appreciate it. "My mom and dad were always really proud. They knew being a vice-president was something, but they didn't really understand it. My sister, who's a housewife, really had no interest. One of my brothers, who now has a swimming pool maintenance business, always felt good. My other brother, who was a heroin addict—he eventually died—didn't care about anything."

But Jake knew, and he was proud of himself. He had a "wonderful" job and he planned to stay in it forever.

Then, in 1983 Burroughs changed its management and though the company offered him a better job, Vigil realized he had to go.

"I can remember when I resigned. They offered me this unbelievable job. I went home and talked to Nancy—I mean, I would have given my life for this job. I could never have imagined being selected for something like this.

"My wife was very scared. It was not an easy decision to make, but I was determined to leave. I really had a total disrespect for the new management. And I felt like the company was done for and it was now just a question of when."

Vigil, to his relief, was immediately approached by two West Coast companies. One, represented by a friend and former boss at Burroughs, was in Oregon, but Jake didn't like its type of computers. He chose the other, a San Jose computer start-up called Elxsi, and joined the firm as chief operating officer.

Elxsi turned out to be a tough lesson in young technology companies. "I was very naive about money. I was told that they were in the process of closing [an investment] round, that they had commitments from the current investors, that they were going to do their pro rata share, that they were going to bring in $11 million in the next round. That it was almost a done deal.

"And I get there and they hadn't started the round and they were broke; in fact, they were trying to get a bridge loan. So it turned out that for two and a half years we were broke. What I learned from that was to respect the balance sheet—to understand it, pay attention to it, and know what its real value is.''

Elxsi was eventually sold off to the equally benighted Trilogy. ''I made nothing at Elxsi other than my salary. My stock was under water from the time I got there to the time I left. We sold the company because we didn't have any choice; we were broke . . . as soon as we closed escrow I resigned.''

Again, two companies recruited Vigil. They represented the two extremes of Silicon Valley: tiny, troubled MIPS and giant, stable Hewlett-Packard.

Vigil chose MIPS. ''I accepted the job. When I came in to sign my offer letter, I started shooting the shit with Vaemond [Crane, MIPS president at the time], and somehow we started about what I would do as first priority and stuff like that. We ended up getting into a lot of detail about the organization—and he drew out an organization chart that was in contradiction to what I had understood my job to be. 'Vaemond,' I said, ''look, I have just gone through two years where I've had to live with founder bullshit, and I'm not going to do it again. So either you give me the job that was described to me or I'm out.' And he said, 'It's your choice.' So I tore the letter up and went home and explained to Nancy what had happened.''

Vigil winces slightly when he considers how much his stock might now be worth had he stayed in 1985.

''So I found myself waking up the next Monday morning with no job and I didn't understand that. I'd never, since I was a kid, been without a job. So I called up Joel Birnbaum, the guy who'd been trying to recruit me to HP, and said, 'Let's talk some more.' ''

Vigil spent the next year working on the Hewlett-Packard Spectrum computer project, learning the workings of RISC processing. Nevertheless, when some friends called and asked him to join a firm they were starting, Jake was ready to jump. Just two years after spending a quarter century at Burroughs, Vigil found he no longer had a stomach for big company bureaucracies.

''I was real frustrated at HP because the culture there was something hard for me to be patient with. Here they had an enormous program they were investing in, hundreds of millions of dollars, and the problems were all very obvious. I could tell them everything that needed to be done to improve things. But because of the culture there, they wouldn't let me."

So Vigil met with the start-up team. The business plan was worked out on the living room table at a member's house. Jake was offered the presidency. He accepted and set out to raise investment capital. One of the venture capital firms he visited was Mayfield Fund, then struggling with how to save MIPS. Grant Heidrich immediately saw the value of merging the two firms—which eventually happened, the new company's product idea becoming the MIPS M6000.

But before that could occur, Jake Vigil would enjoy "a certain amount of vindication" in having Grant call him, say that Crane was about to be taken out of the firm, and offer Jake a vice-presidency at MIPS. This time Vigil didn't tear up the offer letter. He became MIPS employee number 96 (now, thanks to attrition, he is about number 40 in seniority). As for the other four members of the start-up, two still remain at MIPS.

Typically, Vigil quickly buried himself in the affairs of the struggling firm, right down to the details. The title he held then, senior vice-president of engineering and manufacturing, was the same as today, but the responsibilities were more extensive. "We didn't have much money and what we did have we tried to make go as far as it could." Thus, when the facilities manager quit "we couldn't afford to replace him," so Jake took over the job, which led him to the battles over the tunnel. "Miller used to kid me that the only thing that took longer to build around here was the Golden Gate Bridge." There was also the problem of the Vietnamese supervisor on the assembly line, a situation precipitated when Vigil finally found enough money to hire middle manager Judy Sims to direct the operation.

But the biggest challenge to Vigil was the arrival of Bob Miller. If Miller saw in Vigil an unfriendly, unreadable character, Vigil saw in Miller a manifestation of the kind of business creature he disliked most: an IBMer. "When I left Burroughs, it was the IBM guys that I left more than anything. There was Blumenthal, of course, but the staff he had immediately under him were IBM guys and I developed a great deal of disrespect for their style in a very short period of time. They're ruthless. And then I went to Elxsi and there I got involved with [Gene] Amdahl [of Trilogy] and I saw more of it. So then they send Miller in here, and of course Miller's from IBM. I thought, 'Holy shit.' Then on top of that he had a background that was similar to mine—engineering and manufacturing.

"So, before Miller left town on that first visit, I'd already told Grant that I didn't like it. That my first response was nil. But Grant says, 'You need to talk to him some more.' "

It took a series of events to change Vigil's mind about the new president. The first was the meeting the next morning in San Francisco.

Next came Miller's willingness to adjust to the Silicon Valley style. "It took him something like a year to adapt to MIPS. He had a hard time with the informality"—especially on that Halloween with Red Bob walking around backwards in scuba gear. "Employees would come in on dress-down day in the most bizarre clothes and, more often than not, by coincidence, there'd be some important customer here.

"Well, one time it happened and we were in one of Bob's staff meetings and you could tell Miller was pissed and in his own way he was complaining about the behavior of the employees. And Skip [Stritter] said, 'Why don't we get back at them? Why don't *we* dress down?' And Bob said OK and we did, just officers. It was for an all-hands meeting. We showed up dressed like assholes. And ever since then Bob has just been part of it."

The final step in Jake Vigil's acceptance of Bob Miller came with the news of the death of Red Bob. "I was flabbergasted by the news. I called Bob up—he hadn't been at the company very long at that point— and he and Barbara came in. That's probably the first time I saw a personal side of Bob. He was as affected by this thing as I was.

"It was some days later, when we were having a discussion about Red Bob that the decision was made—Bob made it in the end—to see to it that Red Bob's parents got the stock. It was really a nice gesture."

Vigil summed up his thoughts on his boss: "I tell you, Bob's a lot of fun to work with. He's a tough guy and he's very smart, but he's a pleasure to deal with. I always feel that when I say 'Let's talk' that everything is on the table, that there's no bullshit. I've enjoyed it."

To the impending IPO and the sizable reward Vigil will see from it, Vigil reacted with reserve and restrained enthusiasm. He sees Going Public Day less as a time to celebrate than as a challenge to keep newly well-to-do employees motivated. Already, he notes, one employee, Jerry Baudin, an "outstanding technical publications guy," has announced he'll be leaving the firm in 1990. As the potential harbinger of things to come, this worries Jake Vigil. For him, victory is not in going public, but in reaching that point—perhaps at $1 or $2 billion dollars in annual sales—"when the market will say about MIPS, 'Now there is a successful computer company.' "

That will mean years more of hard, hard work, something Jake Vigil doesn't mind in the least. But the bitter times in the 1960s have taught him to be more accepting of his success and recognize he has a personal life as well. Not even MIPS now will keep him from time with his wife and kids.

"I wish I knew of a way that I could leverage off my success to influence people who have the potential. I think there's a lot of people that will never have the luck I had. A lot of what happened to me was sheer luck. I was fortunate that I had the wherewithal to take advantage of it. My brother went into the service, too. Maybe he doesn't have the math aptitude I have, but he's not dumb either, and they sent him to school to be a supply clerk and they sent me to school to be an electronics guy."

He thinks about the racism in his past. "We have to make sure kids get the counseling they need to take advantage of whatever capabilities they have, so they don't piss it away. The world's come a long ways, but it's still got a long ways to go."

As for Going Public Day, Jake Vigil intends to put in his usual twelve-hour day. After all, there is always work to be done. And besides, that's how Vigil celebrates. Having spent thirty-five years "seeing how far I could go," he's at last content with how far he's come.

CHAPTER 16

The Immigrants

ON FRIDAY, DECEMBER 15, Bob Miller held his annual Christmas luncheon with the manufacturing department.

These gatherings were important in Miller's mind because he forever worried that manufacturing, being located in a building two miles from headquarters, felt forgotten by corporate. Even the environment of manufacturing seemed different from the rest of the company. Whereas the headquarters and marketing buildings were located on Arques Avenue, a major artery in Sunnyvale's portion of Silicon Valley, manufacturing's building sat at the far end of a cul-de-sac in Santa Clara, all but invisible.

Inside, the two operations were equally different. Unlike headquarters, the manufacturing building perpetually reminded employees that it was a temporary location, ready to revert to a former use at little more than a weekend's notice to the developer. That was why incongruous design features cropped up in the most unlikely locations.

The most obvious of these was a divider between the office cubicles for quality control people and managers and the more open area of assembly and test. This divider looked like nothing more than an abandoned stream, a thirty-foot raised tray of large river pebbles in which potted plants had been belatedly embedded.

In the headquarters building, such a display, no matter how odd, would remain pristine. But in manufacturing the rules were different. The employees had taken to inking messages on the stones. The two best known, resting nearly side by side, read "In memory of Yosh Sato" and "In memory of your youth/ Ben de la Rosa"—jokes on two of the hardest working and longest tenured employees in the department.

186

The company took pains to ensure that the manufacturing people felt a part of the larger company, but often these efforts only reinforced the difference. For example, a trophy was passed back and forth between the competing headquarters and manufacturing softball teams. And the conference rooms in both buildings were given somewhat whimsical names, but at headquarters they were named after wineries and in manufacturing after resorts.

Miller and Vigil worried about this matter continually, but they also knew the end to part of the problem was in sight. By next spring, if everything went to plan, all of the MIPS operations (except sales offices, of course) would be housed together on the company's new headquarters campus.

On this Friday, however, Miller wasn't worried much about departmental coordination. Rather, he was a little relieved to get away from dealing with the SEC and lawyers and underwriters, escape from the bundle of frayed nerves the executive offices had become, and have a pleasant repast with employees who remained concerned with what MIPS was supposed to be about: building computers.

Or so he thought. However, though their rewards on average might be smaller, the men and women working on the assembly line were just as obsessed with Going Public Day as their counterparts down the road. For many the impact on their lives of these small amounts would be far greater than that of the great riches to be garnered by the company's top executives.

Miller sat down at the table next to a tiny woman with big round glasses, apple cheeks, and a small, soft voice. A board tester and company veteran, she began to ask Miller about the IPO and when it would happen. Miller, knowing about the battles going on that very moment with the SEC and knowing that the entire deal could blow up at any moment, tried to put on a good face. And while he was doing so, he found himself more nervous and upset than at nearly any time in the whole going public process because he knew that this woman, "Connie" Nga Dang, had more resting on Going Public Day than anyone else in the company. She was the one person at MIPS Miller dreaded failing.

Connie Nga Dang is wearing a polka-dot silk dress, pearl earrings, and a gold necklace with a pendant in the shape of a rose. She could be a suburban housewife—except she is wearing a blue lab coat and is seated at a workbench, touching a probe to the integrated circuits on a computer motherboard and checking the results on a glowing oscilloscope screen.

In her soft voice Connie apologizes for her English. She says she has worked for MIPS for three years. "I choose this MIPS company because I have a friend. He work in here. He said this MIPS now is very good in the RISC. They use this new chip. And that's our company, growing up very fast. And I make application in here and I got review and I got a job."

Before joining MIPS, Connie worked for Altos Computer and before that the now-defunct Four Phase Systems. "I work with Four Phase almost four years and then that company, you know, is down and they lay the people off. Depend on the seniority. Therefore I got the layoff."

But change is an old, if unwelcome, visitor in Connie Nga Dang's life. On April 27, 1975, just two days before the fall of Saigon, her husband, a South Vietnamese army lieutenant colonel, told her to take the children and get out of the country. He stayed behind with his unit.

He is still there. So are Connie's brother and five sisters and their families. But Connie escaped with her five children. And, having lived her entire life in Saigon, she suddenly found herself in one new world after another.

First there was processing at Wake Island. Then a long flight to Fort Chaffee, Arkansas. She waited there two months, hoping for word of her husband.

It came as a telegram to Connie's cousin in California. "He said he cannot leave. He could not leave. And I cry. I want to go back to my country then, because with five children, one just 2 year old, one 5 year old, I just worry about how I can support them. Just me. With nothing. I left my country with just clothes only.

"So I ask some of my husband's friends and they said, 'You keep out and stay here. Take care of your children first.' They told me that if I go back my country, maybe the communists kill all my family.

"So I go to Catholic Church and they help me go to Missouri. I live in there about six months. A very small town. Marceline. Very cold in the winter."

Despite the fact that she was a Buddhist, the Catholic Church sponsored Connie and her family in Missouri. Within a couple of weeks they found her a sewing job. "I never use the sewing machine before with the pedal. Electric. Very fast. I was very scared."

During this time Connie learned that her husband had been sent to a

North Vietnamese prison—news that frightened her because she knew that such prisoners often died "because they lack the food and medicine and everything. But I send to my sister in Vietnam and she come to the North Vietnam about twice a year to give him the medicine and clothes and everything he need. He write a letter to my sister and my sister send back to me. I follow that; what he need and I sent it to him."

But in the meantime Connie had to tend to her children and get on with life in America. "Almost the first two years I'm very sick. I go to the hospital many times. Maybe I scared and worry too much about what I don't have, my new life, everything."

After six months in Missouri Connie and her children joined Connie's cousin in San Jose. For two months they lived there, ten to the apartment. The stress continued to take its toll on Connie. She spent three weeks in the hospital, the doctor finally telling her, "look to my children first, don't worry anything my country anymore."

She took his advice. Enrolling at San Jose City College, Connie spent two years studying electronics—coming just two general education classes from her associate in science degree before she had to drop out to get a job.

In time the dream of returning to the Old Country receded. The work was good and the children were growing up to be successful Americans. The oldest daughter married and made Connie a grandmother twice over. One son graduated from the University of New Mexico with a degree in petroleum engineering; the other is a manager in a software company. Her middle daughter earned her bachelor's in microbiology from Stanford, and the youngest, with no memories of her father, studied marketing at San Jose State and planned to study optometry.

Connie's husband expressed in letters his pride in the successes of his children and in the courage of his wife. In 1988 he was released from prison and returned to Saigon where he lived blacklisted from obtaining a real job and dreaming of seeing his family again.

Connie learned to get on with her life and to face the inevitable. In 1984 she obtained her citizenship. She also changed her name: "I changed to Connie because my name is very hard. They just pronounce it wrong. They call me N-yay. And when they call me that, I don't hear it. So I go by Connie now. And my first name now is a middle name."

Connie had found a career at MIPS. "I like this company very much. Yes, a lot of changes in three years. But the first year when I work in here my company look down. I worry. And after that the investor he put the money in here—Kubota—$25 million, and my company wake up and ready to continue with new products.''

Connie knows well that she holds a sizable number of stock options. ''Yeah, sure! If a company stock goes to the $14 and $17, one share, I just . . . how many I have and even if $14 . . . how about $17? How about over? Oh my God! Wonderful. I will have money. I will invest to my house, to my children.''

But first that money will be used to get Connie's husband out of Vietnam. For fifteen years she has dreamed of the reunion. Now it may be just months away.

But she has trepidations as well. So much has changed. The children are grown up now, and though Connie insisted they retain fluency in Vietnamese, they are now very much American. The grandchildren are even more so.

And Connie knows the greatest change has taken place in herself. The dutiful wife has served as head of the family now for many years. She has also developed deep loyalties to her company, often working late and on weekends to get a shipment out in time. She thinks about a friend of hers in a similar situation who earned her Ph.D. and teaches at a college in Massachusetts. ''When her husband come over here, they are so different. Opposite ideas. In my country the woman should stay home, take care of children. It was hard for her and hard for him, too.''

Connie has no intention of returning to the old ways. She has no desire to retire, even though her children are encouraging her to do so. She intends to stay on at MIPS. ''I still here until the company lay me off. I don't want to change. I like company. I want to stay here.'' Nor does she have any interest in returning to Vietnam, except to visit (''I live here forever until I die'').

After working so hard for so long, Connie Nga Dang is about to realize all the dreams of those lonely first days in Missouri. Soon, perhaps, she will have financial security and touch her husband once again. ''I just think about it and I wait and see.''

And the man holding the fate of those dreams in his hands sat beside Connie at the luncheon. And in his heart Bob Miller didn't know if he could make those dreams come true.

There were a number of other Southeast Asian immigrants at the manufacturing luncheon. It wasn't surprising that MIPS had so many Vietnamese employees, as San Jose enjoyed the nation's third largest population of Southeast Asians. They had settled here, often like Connie relocating from another part of the country, because of the strong Asian community in the Bay Area, the comparatively warm climate, and the huge number of entry-level jobs available in Silicon Valley in the late 1970s and early 1980s. During those early years it was not unusual to see a hundred Vietnamese, Laotians, Hmong tribespeople, and Cambodians waiting at a bus stop near a technical training school.

What wasn't as apparent to outsiders was a deep social bifurcation among these immigrants that soon became evident to welfare workers and city social services departments. The split matched the waves of immigrants. The first wave, which came between 1970 and 1975 with the fall of Vietnam, was made up mostly of city dwellers, many of whom were sophisticated and worldly, well-educated and professionally trained, and multilingual. It was this first wave that created most of the glowing stereotype that attached to the Southeast Asian. This group assimilated with astonishing speed into American life, producing high school valedictorians, politicians, developers, doctors, and business-people.

The second wave, which began in the late 1970s and continues to the present, consisted of the boat people. Typically rural farmers and shop-keepers, they had neither the wherewithal nor the inclination to escape before the communist takeover. Cities such as San Jose had greeted these new arrivals with aid programs established for the first wave—and quickly discovered those programs to be all but useless. The average boat person didn't need a preparation program for taking a bar exam to transfer a law degree; rather he or she needed to improve on a third-grade education. Computer programming was a long way off for a Hmong tribesman from highland Laos who just a few weeks before had tried to blow out a light bulb in the refugee camp. And then there was the psychological therapy needed for men who had been brutalized and tortured by the communists or women who had been beaten and raped by pirates in the South China Sea. For this second wave assimilation into American life would be long, slow, and painful. For some, experts predicted, it might take more than one generation.

Among the Southeast Asian employees at the MIPS luncheon were several boat people. One of them was a comparatively tall, thin man of 37 with a wispy moustache, wearing a button-down oxford cloth shirt and Levis. Bao Truong should have been part of the first wave of immigrants, but had been doomed to become a boat person. Now he was struggling to make up for lost time.

When South Vietnam fell in 1975, Bao was an army lieutenant, married, with a baby son. Like most ARVN officers, he was immediately arrested and sent to a re-education camp—a prison, more accurately. Bao's camp was located in the highlands, about seventy miles from Da Nang, a miserable change of environment for a young man of the Mekong Delta. Not only was the weather bad, but the food was rotten and there was no medicine: "I almost died. It was very good luck for me they let me leave after three years."

But Bao soon found that being a "free," sick ARVN vet in communist Vietnam was not much better than being in prison. "My family then was very poor because the communists, they took everything: house, car, everything. My mom alive, my dad is dead by then." While he was gone, his wife found the money to pay their son's secret passage out of the country.

"So mother, three sisters, and I left and there is nothing to work, nothing to do."

As a former army officer, Bao was not only blacklisted from any real employment, but held on a tight leash. "Every day I have to go to see the government men. Check in. Sometimes once, sometimes twice a day. I felt bad. I scared. I couldn't live with the communists. Very dangerous."

Bao heard a rumor that another boat escape was being plotted and that one could buy passage with gold. The family pooled its money: There was only enough for one person. The first thought was to send one of the sisters, as she had a new baby, but she was too frightened. The choice fell upon Bao. "So my family decided I should go, get work and send money."

Into a small motor launch—it was about 52 feet long—jammed 323 people. There were so many they could barely move and the boat rode in the water almost to the gunwales. This overloaded, old craft left its hiding place to set out on a four-hundred-mile journey down the coast of Vietnam and across the Gulf of Siam toward Malaysia.

Disaster struck almost immediately: "The first day the motor die. The engine is stop. So we drift. We just wait to die." The boat drifted for several days. The crowd desperately tried to signal to a passing plane with a single flashlight, but the plane flew on. Unknown to Bao and his fellow passengers, the plane was a U.S. spotter plane searching for refugee boats. It reported locating the overloaded and half-submerged boat, adrift inside the ten-mile limit, and soon thereafter reported spotting Vietnamese gunboats steaming toward the refugee boat, with an unpleasant rendezvous estimated at two hours.

The captain of the nearest U.S. Navy ship made a crucial decision. He ignored the international boundary and raced to rescue the Boat People. "I think I am very lucky," says Bao Truong.

After three months in a refugee camp in the Philippines, Bao came to Los Angeles looking for his son. The search took nearly a year, as Bao had lost contact with the cousin who was taking care of the boy. "When I came here, I don't know where he is. I sent the mail to the Red Cross to find my son and finally they tell me that he's in San Jose. And then they got me his phone number and I call from LA. This was 1980. He was eight years old. I hadn't seen him for more than three years. And then I came over and he is very happy and crying all day and he told my cousin that he's very happy to see me because before that he think that I die in the high mountains."

It seems that in the third year of Bao's imprisonment the government stopped delivering his letters to the family. Thus, the cousin had left Vietnam believing Bao had died and had brought that sad news to the little boy.

Soon thereafter, Bao moved north to live with his cousin and his son. He had already learned some English in an English-as-a-Second-Language school in Los Angeles; he enrolled at Foothill Junior College in Los Altos. After a few months Bao found an apartment and moved in with his son.

Over the next two years Bao earned his associate in science degree and then set out to find work. He joined a Mountain View company, Valley Data Science, as a technician, and when that pay wasn't enough, took on a night shift job at nearby Control Data. "I work two jobs at same time. Because I need that money to help my family [in Vietnam]. I work sixteen hours a day. Sometimes more than that. I had a babysitter for my son." Each afternoon Bao would rush home from Valley Data Science for fifteen minutes, prepare dinner for his son, and then race off to Control Data to work until midnight. "Two jobs for about one and a half years. And so tired for that time. But I had to. I need more money to send to my mother, my sister."

He wrote to his wife until she informed Bao that she'd grown tired of waiting and remarried. A second shock would come when his mother died of cancer.

The only thing to do was to keep working harder. Bao quit Control Data and went back to school at night, studying chemistry and calculus. He dreamed of getting his bachelor's degree, "but I don't have time to finish because too many things to take care of."

When Valley Data Science went out of business, Bao found employment at Altos Computer Systems. It was from there that he was recruited to MIPS by production manager Tu Chau (who would soon leave in the dispute with Jake Vigil). "He ask me because he knew me as a very good technical debug on the board and he told me that 'If you want to, I introduce you to get interview with somebody over here.' And I say, 'Yes, if my salary is up, I will.'

"So, September 30, 1986, I come over here as a technician . . . my title is now Lead Technician.

"The first time I come here I see this company is small, compared with Altos and CDC. But I feel better. I feel good because the design over here is real good and that is why I stay here long. It's not just that though—I can make a lead technician in another company also. I don't know, I just love this company."

The 5-year-old son to whom Bao had to reintroduce himself is now 15 and a junior in high school. They share a room together in a six-bedroom house holding eight of Bao's Vietnamese acquaintances and relations. One cousin just arrived six months before after escaping Vietnam.

Bao was driven to give his son the life he missed. In the process, he gave up even more. He had little time to go to the Buddhist temple and "no time to go to the Vietnamese nightclubs. If I go out my son he feels lonely and then he cannot do his homework. I have to stay home and teach him how to do his homework. We play pinball together and sometime go out to movies. More time for him lets him do better."

The boy originally attended Fremont High School in Sunnyvale, but Bao pulled him out: "That school is too many Vietnamese guys. Some no good. His friend always call at night, sometime midnight, and wake all the people up. I told him they never call back again after 10, but they still call." The boy was sent to Santa Clara High: "My son is doing real well in school. He told me that if he finish with the high grade he can go straight to university. He love to go to UC Davis. Medicine. But sometime they change mind."

But university tuition is expensive. That's one reason Bao was look-ing forward to Going Public Day: "I always dream that our company go public. But don't know when, but we have confidence that we will go. Right now the customer is more than before. It's good work and we have more design, more product. So I think have to go public."

In his dreams Bao divided up his windfall. "At that time I can get money to buy house. And send money for my sisters. One got marriage last two years and they have a kid, so it's so hard. I hope to get the other two sisters out. It's so hard." With his son off to college and money in the bank, Bao might also find the time to get a girlfriend. "Me? I'm looking for. One day I have to have. I cannot live alone."

That day might come in an unplanned way. Just at the moment he was about to be rewarded for his decade of sacrifice, Bao found he might be burdened once again. He received a letter from his ex-wife telling him that she had escaped Vietnam and was in a Philippine refugee camp. "She says she is very happy to wait for me. I told her that 'you already got another husband.' " Bao didn't know whether the second husband was dead, divorced, or merely left behind. "I didn't ask her. I don't know what to do. I ask my son, 'If you want, you can live together with your mom. And then we'll see if we can all live together.' " Bao's life had once again been turned upside down.

So it was that at the MIPS manufacturing division Christmas luncheon, held less than a week before the company's planned Going Public Day, beneath the holiday cheer and the pleasantries there lay anguish. The company president made happy predictions while he feared that he might not fulfill them. And hanging intently upon each of his words were two employees—two immigrants and new Americans—whose minds were filled with thoughts of people rescued and new lives begun, of redemption and reunion, happy or bittersweet.

CHAPTER 17

The Last Battle

SIX MONTHS HENCE, too late to help the beleaguered team at MIPS during the final days, *Inc.* magazine would poll CEOs of newly public companies about the IPO process. It found the most common fears these executives remembered about the experience were: I won't be an entrepreneur anymore, I'll embarrass myself on the road show, I'll be forced to live quarter-to-quarter, my prospectus will be used against me, and I'll become the target of a hostile takeover. The top four most troubling consequences of going public, the CEOs said, were the cost and time of dealing with Wall Street and shareholders, the emphasis on short-term results and ever-increasing expectations, the lack of secrecy, and constant outside criticism. The upside was enhanced credibility, visibility, more options for future financing, better employee morale, and improved recruiting.

Asked how the IPO had made them better managers, the most common replies by the CEOs were that they had become more disciplined, efficient, focused, financially savvy, more analytical, and better communicators. But they also added that the long days and the emotional roller coaster had been physically and emotionally draining—and that the new pressure of being public never let up. "I feel like a squirrel in a carousel," one CEO would tell the story's author. "I just keep running."

After their successful road show, the presentation team returned to MIPS feeling jubilant. The news at home was equally good.

A few months before, on a trip to New York City, Miller and Jobe had been walking along the street when Jobe suddenly stopped before the display window of the Beaufort Gallery on the Park, a purveyor of bronzes, carpets, and art objects. His eyes lit up at the sight of his favorite sculpture, Frederic Remington's *Broncho Buster*. Though he was a wealthy man, Jobe could not bring himself to buy such an indulgence.

Miller put his hand on the Texan's shoulder. "I'll make a deal with you, Bill," he said, "if your sales team gets MIPS over $100 million in revenues this fiscal year, I'll buy that Remington for you."

"It's a deal," Jobe replied.

Now, on his return from the road, Miller was informed by Jobe that it looked as though MIPS would make its goal.

Miller was ecstatic at the good news. Reaching $100 million would be good for the new stock and was a major step in the evolution of the company. Any investor, customer, or competitor had to take a $100 million company seriously.

But if Miller was pleased, he was not really surprised. He trusted Jobe to come through. That was why *Broncho Buster* was already sitting in its wooden crate in the corner of Miller's office.

Of course, just to be sure, Miller had made a point to show Jobe the crate.

So, with a week left before the planned IPO date, MIPS looked perfectly positioned to conduct the last great stock offering of the 1980s. Too perfectly positioned. And, like the new financial decade it would inaugurate, MIPS's sense of assuredness was about to be tested under fire. For Miller, his image of the MIPS airplane tumbling, burning, down Wall Street, would grow more vivid by the day.

The first concussion had actually come a month earlier with the pricing meeting. Miller expected this one. Stock prices are typically set just days before the issue, when the state of the market and the health of the company are pretty well known. Pricing sessions often become the moment when the first hints of distrust between company and underwriters surface. Wars can break out over a dollar a share difference, lifelong animosities can develop over four bits. Underwriters see the pricing session as the moment when their wisdom and expertise in the stock market come to the fore and when they often have to pull company executives down out of the clouds to reality, force them to abandon their greedy personal dreams of wealth, and face the fact they are about to be a public company, answerable to shareholders. The company executives, in turn, often come away from the pricing session embittered.

Until this moment the underwriter may have seemed to be their greatest advocate, but now, when it is too late to turn back, the underwriter turns on them; indifferent to the company's needs, the underwriter now takes care of its own image, low-balling the price to guarantee the maximum number of shares sold to look good in the proposal to the next sucker.

Miller had an idea of what was coming and developed a strategy. He chose as a meeting site a less-than-neutral location: his own house. And he decided to be willing to bet the entire offering to get what he wanted.

Barbara Miller was there, offering food and coffee to the feuding groups as they split up and caucused in different rooms, regrouped, and argued some more. She knew Bob wasn't going to settle for a low pricing, especially not after some of her friends on Wall Street had called and said, "Boy, when that stock comes out, it's going to go out at a premium. Everybody down here on the floor is talking about it."

So, when the Morgan Stanley people announced their "strong recommendation" of a $13 to $16 range, Miller nearly blew his top. "We had a little meeting, including calls back to New York City. [Headquarters] had obviously told Quattrone to get $13 to $16. And I said, 'At $13 we don't have a deal. We're not going to go out.' And they said, 'Well, we'll have a gentlemen's agreement that we won't really sell it at $13. We'll just put $13 to $16 on the prospectus.' And I said, 'I think any number you put on that prospectus you should be willing to sell the stock at. So that's it. Let's just call it off if you guys really believe in that.' "

The meeting ended with the formal estimated price of the MIPS stock at $14 to $17, but not before, according to Ludvigson, Quattrone had theatrically gotten down on his knees in Miller's living room and begged for the $16 price ceiling.

Then had come the wildly successful road trip and the subsequent glowing reviews from analysts and now the upbeat sales numbers. It should have been time to start chilling the champagne . . . and yet.

And yet, there was an unpleasant and growing murmur about the MIPS IPO emanating from the Securities and Exchange Commission building in Washington, D.C. Sonsini and Latta had both warned the MIPS team to expect the SEC to challenge sections of the red herring and to demand rewrites, further elaborations, or more obvious warnings to potential investors.

That was all in the game; that was the SEC doing its job. And it was even expected, in the aftermath of Boesky, Milken, and the go-go market of the 1980s, that the SEC might lean on MIPS, since it was the biggest tech offering in a while, in order to put the fear of the God of Securities into the next wave of firms going public. Besides, the SEC might see it as a good precedent to set for the 1990s. The MIPS people weren't worried—theirs wasn't some fly-by-night company trying to pull the old cut-and-run; there were no big skeletons in the company's closet; the company could answer any question the SEC might ask.

But by early December even the lawyers were showing their concern. The standard drill was that the company submits the red herring documentation and the SEC comes back with a list of questions. The company then shows its earnestness by answering those questions in the most complete manner and in the shortest time possible. The SEC ponders the answers for a while and then comes back with a new list of questions that are refinements of the first. The company and the SEC volley back and forth for several iterations until the last point of difficulty is cleared up, the SEC declares the offering "effective," and the company goes public with the sale of the stock. Not an easy process, but certainly straightforward.

Until the late 1980s going public was slightly more difficult. In those days the company also had to file a pricing document just before the IPO. It was that document that often led to the red-eye plane flights to Washington. With the change in procedure, the initial public offering was made similar to a regular stock offering. According to Bob Latta, "the SEC doesn't see the pricing information until the final prospectus is filed; which is a couple days later because it's got to get printed. And it takes twenty-four to forty-eight hours to get those fifty thousand copies from the printer." This intentional ignorance of pricing is proper, says Latta, "because the SEC is not supposed to be a fair, but only an equitable, judge of an offering. Its job is to assure full disclosure; so it doesn't need to know price because price is irrelevant to what it's doing."

About half of the states, in what is called "coordination," automatically clear an offering once the SEC does. The other states want to know the price, as they choose to judge the fairness of the offering as well. Latta frowns, "It's a non-Adam Smith, protectionist orientation those states have." But the impact of those state judgements is still minor compared to that of the SEC.

With MIPS, the SEC was changing all of the rules of the dance. "Usually," says Latta, "what happens is you get the first [SEC] comment letter and it has thirty or forty comments in it. You respond to those comments and most of your comments stick. Some don't, and of those, on some you choose to play hardball.

"So, let's say you start out with forty. You winnow it down to ten or five. Then you give them the answers on those that they really wanted in the first place—that you were trying to get away with not answering. They accept and that's it.

"Well, on the MIPS deal we got about seventy comments in the first letter. Then we got two more sets of comments—and one of them had nothing to do with the prospectus! It had to do with jumping the gun on publicity. So we got close to a hundred comments. And then each one went through three or four iterations. They were just raking us over the coals. We got more iterations of comments than I'd ever gotten before."

With a crudeness born out of frustration, Miller likened the growing battle with the SEC to "the turd in the punchbowl. You don't know where it came from and you don't know what to do with it."

Latta: "The number of comments and the distribution of them and the way they were, it was pretty clear that the SEC was trying to slow down the deal. Why? Because they felt it was overheated. And they were right. It was overheated. This deal was getting much more publicity than they were used to."

Miller: "I was worried that if the SEC really was in the punishment mode, they could go back and really hit us on the stock option price. Not that it would be legitimate, but they could position themselves well. They'd done that with other companies where they'd said 'for the last two years stock option pricing hasn't been any good. We want you to pay X number of dollars per share.'

"And so I kept waiting. And, of course, what they kept doing was introducing new issues. It wasn't like normal; they didn't keep working the same set of issues. No, they'd say, 'These are the X, Y, and Z issues, but we have more and we're not going to tell you what they are.' And I was just waiting at any moment for them to demonstrate that they were really pissed and hit us on stock option pricing. And that would have hurt [company profits]—and we would have really taken a hard position on the matter to justify our stock options and that would have taken time. And we didn't have time."

But the stock option challenge never came—a clue that the SEC didn't want to kill the offering, just cool it down and buy some time.

But MIPS didn't have time. Says Latta, "Clearly, the SEC staff thought, 'Oh, this is just overheated. It needs to cool off for a week or two.' They felt, 'What's the big deal? Christmas is a shitty time of year anyway. Let's just slow this deal down until Christmas. They'll never bring it out between Christmas and New Year's. So, we'll see it the first week in January. What's the big deal?'

"Now, no one ever said that to us [the SEC also does not talk to the press], but my hunch is that that is what they were thinking, 'Look, this is a lousy time of year. At the end of the year the market's got nothing better to talk about than MIPS—whereas in January you get the January Effect. This deal will cool down. Lots of fun stuff happens in the market in January anyway, so it won't be the one big deal in front of everybody's nose. So, it'll be a better time to bring the deal out.'

"The thing the [SEC] couldn't figure out was why we were working so hard to push the deal. They didn't realize that if the deal had not gone that week, it would have been disastrous. If we'd had to wait until January, we'd have had to close out the fiscal year. And no way could we have gotten that done before the end of January. Then we would have had to amend the prospectus. We'd have had to recirculate it. We would have had to do a new road show. It would have been middle to late February before the deal would have been brought out. I don't think the staff at the SEC even thought about that."

Caught in the middle was Ludvigson, who, if the IPO suddenly collapsed, would have to shoulder most of the blame. One morning, exhausted, he would complain, "The problem is you don't know if they [the more difficult the situation became the more the SEC was referred to as "they"] are just being cavalier or what; whether the guy is overloaded with work if he's trying to jerk us. It's hard to tell. I think they really try to do a diligent job, but on the other hand, when you get somebody ticked off, they tend to do whatever they want."

Once-removed from the fray, hearing only the reports from the front, Miller grew increasingly angry. The IPO was the culmination of the first phase of his grand strategy to turn MIPS into a great corporation. And now that strategy risked ruin not from some mistake on his part, but from the death of a thousand cuts inflicted by the SEC.

Adding to his fury was the realization that other, more questionable companies were happily going public during this period when the SEC was coming down hard on MIPS. "I saw the prospectus of a company that went public about the same time we planned to. Well, I'm reading this thing and I see the chairman of the company was part of a divorce trial in which a restraining order was issued against him, which he violated and got thrown into either a jail or a mental institution for six days. There are three pages of lawsuits ranging from not paying their suppliers to not paying their taxes, from defaulting on bank loans to tax infringement. The company has only $57,000 in cash. Fifty-one percent of their revenue is going to a Bahamanian corporation owned by one of the board members. And all the directors issue themselves eleventh-hour stock options before the IPO at like 1 cent a share.

"And these guys go public! I'm saying to myself, what the hell is going on here? I mean, here's this bizarre little company and they make it through the review process. Meanwhile, we don't have a single lawsuit, no debt, and the SEC is busting our chops."

But proving its seriousness to go public in December didn't at all help MIPS's case with the SEC. Latta: "As I said, I think the [SEC] staff thought it was a week's delay and we knew that it could be two months' delay. And so they were sort of saying, 'What's the big deal?' and we were saying, 'It is a big deal!'

"I think they were stunned when they would lay seventy comments on us on a Friday and walk in Monday morning and find a complete amendment with a fifteen-page letter in response. You could tell from the voice of the examiner when he would call us that Monday morning that, in so many words, he was saying, 'Hey, you guys need to get a life.' He would be stunned.

"And, of course, the harder we pushed, the more suspicious and the more concerned the SEC got. Once you get a guy like that suspicious, there's nothing you can say to make him feel better other than 'I'll talk to you in January.' And that was the one thing we wouldn't say."

As the December days passed, it became increasingly apparent to the MIPS IPO team that the seemingly endless supply of new questions from the SEC was not the problem, but only its symptom. The SEC's real gripe was the extraordinary coverage the MIPS IPO was receiving in the nation's press. No amount of protestations from the company that it was trying to stop the stories, that any company quotes predated the quiet period, seemed to have any effect on the SEC.

Latta: "Every time things would start to calm down, another big article would come out. And the press problem was two-fold. First, there was just too damn much of it. Second, it didn't all come out at once, but trickled out every three or four days.

"See, the problem is that the company can be completely blameless and the SEC can still decide to hold the deal. It has the power to deny what is called 'acceleration.' If you want to be effective, the SEC has to accelerate your application. If they don't accelerate, you don't go effective. It's not that they are stopping you; it's that they're refusing to allow you to accelerate. It's a fine distinction. But from a political standpoint, it's much more palatable.''

What this meant was that if the newspaper and magazine articles kept appearing, the SEC could deem the MIPS IPO overheated and put it into a sort of bureaucratic limbo for a time. MIPS, of course, would lose its window of opportunity.

But it was even worse than that. In Bob Miller's mind he faced a nightmarish scenario in which the delay in the MIPS IPO would only generate a new wave of press coverage, this one speculating on what terrible new development or discovery had delayed the offering. That might cause even more delays until months hence when MIPS stock, now badly crippled by rumor and innuendo, finally limped into the marketplace. ''And meanwhile, we're still in the quiet period. We're not allowed to say a word in explanation.''

The articles continued to appear, each one leaving a crater and scattering debris. The December 10 *New York Times* piece, the one the road show team read while on tour, turned out to have a fuse on it for a delayed explosion. The article and an ''Investing'' column by Lawrence M. Fisher entitled ''Finally, a Hot High-Tech Offering'' began with ''In a slack market for initial public offerings in technology, many analysts are toasting this month's coming debut of MIPS Computer Systems, Inc.''

Any other time MIPS would have cheered such an article. Silicon Valley firms paid public relations firms hundreds of thousands of dollars to try, most often without success, to get this kind of coverage in the *New York Times*. But MIPS could only wince and, in an ironic turn, find solace in the caveat of the article's second sentence: ''Investors might find that it is best to join the party now, buying during the offering but maybe selling before others take a sober look at MIPS's long-term prospects.''

The bomb with the delayed detonation lay near the end of the article. It was a quote from John B. Jones, an analyst with San Francisco's respected Montgomery Securities, who was reported as saying: ''It's a rich deal, but it may well be the street is willing to pay for it. It is a company with a lot of stability, given the relationships with DEC and Kubota.''

Not an unusual quote from a securities analyst covering the computer

industry, nor especially inaccurate. There were upbeat comments from
the other analysts (from Soundview Financial, Alex, Brown & Sons,
and Wessels, Arnold and Henderson). Normally, this would be no big
deal—analysts are often used by reporters as quotable experts—except
that every one of these securities firms was part of the MIPS underwriting syndicate. And this was the quiet period. The SEC summarily kicked
them all out of the syndicate.

A very bad sign.

"You have to put yourself in the SEC's position," Latta says,
"You're them and you haven't had a good, hot technology IPO like this
since 1983. Secondly, nothing has had this much hype probably since
'86 or '87. Finally, you've got to remember that the staff of the SEC,
except at the top, turns over every two or three years. So, the guys that
are there aren't the guys that are used to this. It's not like the wild and
woolly days of the early 1980s. So they thought they had sufficient
grounds."

Three days later the dreaded *USA Today* article appeared. It was titled
"MIPS: From Ugly Duckling to Swan" and began with an atypically
long lead: "There hasn't been a coming-out party for a Silicon Valley
high-flier in years. But get a load of MIPS."

Despite all the pleas by Bev Jerman, reporter Rebello had made only
a single concession to the company's quiet period—a paragraph halfway
through the story that read: "In interviews before MIPS filed to go public,
management mapped its story. It goes like this: from fall to rise."

That was something at least. But the article also contained a quote
from Michael Murphy, editor of the *California Technology Stock Letter*.
"It's a very hot deal," he was quoted as saying, adding that Murphy
expected the 4.25 million shares available for sale to open at $17 and
"run right up to $20 to $21."

"I think [Rebello] singlehandedly cost the deal a week," Latta com-
plained. "See, we all knew it was coming. So Larry Sonsini had to
make a deal with Howard Morin [SEC assistant director] that said,
'We'll let MIPS go a week after the *USA Today* article if there's no more
publicity.'

"That was the first of several times that Sonsini was critical to the
deal. He essentially told Morin, 'Look, this isn't the company's fault.
The company's not to blame. You've got to let these guys go out.
Everybody complains about how the Japanese are cleaning our clocks.
Well, look at how easy it is for the Japanese to get capital and look how

hard you guys make it. Here we've got a bona fide superstar, one of the few bona fide superstars on the U.S. horizon, and you guys are denying them access to the capital market.' ''

Latta would henceforth call those statements Sonsini's ''Bob Noyce speech,'' after the Silicon Valley pioneer and advocate of American high-tech competitiveness.

As the skirmishing rolled into the final week before Christmas and the company's deadline, Sonsini would play an increasingly vital role. Sonsini, at 49, was, in the words of one newspaper, ''a mythical figure in Silicon Valley, often called the best high tech lawyer in the country. . . . Longtime clients, including some of the valley's most powerful CEOs, talk about him the way people talk about the cardiologist who just pulled them through a triple bypass.''

Sonsini had founded Wilson, Sonsini, Goodrich & Rosati in Palo Alto in 1966 with John Wilson, Roger Mosher, and future congressman Pete McCloskey. It had grown to become the nation's best-known law firm for electronics companies and their entrepreneurs. In the process Sonsini had made himself (according to Forbes in 1988) the thirty-eighth richest corporate lawyer in the United States with an annual salary of $1.2 million. He owned a mansion in Woodside, wore expensive tailored suits, and remained the quintessential workaholic, putting in long days in the office or on the road.

Self-taught in the processes of going public, Sonsini had now handled more technology IPOs than any person alive. Two shelves and a credenza top in his office were covered with the little lucite cubes, each containing a miniature prospectus, given as gifts when companies complete a successful stock offering. (When the October earthquake hit, Sonsini was unique in suffering furniture damage caused by too many falling IPO trophies.) Among them could be seen such names as Rolm, Apple, and Seagate. In one extraordinary week in 1981 Sonsini and his team took four companies public. ''I went three days without sleeping,'' he told a reporter. ''. . . It was like the Wild West. We were kind of doing it with mirrors.''

Thus, it could be honestly said that nobody connected with the U.S. electronics industry knew better how to deal with the SEC. And Sonsini used every connection he had. During the delay period he called the SEC at least three times, dealing not with the examiner on the MIPS case, but directly with Morin. Ludvigson said later, ''We just think the guy deserves *hero* kinds of awards.''

Said Latta, Sonsini's junior partner, "I think what was critical was Larry's image with the SEC. There are probably only five or six other attorneys, all of them on the East Coast, who could talk the way Larry did to an assistant director of the SEC. And I think that they figured, well, if Sonsini's stumping for MIPS, it must be a pretty good deal.

"You see, Morin is sort of a contemporary of Larry, so they've seen each other work for a long time.

"I'm sure that Larry brought a few chips to the table, but they were spent well. It'll probably cost him. Let's put it this way, the next time Howard Morin needs a leading securities practitioner to sit on an SEC panel, you know Larry's going to be sitting there."

Those three phone calls by Sonsini, none of them longer than fifteen minutes, turned out to be as important as all that had come before.

CHAPTER 18

Deus ex Machina

THE WORK WEEK BEGINNING DECEMBER 18, 1989, MIPS's last chance to go public on time, began quietly compared with what had come before.

The press had been blissfully silent since the *USA Today* debacle the previous Wednesday. If it could just stay quiet until this Wednesday, the unwritten agreement between Sonsini and Morin would hold and the SEC would at last let MIPS go effective.

The once seemingly endless lists of comments from the SEC had been whittled down and no new surprises seemed in the offing. Not that the process had become any easier. Ludvigson and crew stayed late Monday at Bowne printers filing amendments on the previous SEC comments. They finished at three o'clock Tuesday morning, and the filing was transmitted at five. Ludvigson stumbled home for a few hours of sleep, but he was upbeat: "You get a real adrenaline rush from doing this stuff"; after all, the SEC promised to come back with final comments later that day.

It would be his last moment of optimism for three days.

The comments that came back from the SEC examiner David Thelander on Tuesday morning weren't final at all. "We were expecting to get our final comments," an exasperated Ludvigson would say, "maybe even get approval to go. And what we got on Tuesday was a whole raft of new comments on different issues—and the examiner's telling us he just didn't have a chance to look at the amendments we'd submitted. He promised to call the team Wednesday morning at nine with his comments on the newly filed amendments."

The stunned team set about answering the new comments. "We got all those taken care of and ironed out." Then they broke early Tuesday night to conserve their strength for the next day.

As promised, at nine on Wednesday, December 20, the examiner called. "And his comments were easy," says Ludvigson. The team was jubilant. "It looked like we were over the hill. We were rolling! I called Bob and said, 'Geez, it looks like we're going to make it. Let's go. We're going to have to have a pricing meeting.' And he says, 'Well, I think I'll come down.' "

This final pricing meeting would set the exact price at which the stock would open trading. It was a brief meeting with all the principal players gathered at Bowne. The opening price was set at $17.50. After all these many months, only now, on the eve of the IPO, did the MIPS management finally learn that this would be a $70 million offering.

Everyone was ready to celebrate. The final changes were made in the document and it was faxed off to the examiner in Washington. Just to make sure, the MIPS team called, and Thelander confirmed that the papers had arrived and said he would call them back in fifteen minutes.

As Bob Latta recalled, "Wednesday we're at the printer and it starts off going great. We send in our responses to their big, long list of comments. We get a very light response back from the SEC. We spend all morning turning pages for our response. By lunch we're in Fat City. We fax the changes to the SEC and we're thinking, hey, if everything goes well, not only are we done, but instead of going effective tomorrow morning, under a new rule we can go effective this afternoon! And wouldn't that be wonderful, because that means that there's nothing in our way between now and going public tomorrow morning but maybe the plane carrying our documents going down over the Midwest somewhere. And, in fact, if we were effective, even that wouldn't stop us. We'd just call [Morgan Stanley] in New York and say, 'Bring the deal.' So, we're trying to pull off this real smart ass move of getting effective by the end of the day, which is unheard of in an IPO, but what the hey, why not try something creative?

"So now Miller's on his way up to the printer, the first time in the whole process he's been there. And Ludvigson's trying to get it all done before he shows up, right? So we fax the stuff off and we're thinking this is great, life is sure wonderful.

"After lunch, Miller arrives and he, Ludvigson, and the underwriters go into one of the rooms and they start talking pricing. Meanwhile, us peons are feeling pretty good. We're working out details like exhibit buy-ins and shit like that waiting for the examiner to call back.

"But he never calls back. The pricing meeting is still going on. It lasts an hour or so, from 1:30 to 2:30. Meanwhile, we're calling the examiner every fifteen minutes, because the SEC closes at 5:30 eastern time.

"I figured that if I could get the stuff to the file desk at 5:30, I could prevail upon the examiner to stick around for a little while and look at it. I knew he wanted to get the goddamned thing over with, too. But, 5:00 [eastern time] rolls around and he's not returning calls. That was strange, because he'd been pretty good about things. So we figured he was up with Morin.

"Now, it helps to understand how all this works. David Thelander, the examiner, was a young guy. He'd been in a law firm in New Hampshire or Vermont for a couple of years and then he'd come to the SEC. So, he's probably four years out of law school. It's not atypical for a guy to do that. They'll go to the SEC and then try to get a job at a big firm out of there. Now, Thelander was a good guy, he'd busted his ass on this thing."

Figuring that Thelander would be responsive to such a last-minute gesture, the trick would be to grab the young man the moment he walked out of Morin's office. So Latta and his team set a tripwire. "Just in case, an hour before, we had telecommunicated a full package to the Bowne office in D.C. We had extra signature pages for amendment 3. We had original accountant's consent. Original legal opinion. All there just in case. And we had them box the amendment by long distance, walking them through it over the phone. Then we had Bowne send two guys over to the SEC in a car with a car phone. One of those guys then stood in the lobby within eyesight of the other guy, who was parked illegally out front. This man on the car phone was connected with the guy in his office. And the guy in the office was connected with us in San Francisco.

"So, we've got this tag team, with the guy in the car making hand motions to the guy in the lobby with the file package. The clock's ticking toward 2:30 our time and we're waiting for the examiner to call. About 2:25 the guy at Bowne is asking, 'Should I file? Should I file?'

"And that's when the examiner finally calls back. We say, 'Okay, great, we've got an amendment that we want to file right now.' And that's when the examiner says, 'Don't file it. There are more comments.'

"Damn. So much for trying to file by remote control. They're kicking the Bowne guy out of the building by this point, so we call off the plan.

"So now we're thinking, 'Shit. What can the comments be now?' "

At three o'clock, six o'clock in Washington, the phone rang again. It was Thelander, but this time he had Howard Morin with him.

Ludvigson, out of the pricing meeting, received the call: "I'm out of the meeting, feeling all relaxed and all of a sudden the phone rings. I pick it up hear, 'Hello, this is Howard Morin.' Then it's like, 'Oh shit! Where are the fucking lawyers?' Then I start buying time until they get there."

"We weren't expecting Morin," said Latta. "Normally, you never talk to an assistant director of the SEC. In fifty offerings I can count on one hand the number of times I've talked to an assistant director. You deal with the examiner and then the branch. But, except for a few of the phone calls about gun jumping, we never even dealt with the branch chief. Now, there are ten branch chiefs and they report to only four or five assistant directors. So it was like an entire layer of SEC management had been cut out of this deal.

"That meant we were getting special treatment—and this isn't the kind of special treatment you want."

The phone conversation was carried on the speaker phone. Within moments the two lawyers were joined by, among others, Miller, Ludvigson, and Sweeney from MIPS, Strandberg from Morgan Stanley, and Zwicker, Wall, and Brad Harries from Cowen—a dozen men jammed into a room designed to hold six, and all of them expecting the worst. Says Ludvigson: "The number two guy in the SEC calling is not good news. And he was pissed."

Here is part of the recorded conversation, Morin speaking in an aristocratic Southern accent:

MORIN: The reason why I'm involved in this telephone call is that there was an article in the December 11 issue of *Corporate Finance Weekly*, that there was an article dealing with the MIPS IPO. Are you familiar with *Corporate Finance Weekly?*

LATTA: No, unfortunately I'm not familiar with that publication.

Latta commented, "Turns out it's the Bible of investment banking. The Morgan Stanley and Cowen guys knew of it. Strandberg turned white."

Ludvigson recalled, "I'd never heard of it, either. And he's really playing it up, and I'm thinking, 'All right, who screwed up?' I'm looking around, trying to find the guilty culprit. I don't think it's me. I didn't talk to anybody. It could be Bob, but probably not. Then he said it was the guy from Morgan Stanley and I just about dropped over.''

MORIN: In any event, we get it as a matter of course. And in any event, in that publication, which I think is fairly widely distributed among law firms as well as, I'm assuming, brokerage houses and possibly other entities. In any event, I'm going to read it to you. Some quotes are in here apparently by some broker dealers who are not engaged in the offering. That's in the first paragraph.

Second paragraph: ''The Sunnyvale, California-based computer system manufacturer is expected to price the issue at 14-17, said Frank Quatron [Morin mispronounced Quattrone's name every time he read it], principal at Morgan Stanley, which will handle the books. Cowen and Co. will co-manage. . . .''

Then it goes on to indicate what the nature of the offering is: ''This issue is expected to do well because MIPS is an industry leader in reduced instruction set computing (RISC), Quatron. RISC technology can be incorporated in both computer hardware and software and performs microprocessor operations and in a significantly more quick and efficient manner than existing technology, *he said*. With RISC you get a lot more bang for your buck. It's the new platform for the computer industry. The company is perceived in the industry as a winner because its revenues come not only from the sale of its products, but also from licensing arrangements for its technology with the leading computer and semiconductor companies around the world, *he said*. The company will use the proceeds for working capital to acquire equipment and possibly business products or technology. The company decided to do the IPO now because the perceived market for emerging growth company common stock is improving, quotes from Quatron said. Morgan was chosen to lead the issue as a result of a mutual courting process, according to Quotron.'' Or Quatron, I'm not sure how you say it. Q-u-a-t-t-r-o-n-e.

Latta: ''While this is going on, Brad Harries runs out to get a copy of the article faxed to us at Bowne. Meanwhile, Morin is just butchering Quattrone's name—including calling him Quotron [the brand name of a stock terminal], which is an interesting slip. And every time he gets to the end of a quote, he comes down hard with *Quatron said*. He was pissed. We're all looking around the room, like 'Oh shit.'

"Quattrone's not there; he's in Philadelphia at his in-laws. But we know he's a super underwriter, the last guy I would associate with this kind of embarrassment. I mean, if I had a company to take public, I'd use him. Turned out later he'd talked to the reporter off the record."

MORIN: That's the gist of the article and based on that, we have the same concern that we had with respect to the quotes being made, or that were made, by the other investment bankers that were to participate in this offering. . . .

    The bottom line, our position is that there is either remedial disclosure concerning that article and the circumstances surrounding its release or Morgan is out.

Latta: "Now he knew there was no way we could fire the lead underwriter. He was just showing us how angry he really was. He was having fun."

Ludvigson: "Losing your underwriter is not a viable option. You can't do that at the last minute to your underwriter."

Latta: "Now, there's no such term as 'remedial disclosure.' It's not a term of the art, but something Morin had just made up. So I had to find out what it meant."

LATTA: Are you thinking in terms of the comments that we got from David [Thelander] the other day with respect to Alex Brown and Montgomery Securities? Is what you're looking for, something in the risk factors discussion about how the article and interview came out?

MORIN: What it was and remedial disclosure. And as far as where you place it, I guess to be consistent, it might sit well under the same risk factor dealing with the pricing, the dollar amounts dealing with the contract. . . .

Latta: "Now putting this new disclosure in that risk section was like putting an apple in an egg carton. Weird."

Latta spent the next five minutes trying to get a more complete explanation of what would be required in such a "remedial disclosure."

The most he could get out of the two SEC officials was that the language would have to be stronger than the earlier disclosure with the syndicate members.

Latta: "Finally I said, 'As you know, we would like to price, we've been engaging in a pricing meeting, and we would like to go effective tomorrow morning. If the other comments are not that substantial, we would like to go effective tomorrow morning. But there's no way to get this language to you.' And Morin said, 'Okay, here's my home phone number.'

"Now, that was unprecedented. I'd never heard of an SEC official giving his private phone number."

LATTA: We'll get on a plane tonight with amendment number 3.

THELANDER: And number 4.

LATTA: Actually, I guess we never filed 3.

THELANDER: Right.

LATTA: So John will file 3 at the file desk and bring a courtesy copy to you and give the final pages for the confidential treatment. We'll also give you a market copy showing the changes on page 23 on the private label issue as well as the risk factor.

THELANDER: Bob and Dave, when do you intend to go [public]?

LATTA: Tomorrow morning.

THELANDER: [A pause in disbelief] Okay.

LATTA: . . . Thanks for your hard work. I know this has been a pain in the ass for you guys.

THELANDER: It certainly has.

LATTA: See you in the morning.

"You ever hear the story about how hostages start liking their captors," said Miller, "that's how we felt when we realized that Morin actually wanted to help us."

Added Ludvigson, "One of two things happened. He either really is the kind of person who is interested in helping or we had finally worn him down and all he wanted to do was be rid of us. I don't know the man so I'm not sure which of those two it was. But thank goodness he was cooperative.''

"I think they got tired of us," said Latta. "They would hit back these lobs and think they could go hide for a couple of days. Then our working group would work all night and the sucker would come rocketing back to them. I think they finally just felt, 'All right. Shit. Let them go.' But I'll say this, Morin was a reasonable guy and I don't know why. I guess he'd say he was just doing his job and part of that job was getting us effective.

"I also think he started to realize what Sonsini told him earlier, which is that the longer he delayed this thing the more press there was going to be. Instead of there being press on the offering's going effective, there'd be press about the SEC's holding the offering up—and nobody wanted that. He must have realized, 'Hey, it's not going to stop.'

"Now, I have to say that I think all of the SEC's actions up to this point were defensible. I mean, there was a lot of publicity. So I can understand why they reacted the way they did. The company did give some interviews and pose for some photos and did some things they didn't have to do. So maybe MIPS was 15 percent to blame, but it didn't do anything that was inconsistent with what most companies do going public. But from the SEC's point of view, they're seeing all these articles coming out, and some of those articles clearly could not have been written without the company's participation. So they're saying, 'Hey, you guys could've kept your mouth shut.'

"Luckily, Howard Morin's a very reasonable guy, a classy guy. There are a lot of bureaucrats who aren't. What surprised us, especially Sonsini, was how emotional Morin got about the deal. I mean, he was really pissed. He was pissed as early as two weeks before, when we were getting all those gun jumping comments. So that says something: A guy like that doesn't get pissed often unless he thinks there's been some bullshit going on.''

And if Howard Morin didn't have reason to think so before, he might soon enough. Very likely one reason for Morin's shift in attitude was that his deal with Sonsini for no more publicity on the IPO had held up. The *Corporate Finance Weekly* article had actually appeared December 11, two days before the *USA Today* piece, and had only just arrived from the clipping service. Thus, the deal still held.

The room was sober, but determined. To break the ice, Brad Harries stood up and announced that if Morgan Stanley was going to get thrown out of the deal then he'd better go get the Cowen style guide for prospectuses—a joke, since this was Cowen's first IPO and it had no such guide. The laughter was dark.

Ludvigson quickly sat down to write a first draft of the addition to the risk factors section. Strandberg suggested that he should clear the addition with Morgan Stanley's lawyers. Ludvigson: "I looked up at him and said, 'What makes you think you have a vote?' "

At that moment, as if in a scene from a French farce, Harries, now ashen-faced, came running back in with a flimsy fax copy of an entirely different clipping.

Latta: "I'm on the office phone to find out where Sonsini is to track him down and have him call us. And only then do we finally sit down and find out what the hell Brad's so excited about."

It was the worst article imaginable, from the Dow Jones News Service, dated and timed literally minutes before, and entitled "MIPS Computer Systems Common Priced." It read: "New York—DJ—An initial public offering of 4.6 million common shares of MIPS Computer Systems Inc. was priced at $17.50 a share. Of the total amount, which is offered on a global basis, 3.6 million common shares will be sold in the U.S. through underwriters led by Morgan Stanley & Co., Inc. Gross spread is $1.13, selling concession is 62 cents and reallowance is 10 cents. Delivery is scheduled for Dec. 29."

About the same moment the story was being read to the stunned MIPS IPO team members in the crowded room at Bowne printers, it was also being read in every major newsroom around the country, including across town at the *San Francisco Examiner*, which immediately set about writing an article for its "Off the Ticker" column. It read in part: "Interest in MIPS Sparked. MIPS Computer Systems, Inc. fielded a flurry of media calls late Wednesday, following a Dow Jones report that said the price of the company's initial stock offering would be $17.50 per share. Steve Bennion, the company's treasurer, declined to comment on the report, saying the company was in a 'quiet period' mandated by the Securities and Exchange Commission. . . . Analysts say MIPS is one of the hottest high-technology stock offerings in recent years, and many think it will do as well as such recent technology hits as Compaq Computer Corp. and Sun Microsystems."

Now the world knew. Employees at MIPS who followed the market closely knew, too, and they began calling their fellow workers. A number of employees in the manufacturing, engineering, sales, and corporate offices received phone calls from relatives and friends around the country telling them the news.

It was the absolute nadir in the long, difficult story of MIPS's struggle to go public. The entire world now knew when MIPS was planning to go public and at what price. Meanwhile, the SEC now had an irrefutable reason to kill the offering. The resulting bad publicity would no doubt go into an uncontrollable chain reaction and the fall-out from the resulting explosion would last for years.

And, on top of that, hourly reports were coming into the room saying the New York stock market was down more than forty points. The next recession could be just days away.

The group in the meeting room at Bowne sat in a daze. Latta: "It was like we were snakebit. There's this thing called the Telerate System. It's a wire system that the bankers use to distribute pricing information to their syndicate members. So some smart ass at Dow Jones is watching for it, sees it come across the Telerate System, and puts it on the wire. Now this could have happened to any offering, but for some reason the sonuvabitch threw it out on MIPS.

"So now we're shitting bricks because we're thinking, 'Great. We get Morin happy about the Quattrone article and then he walks in tomorrow morning, sees an article in the *Wall Street Journal* about MIPS being priced. He's going to say, "Those sonsabitches can't price this deal. I haven't let it go effective yet." ' I mean, it's just throwing it in the face of the bureaucrats. It's the worst thing you can do.

"Now we're really going. We've just gone from quicksand into something worse—and we're not sure which one to be more worried about. And only three hours ago we were euphoric thinking we were going to get effective a day early. So it was pretty fucking depressing."

Not in attendance on this day, to everyone's surprise, had been attorneys from Morgan Stanley's counsel, Davis, Polk. "They did a great job on the offering," said Latta, "and they were very active by phone. But they should have had someone there that day, an associate at least, if not a partner. I guess it was because it was Christmas and nobody wanted to fly out."

Now the assembled team got the perverse satisfaction of calling Davis, Polk to give them the bad news. Said Latta, "The last time we talked to them, they thought the deal was over. Now we got to call them up and ruin their day. And so now it's their turn to shit bricks because it's their client that's going to get splattered on this."

Not that Wilson, Sonsini's reputation was secure from this possible disaster. "We represent Morgan Stanley, too, when we're not corporate counsel. So we don't want Morgan Stanley to get splattered either. And they're good guys. They don't deserve this.

"So what the hell do we do now? Well, we start drafting up this real disclosure, and then we also start a guy drafting the remedial disclosure. And we get another guy trying to find out what the fuck happened with this Telerate thing.

"Then Larry [Sonsini] calls in. He's calling from [IBM headquarters in] Armonk [New York], I think. We read him the disclosure. He likes it. We tell him what happened on Telerate, that we're innocent, that it's not our fault. He likes it. He says he'll call us from the airport."

Ludvigson: "Sonsini called in to see how we were doing and he got knocked over by all the news—to which he kind of just said, 'Oh shit.' Then he said, 'Let me call Morin.' He's known Morin for twenty-some years. They grew up in the trenches together. So while it's not a personal relationship, there was years of a working relationship.

"So he called Morin, to find out where he was at, how angry he was, what we had to do . . . and also to tell him about this other 'little' issue with Dow Jones."

Latta: "Larry calls us back from the airport. We conference with Morin, and Larry, with a little prompting from me on some details, walks Morin through the Telerate problem. Morin's at home by this time and already had dinner. He picks up the phone, I guess downstairs, asks us to hold and goes to a more private phone. And he seems to be in good spirits."

Ludvigson: "So we've got this conference call with a guy in D.C. and a guy at JFK. In the background, behind Sonsini, you can hear loudspeaker announcements of flight departures. And we've got a dozen people all clustered around this tiny microphone you could hardly hear out of and negotiating with Morin on how badly he wants to screw us."

Latta: "Larry's pitch to Morin was great. It was a call to the flag, a pledge of allegiance. It was *beautiful*.

"Morin's pretty cool about it all. 'So, how many people have this information?' Strandberg from Morgan Stanley pipes up to tell him that, as a syndicate member, 'this is how we always do it. All we can tell is that Dow Jones must have picked it up on the Telerate System.' But Morin wants to know the names of all the people who have this information. He wants us to put it in a letter to him for tomorrow morning.

"But Larry keeps talking to him, saying that this is standard business practice . . . this, that and the other thing. 'We can tell you that it's all the syndicate members and you have the syndicate list in the prospectus. You can see who it is. We don't really need to do this long letter to you.' He talks him through it. Morin starts getting comfortable with the breadth of the dissemination, that it's not that broad.

"Next, [Morin] expressed his concern with the pricing. He was concerned that [the Dow Jones article] was going to be used as a trial balloon on price. That there was some evil intent here to put up a trial balloon and see if it stuck at $17.50. You can understand his concern—he was already bugged that we had increased the filing range [to go up from the published $14 to $17 to cover the $17.50 opening price]. He didn't want us to be benefiting from our hype. Luckily, in a real heart-to-heart with the examiner the previous Friday, we'd warned the SEC this might happen.

"Then Morin asks, 'Were you planning to file under rule 460A?' That's the rule that allows you to file an amendment without putting the price in. Now, Larry's standing in a noisy airport in New York and I can't be sure he's caught the subtlety of the question. What Morin is saying is 'Are you going to file without price?'

"So, before Larry can respond I said, 'You know, Larry, we could put the price in the document tonight instead of filing under 460A.' In other words, we can do it the old way of dropping in the price before we file. And Larry, BOOM, picked up on it in a second. I mean, I set the ball up and he just slams it.

"Larry says, 'That's right, Howard. We could drop the price in tonight and that would comfort you in knowing that this is not a trial balloon because the price would be set and therefore there could be no damage whatsoever caused by this early release.'

"And Morin says, 'I like that. Let's do that. I think that handles my concern on that issue.'

"So then Larry says, 'Bob, why don't you read the remedial disclosure?' I finish reading it and Morin says, 'That sounds good.'

"And Larry says, 'Howard, do you think we have to use Mr. Quattrone's name?' And Morin replies, 'No, I guess we don't have to.' And Strandberg lets out a big sigh and folds his hands like he's praying and mouthing the words, 'Thank you, Larry. Thank you, Larry.' That's because Quattrone's his boss. Strandberg did a super job, but he's an associate and this is scary shit. This is bad stuff for Morgan Stanley.

"So that's the first bullet. And so then Larry says, 'Furthermore, Howard, do you think we need to mention Morgan Stanley by name? Can't we just say "a member of the syndicate"?'

"But Howard didn't jump at that. Then Larry changes it to 'Can't we just say "one of the managing underwriters"?' And so now the Cowen people are looking pissed [because it might appear to be them]. And Howard says, 'No. I think we have to mention Morgan Stanley.' Strandberg looks like this [Latta makes motion like he's been electrocuted]. But he says, 'Okay.' And we sign off."

MIPS might make it public after all. "At that point we just got to work making the changes. We had to drop the price in everywhere and then handle all the resulting ricochets through the document. It was now just a sprint to get the stuff ready."

Miller left about this time, Sweeney a little later, both heading home to wives and infants. At Bowne, it was chaos, as the remaining team raced off in every direction to get everything in place before the last flight to Washington at 10:30 P.M. At 9:00 a call was placed to the Manhattan residence of William Osborne, the Morgan Stanley director of equity capital markets, to bring him up to date on what had happened. But Osborne was at a Christmas party and the call only managed to wake up his wife.

Soon after that Latta agreed to carry the papers and was sent racing off to the San Francisco airport, the rest of the paperwork pursuing him. At midnight another team member was dispatched to the San Francisco airport to intercept the first West Coast editions of the *Wall Street Journal* and the *New York Times*.

By then, Dave Ludvigson was driving home for three hours of fitful sleep. He awakened every half hour, expecting Latta to call the moment he touched down in D.C.

But Latta never called. "I woke up at four thinking he must have gotten diverted. That there was a snow storm or fog or something in D.C. That the whole deal was going to crater again."

Unable to sleep any more, Ludvigson got dressed and headed for Bowne. In his mind he gave the chances of going public that day just fifty-fifty.

THE MOMENT

Washington, D.C., 8:40 A.M. EST

LATTA: "It's now twenty to nine and I'm starting to panic. At 9:30 the market opens. I know if I have to wait until the courtesy desk opens at 9:00, the copies won't get to the examiner until 9:30. Then he's got to read it, bless it, pow-wow with Morin—and it'll be 10:30 before we're effective. And that's not what Morgan Stanley wants. They want to go at 9:30.

"I don't know what to do. I can't keep leaving strange messages for Howard Morin with Sally and Suzie. Maybe it's the phone, I decide. Maybe it's fucked up; maybe it fucks up consistently just on certain numbers. Somewhere out there in the Virginia suburbs Sally and Suzie are going to wake up with some pretty strange phone messages.

"So I trot back to the SEC to see if maybe there's a phone there I missed. But there isn't. Just a dozen lawyers standing around waiting for the desk to open.

"So, with no other choice, I run once more out into the cold and start making concentric circles again around the SEC looking for another phone."

Ludvigson: "On the way into San Francisco I call Morgan Stanley to see if they've heard from Latta. But nobody there was answering the phone. So I get to Morgan Stanley about a quarter to six and start pacing the floor waiting to hear."

Latta: "I finally run into this Roy Rogers restaurant that's on the ground floor of the SEC building itself. There's this waitress there,

Bertha or something, and I ask her. 'Why, honey, there's one right over there across the street.' It figures the waitress in the Roy Rogers would have the best intelligence information in the building.

"Turns out I've been looking at this phone the whole time. It just doesn't look like a phone. It doesn't say 'Phone.' It's in this stupid little green and white colonial letterbox with its back to me.

"And it works. I dial—and get Thelander right away. I tell him I've got the papers. Is he ready to look at them?

"He says, 'You're in California. Are you going to have the printer deliver it?'

"And I say, 'No, I'm standing outside of this building and I'd like to hand it to you.' And he pauses, a sort of I-don't-really-want-to-walk-downstairs-and-get-it pause, and I said, 'AND, since I'm a California boy, I'm freezing my ass off out here and I'd really like to come inside and give this to you.'

"So I meet him in front of the reception area and hand it off. He takes it upstairs. It's now about a quarter to nine."

Ludvigson: "Latta finally calls at about a quarter to six and says he's there, has the package on file, and is going off to find people.

"Strandberg has shown up by then. Miller arrives about fifteen minutes later. So we're all waiting there at Morgan Stanley for Latta's next call.

"Osborne calls from New York and says, 'Well, where are we? We've got everybody ready to go and it smells like it's going to be good and the market's going to open well and I really want to get you guys out.' I knew if I didn't tell him something, if he thought we were still hanging out there, he'd start panicking. So I told him, 'Shoot, I don't know. . . . We'll start trading by ten o'clock New York time. Don't worry.'

"Literally, two minutes later a guy from the trading floor in the building where we are in San Francisco comes running into the room and says, 'Hey, I hear you guys are ready to go and you're going to start trading at ten.' Miller and I thought, 'Oh God. Just what we need.' "

Latta: "So I'm waiting. At 9:00 the reception area opens. There's a bank of about ten phones there. I call Strandberg and say, 'Look, I finally got it to Thelander at a quarter to nine. Hang tight. I don't think we're going to make 9:30. I think it will be more like 10:30.' He's disappointed, but says, 'Okay.' After all, we're not in a position to be choosers; we're beggars at this point. Who knows what Morin is going to do?

"At 9:15 I call the examiner and give him the number of the phone in the reception area. I ask, 'How's it going?' He says, 'Mr. Morin's reviewing it.'

" 'Fine.' I'm back to waiting. By now a whole bunch of lawyers have come into the waiting room. They've gotten there when the courtesy desk opened at 9:00 and now they've come up to the reception area. Well, I know that I'm a step ahead of them all the way along. My examiner's already gotten my package, so I should be the first to get called, right?

"Wrong. I'm the last guy to get called. They all get theirs—'It's effective, thank you, goodbye'—they're happy; they're gone. And I'm still there wondering what's going on.

"Finally—it's like 9:40 now—the examiner finally calls.

" 'You're effective,' he says. "I have some last minute stuff to go through on the exhibits, but we can talk about that later. I'm not going to hold you up for that.'

" 'No further comments?'

" 'No. You are effective at 9:45 this morning.'

"I hang up and immediately call Strandberg. Ludvigson and Miller are sitting there with him. I say to Strandberg, 'You're effective.' It surprises them, because I've got them waiting for a 10:30 call. I can hear whooping and hollering and Strandberg saying, 'Thanks a lot. We have to call the syndicate. Bye.' Click.''

Ludvigson: "Latta's call comes in at 9:46. We were standing there in the conference room at Morgan Stanley. 'You're effective.' ''

Latta's call took about one-sixtieth of a second to reach the team in San Francisco. It took the same amount of time for Strandberg's telephone call to retraverse the continent to New York and reach the desk of Will Osborne at the Morgan Stanley headquarters offices on the thirty-third floor—the equity trading floor—of the Exxon Building in midtown Manhattan, across from Rockefeller Center.

The thirty-third floor was physically and psychically divided into two sections. The smaller section, that of Osborne's equity capital markets group, was, at least in appearance, subdued and calm, like the business office of a bank. It was at his desk on one side of this section that Osborne received the happy news. Then he too made a call, this one only requiring about a microsecond as it crossed to the other side of the thirty-third floor.

In this section was the trading floor, surprisingly tiny for its power, noise, and frenzy, segregated from the quiet section by only a few filing cases and a kiosk bearing the latest Morgan Stanley red herrings, including MIPS's. The trading floor had blue and white walls, a nicotine-stained ceiling, a hard brown carpet, and banks of anonymous desks, each with a glowing Davox 2900 stock terminal and a chrome and cloth chair. It still smelled slightly of yesterday's daily delivery of Chinese food and deli sandwiches.

These desks were personalized with a few items that were telling about the lives of the traders who worked at them: Far Side daily calendars, vacation momentos, goofy joke items, a bottle of A-1 steak sauce wedged in a bookcase. But there were few of these items compared to the offices at MIPS. Rather, like the beat reporter section in the newsroom of a major newspaper, these desks seemed to have no permanent owner; they wore their anonymity proudly beneath their inevitable piles of paper.

And everywhere noise: of telephones, of shouts across the floor, of hurried conversations between traders, of reactions to the latest news crawling across the trading board mounted above the north wall windows. The traders were nearly all young men ("Chauvinism in action," one secretary would complain), wearing yellow ties, sporting sharp haircuts, and exhibiting an almost infinite supply of nerves.

Osborne's call went into the heart of this frenzy. It also went to a group of desks at the west side of the trading floor, the international section, to the east side of the trading floor, the block trading section, and beyond that to a sinister-looking glass room where computer brahmins directed programmed trading.

Within five minutes of Strandberg's call from San Francisco, the young men began trading MIPS's stock.

Three floors below, Morgan Stanley executive offices also soon heard of the MIPS IPO. In contrast to the chaos and impermanence above, the thirtieth floor was a place of wood paneling, Oriental carpets, Chippendale chairs, and chinoiserie cabinets—"a soap opera set," as one "Dynasty"-watching employee described it. At this time in the morning cooks and waiters were rushing about preparing elegant meals to be served on fine china in the half-dozen executive dining rooms a few hours hence. The Morgan Stanley executives, corporate descendants of the men in the sober portraits that hung on the walls, looked out over the

Manhattan landscape and discussed the news about a young computer company beyond the horizon in California.

Latta: "I called Segre [at Wilson, Sonsini] and let him know what was going on. The National Press Building has a shopping mall in the center with lots of stores, so I killed a half an hour there buying a Christmas present for my wife. Then I went back to Bowne, picked up my shit, and got them to order a car for me.

"I still had some time to kill before my flight out of Dulles. So I had the Bowne car stop at the Vietnam Memorial. I'm an army brat and I grew up with that kind of stuff, so I wanted to see the place. It was four degrees and pretty windy, when I was walking around the Memorial, but for some reason I wasn't cold now."

Ludvigson: "I called Zwicker [at Cowen], who was the other banker on the deal. He said it was going to open at 20½ and that it would trade at 19½. Then he said, 'Wup, it just came across the screen. It's trading at 20½!'

"I turned to Bob and said, let's go. So Bob and I and Strandberg and one of the other Morgan guys, Ken Rivera, went out on the trading floor at Morgan and watched the computer terminal running the changes in bid and ask prices."

Miller: "I remember when the word 'MIPS' came on the screen, Ludvigson and I turned to each other, shook hands, and said, 'We made it.'

MIPS Computer Systems, Inc. was now a public corporation.

THE DAY

CHAPTER 19

The New American Dream

THE ELECTRONICS INDUSTRY is now America's largest manufacturing employer, exceeding steel, automobiles, farm machinery, and every other type of manufacturing once considered synonymous with the Industrial Age.

At the same time it can be said that the single most distinguishing characteristic of commerce in the United States after the Second World War has been entrepreneurship. Certainly it has been entrepreneurship that has taken the fruits of American technology in the electronics age, many of which have permanently changed human society, and converted them into thousands of companies. It is because of entrepreneurship that most of the five hundred largest American manufacturers are companies that did not even exist twenty years ago. And it has been entrepreneurship that has served as the last bulwark against the depredations of foreign competition.

It follows that the Going Public Day of a young electronics company, the day when entrepreneurship is rewarded for its sacrifices and risk taking, is now the emblematic moment of the new American Dream—the day of payoff for gratification deferred, years of eighty-hour work weeks, broken marriages, lost career opportunities, grandiose dreams, struggle for personal freedom, huge financial investments, and unshakable loyalty. It is the day when the loyal secretary may become wealthy, the rebel post-adolescent may join the ranks of the world's richest men, the young immigrant may fulfill every fantasy about America heard in the Old Country.

In an egalitarian society that too often exhibits cruel inequalities, Going Public Day often represents a return to first principles. Certainly

231

those at the top of the firm receive greater rewards than those at the bottom, but all receive rewards far beyond those conferred by the society outside the firm. Loyalty, pluck, endurance, faith—all of the qualities Americans profess to hold precious—are recognized on Going Public Day to a degree rarely found elsewhere in the society.

It is estimated that in the instant MIPS went public, twenty employees and directors made more than $1 million. Perhaps two hundred more saw their net worth increase by $100,000 to $200,000.

On Going Public Day the individual employees are rewarded for sacrificing years of their lives, for spurning higher-paying jobs elsewhere, and for taking a risk on an enterprise with little chance of survival, much less a payoff. Executives are rewarded as well for taking a flyer on a deal that might sink their reputations. Venture capitalists are rewarded for betting millions on a few pieces of paper and a handful of inexperienced founders.

Most of all, Going Public Day rewards, often with extraordinary riches, the entrepreneur. And that is only fair. It is the entrepreneur who has performed the most magical feat of all: He or she has converted a dream into a real company, producing real products that may change the lives of strangers around the world and providing employment to hundreds of people.

Each Going Public Day is the celebration of a small miracle. The odds against a start-up's surviving more than a couple of years are huge. The odds against that firm's being successful enough to reach the $50 million or $100 million it takes to become a publicly owned firm are astronomical.

In Silicon Valley, the heartland of American high tech entrepreneurship, of the ten thousand or more companies that have been founded in the last three decades, no more than a hundred have gone public. This singular list contains many celebrated names: Hewlett-Packard, Varian, Intel, Fairchild, National Semiconductor, Apple, Tandem, Amdahl, Commodore, Atari, Sun. Now MIPS would join that select list.

Going Public Day also has a ritual value that reaches beyond the individual company into the community itself. A place like Silicon Valley exists on hope, on the belief that anyone with enough ambition, guts, and brains can make it. It is this belief that draws immigrants and ambitious young graduates to the valley and keeps them there even as they watch companies fail. It keeps them there in the face of traffic congestion, pollution, expensive real estate, an exorbitant cost of living that seems forever to grow faster than their salaries. It is this hope that enables them to commute seventy miles and ninety minutes each day to work from their distant homes in California's Central Valley. And most of all, it is this dream that keeps them going in a gypsy-like, rapidly changing, youth-oriented career that may move them to a dozen employers in two decades and make them obsolete before they are 50 years old.

This dream must be regularly renewed, lest it fade and leave visible only the dark side of high-tech life. Every few years there must be that spectacular reminder that the merry-go-round still offers its riders the brass ring. The stories of Hewlett and Packard, Noyce, Jobs and Wozniak have enduring power, but must constantly be made current with new, even if lesser, stories of later-day entrepreneurial successes. When MIPS went public, Silicon Valley was living on the aging stories of T. J. Rodgers at Cypress Semiconductor, Finis Conor at Conor Peripherals, and the crews at Octel, Quantum, and Oracle.

Now, to the considerable relief of many aging and new Valleyites, came the over-the-hill gang from MIPS with their story of the company brought back like Lazarus from the dead and of the billion dollar management. Throughout Silicon Valley people would open the *San Jose Mercury-News* or the *San Francisco Chronicle,* read of MIPS's spectacular opening market price, and say to themselves that someday they'd find a firm like that and strike it rich. It could be done.

For some those thoughts would be darkened by desperation. One cannot grow old in Silicon Valley. Until the government mandated the 401K program, valley companies like Apple Computer had no pension plans. Gyms certainly, day care centers perhaps, but no one gives out gold watches in Silicon Valley. A middle-aged public relations woman, a 25-year Silicon Valley veteran, would say about the stock she owned in one of her clients that was planning to go public, "You don't understand. This isn't a bonus. This is my only chance for retirement."

If holding founder's stock on the day a young company goes public is the modern American Dream, then Going Public Day is the nexus of hundreds of individual dreams, all converging on that instant when the company's name appears on the stock ticker.

Then the dreams again diverge, imperceptibly at first, but with an ever-broadening sweep. Some employees, in pursuit of new dreams, leave the firm within weeks or months. Others stay several years before being carried off in the cyclone of electronics industry life. A few, sometimes the least likely candidates, stay for decades, long after the principals of the firm are dead or retired, until, like ancient drummer boys, they are the last surviving veterans of the company's entrepreneurial battles.

Going Public Day is probably the most profound turning point in a firm's history. Before that point of inflection the people it hired were, by necessity, entrepreneurial to some degree. They were willing to bet the come, to take the high risk and the reduced salary in exchange for equity in the big score. After Going Public Day the newly hired people are drawn to the firm for entirely different reasons. They are not as willing to take risks; they are more conservative, more political. With no founder's stock available, these new corporate types have different goals than their entrepreneurial predecessors: they want money and power.

In the final weeks before its IPO, a company begins to look like an exhausted marathoner. Growing at a breakneck pace while simultaneously going public takes its toll. Top to bottom, the company is worn out, ready for a vacation, and Going Public Day serves as a perfect mental finish line.

Not surprisingly, many newly public companies go through a difficult period as they adapt to being big corporations. Suddenly, what used to be scarce, money, is abundant, and the challenge becomes not to overindulge every pent-up whim. Too many new corporations immediately launch into new markets, design new products, or build extravagant new headquarters buildings . . . only to find themselves overextended and in trouble.

Sudden wealth can be a problem for the individuals, too. The parking lot transformations after an IPO are famous. Within six months and full stock vestment, the Fords, Hondas, and Toyotas are replaced by Mercedeses, Porsches, and BMWs, as well as the occasional Rolls-Royce and Ferrari. It can be hard to stay motivated to work till midnight when several hundred thousand dollars are sitting in your bank account.

Finally, there is the entrepreneurial spirit itself. The wildcatting era of the company is over. Those who thrived in those rough and tumble days often find themselves confused and frustrated when the company announces a dress code or publishes an employee manual or begins filling up the executive offices with young Harvard M.B.A.s who've never had to make a payroll. Then, the early days of the firm, no matter how hard and unpredictable, take on a rosy cast, like memories of a pre-empire republic.

This frustration with corporate life can be experienced by veterans from the rank and file right up to the president's office. Soon there will be annual reports and quarterly earnings announcements and shareholder meetings and proxy fights and all the rest of the exposure that comes with being a publicly traded corporation. Some company presidents begin to feel restless, bored, dissatisfied with their work. And some companies begin to feel dissatisfied with their president. One of the saddest sights in Silicon Valley life is the entrepreneurial founder who has become a liability to the mature firm he created and has been unceremoniously dumped on the street.

Of course, all of these potential problems, if they ever did arrive, lay in the distant future for MIPS. For now the company was blissfully happy. Everyone tried to work, but beneath attempts to take care of business lay a giddiness that threatened to burst out at any moment. This euphoria wasn't due to the money alone, though obviously that played a major role. For most of the employees the big payoff they'd just earned would still seem unreal for days. Rather, much of the excitement came from being a participant in a success story, from having achieved a long-sought goal.

Exhausted though it may be, a company will probably never run better than in the weeks before Going Public Day. Morale is high. Turnover is low. Productivity, despite the distractions, is excellent. Most of all, for perhaps the only time in the firm's history, every employee shares a mutual and immediate goal. On this common ground, assembly people and vice-presidents speak to one another as equals, as travelers on a shared adventure. And on Going Public Day the company becomes, for that one day alone, a place in which every inhabitant is awarded the winning prize.

As the six hundred members of MIPS assembled at the company's offices, their dreams converged. By the time they left, their dreams had already begun to fly off on myriad trajectories.

CHAPTER 20

Morning—Getting the News

AFTER A FEW MINUTES of congratulating one and all and a few more of watching the MIPS listing on the Morgan Stanley terminal, Miller and Ludvigson returned to business, analyzing the patterns in which the young stock was being traded.

Ludvigson: "We were on the phone with Osborne frequently to try and figure out the size of the blocks that were coming across and whether any of the prime institutions were selling. The opening flurry of activity in the first fifteen minutes looked like it was largely retail activity—one thousand, two thousand shares, that kind of thing. There were a couple of big orders that popped out. The price was at 20½. Then it blipped momentarily to 21. I'm sure some poor sucker, with a buy order placed at Schwab for the first possible buy-in, got nailed on that one."

Breakfast was a few rolls at Morgan Stanley. Miller left about half past eight, saying he wanted to get back to the office. Ludvigson stayed to make a few phone calls to let people know what had happened. He had already called home, having done that even before coming down to the trading floor and just after he'd heard the news. "I called home first thing because my kids go off to school at 7:30. One's 14, the other's 12, so they understood what was going on. They were excited. They were more excited than I was."

He also called Sweeney at MIPS "a couple of times to tell him where things were at, what the trading pattern looked like, and all that so he could not only feel a part of it, but also understand in case any questions came up."

He left Morgan Stanley a few minutes before eight, heading out of the city against the morning commuter traffic. He reached Sunnyvale about half past nine. Waves of exhaustion were rolling over him as he sat at his desk, his head cradled in one hand. In a few hours he would have trouble completing sentences and keeping his train of thought. "I'm so tired," he mumbled.

Meanwhile, Miller had not gone back to MIPS, but rather had met with Boesenberg at C&I Photography just down the street from company headquarters. A photographer was waiting in one of the studios. The two executives, barely able to contain their laughter, straightened their ties, buttoned their suit jackets, stepped in front of a grey backdrop, and pointed at a line chart they held between them. "This is going to be great!" Miller announced. The camera clicked.

The big chart the two men held showed MIPS's earnings shooting almost vertically upward in the years to come. It was titled: MIPS's Skyrocketing Earnings Projections. The printed and cropped photograph was to be glued on a real cover of *Fortune* Magazine, with the fake headline, "MIPS: THE IPO OF THE CENTURY" and the tag line, "Silicon Valley's hottest high tech company discloses the future and goes public." A score of dummy *Fortune* magazines would then be prepared.

On Friday morning, at the executive staff meeting, executive secretary Sher Parker suddenly walked into the conference. She was ashen faced. She handed a pink telephone message slip to Miller, who looked at it with an expression of great dismay, folded it, and handed it back to her, saying, "Pass it to Dave."

Ludvigson: "I'm sitting in the front of the room with Boesenberg and I get this phone message. I open it up and it says, 'SEC has suspended trading because of publicity. *Fortune* cover article out.'

"I can't believe it. I'm in shock. I pass the note to Boesenberg.

"Just then Bobri Roberts rushes in carrying in a stack of *Fortune*s. And there's the cover picture. It's impossible. It can't be happening. My mind is doing like binary processing. Half of it's saying, 'What can we do to save this deal?' And the other half is saying, 'Wait a minute, something's wrong here.'

"That's when I look up and see that Boesenberg is taking my picture. Then everybody starts laughing."

*   *   *

By the time Miller and Boesenberg returned from the photo studio, most MIPS employees had arrived, and all had heard the good news. Many had been called in the wee hours of the morning by friends and relatives watching the morning stock reports on television.

Joe Sweeney had held down the fort at MIPS while the others gathered at Morgan Stanley. With a newborn baby at home he was, if it was possible, even more exhausted than Ludvigson.

Sweeney reached MIPS at quarter to six, running into a long-time MIPS employee, Dan Freitas, in the parking lot. "It was very early for me, but it was Dan's normal time. He asked about the IPO and I told him that we hoped it was today. That it should be today."

He was at his desk by six, like Ludvigson having gotten about two hours sleep. That made a total of ten hours sleep for the week so far. "How'd I sleep last night? A perfectly restful three and a half hours."

By half past six the calls began coming in. First Ludvigson, then Miller and Ludvigson, finally Latta from D.C. "We all exchanged information back and forth on what was going on."

Then, just before ten o'clock Miller called to say MIPS was effective. "I remember him saying something like, 'We made it. It took a lot of hard work, but we've made a big step.'" A few moments later Latta called with the same news. "He was pretty happy."

Perhaps fittingly, Joe Sweeney, the corporate counsel, secretary, and co-author of the prospectus, was the first person at MIPS to hear the news. He immediately typed out an electronic mail announcement to appear on every employee's computer. Within minutes a small crowd had gathered outside his office door. He joined them. Then he went back into his office to answer telephone calls. He worked through lunch.

"I'm going home tonight and spend some time with my wife and baby and try to get human again."

In the lobby, with its new Christmas tree to celebrate the season, Joe DiNucci took it upon himself to greet each arriving employee and congratulate them on the good news.

On this morning, on a date he would find even easier to remember than most others that held a permanent residence in his brain, DiNucci was fully experiencing the IPO process he'd once, as a corporate man, downplayed. Standing in the lobby, he gave the news to every MIPS person he saw, from receptionists to fellow vice-presidents. He shook hands and slapped shoulders and told jokes.

"I heard the news this morning at 7:30 when I walked in the door. I broke into this ear-to-ear grin and called home and I got to speak to my wife's answering machine. I left a message telling her she was hearing the voice of a happy person.

"It's really fun right now. I mean I'm bumping into guys like Stritter and Hennessy and the other guys who started the place and they're just like standing there, like human beings. They did it."

DiNucci looked like a man who'd been with the firm for twenty years, rather than just nine months. And he looked like a man who'd just been given a second chance at independence.

By 9:30 everyone in the company knew the good news. Hundreds of telephone calls had been made home and elsewhere. They'd been matched by nearly that number coming in, from people who wanted to be investors, congratulators, reporters, and con men. Most were referred to treasurer Steve Bennion, who barely found a moment between ringing calls to talk to his fellow employees.

Throughout the two wings of the headquarters building people could be seen forming little knots of conversation, laughing, and then moving apart. The mood was still sober, as if coming off the pressure of the preceding months too quickly might create a company-wide case of the bends. Still, one could hear intermittent outbursts from passing pairs of employees:

"Can you believe it?"

"We did it. We fucking *did* it."

"I'm going to splurge and have that extra diet Coke for lunch today."

"It was scary when the price was at $21 for a moment, then went back down to $20. I've never lost that much money so fast. I think I'll make a trip to the liquor store on the way home and get some Dom Perignon."

"I didn't even need my calculator. It's easy to multiply by twenty."

"I'm just relieved. The suspense was starting to get unbearable."

In the engineering section and in John Hime's office, terminals had been set up to carry stock prices. Employees would regularly walk past and check the numbers, cheering when they rose, talking bravely when they fell. The $21 high couldn't hold for long, and by eleven o'clock the price had dipped back under $20. Nevertheless, the employees knew that even with that price, they were working for a $400 million corporation—and they had made nearly 20 percent more money on their options than they had expected. That fact only added to the growing excitement.

Down the road in manufacturing, someone had posted the same sign on pillars all over the building. It read, with the humor of infinite optimism:

COME ON BABY

SPLIT! SPLIT!

SPLIT! SPLIT!

SPLIT! SPLIT!

Throughout the morning of Going Public Day, exhibitions of excitement were controlled. Because the actual date of the IPO could not be known in advance, planned meetings had to be attended, schedules filled, and work completed that day before any celebrations could begin.

Dave Ludvigson, though visibly exhausted, spent the morning on the telephone with the bankers and the lawyers finalizing the word of the formal prospectus. He had to study a contract for a new telecommunications complex and then review the status of the 1990 budget. Skip Stritter was off site at a meeting. Bev Jerman and Joanne Hasagawa discovered that BusinessWire, the wire service carrying the announcement of the IPO to magazines and newspapers, had printed the wrong area code on the company's telephone number. They scrambled to get a corrected version out by eleven. Then they had to rush into a meeting to plan the company's first annual report.

Still, every employee in the company exhibited a level of distraction that was proof that this was no regular day in the company's life. Over in legal, Babs Louie, the company's unofficial recreation leader and cheerleader, admitted to "crying at inopportune times."

The news of the IPO appeared to have little effect on three of MIPS's employees. They seemed to shrug it off as a distraction or even an irritation. These were the dynamos of the company, the running at red line, eighty hours a week types upon whom Silicon Valley was built.

Nobody at MIPS that morning seemed to be working harder than the director of customer marketing, Andreas Kyriakou. The tall, thin blond man was either on the phone with a vendor or rushing out to the lobby to meet one. The bottle of champagne on his desk was not to be drunk to celebrate the IPO, but to be given to a young salesman as a reward for his first sale.

Kyriakou's energy came not just from career building, but from an outsider's amazement at finding himself in a place as odd and compelling as Silicon Valley. A sign on his wall, a "No Nookie" award, was given to him as a department joke after a sales trip to London. It seems he had been about to score at a club called Stringfellows when his fellow employees dragged him off to catch the flight home.

"I felt the fair thing would have been to give the award to the other guys," Andreas says.

He was born in Vienna in 1952. His Greek father imported chrome ore from Turkey and Greece into rebuilding Austria and Germany and made it very big. He is now retired and living in Athens. His mother lives in Vienna, and that's where Andreas spent most of his youth, with summers in Greece with his father.

"By the time I graduated from high school—gymnasium, as they call it—I was a real rock and roller. Even now rock and roll is something I'll never give up; although nowadays it doesn't show on me as much.

"Vienna wasn't as cosmopolitan as it is now. Then it was a lot of old ladies left over from the war and it was depressing and anything new and young was not well received. I joined a band called Nostradamus, because I was a real student of him. I was the drummer. It was hard rock, Jimi Hendrix-type music.

"While I was with the band, we played in Copenhagen and there I ran into this American, this real Jewish-American princess from Sarah Lawrence. She came back with me to Vienna, but then ran off with the guitarist in the group. Then, just before my twenty-first birthday she came back to me."

But the summer was ending and the girl returned to America and school.

"I worked for four months with two days off and finally got on a student charter flight to New York with $400 in my pocket. She met me at the airport. It was Christmas Day 1972.

"She was on winter break and had rented a house with a group of women in White Plains. I get there and the ladies are all on the floor drinking beer and playing cards. One of them hoisted my suitcase over her head and carried it up to her room. And that was my welcome to America. It was great.

"It was fine for a month and then my money started running out and school was starting. So she went back to Sarah Lawrence and, it turned out, back to her affair and romance with her literature professor. Meanwhile, my money ran out and I had to find my way in New York."

He worked as a painter and plasterer and for a while as the maintenance man at an East Side mansion. His English, first learned in school and from deciphering Beatles records, grew ever better. At night he played rock and roll "without much success."

Hearing of some Austrian friends in Los Angeles, Andreas joined a rideaway program and made the trip in a Dodge Charger in less than seventy-two hours. Not long after that, he caught a plane to San Francisco.

"I'm walking around the city, looking at the sights, and as I cross the street, a guy nearly runs me over. I look over—I swear this is true—it's the guy who owned the nightclub in Vienna. The police had raided it and shut it down and now here he was."

Soon the two men were in the antiques business in Los Angeles, importing container-loads of old furniture from Germany and France and selling it to Beverly Hills socialites. "I rented a big store right on Melrose and LaCienega and did the LA thing for a year. Made some bucks."

Andreas moved back to San Francisco, ran out of money again, and found himself once more doing odd jobs. But he also enrolled in a vocational school. Andreas's initial goal was to learn how to fix a broken electronic music instrument he owned, but soon he found himself interested in basic electronics.

Within two years Andreas was teaching the course. He also gained a wife and, in time, a son. Still pursuing his interest in electronics, Andreas moved to Silicon Valley and took a decade-long job at Rolm, then still in its glory days before the buy-out by IBM. It was at Rolm that Andreas first learned of MIPS.

Now, eighteen years after coming to the United States in pursuit of a girl and eighteen months after joining MIPS, he was putting in long hours at work, was divorced, spent what little spare time he had with his boy and with his music, and was enjoying his insider's look at the American dream.

And the IPO? "A matter of being in the right place at the right time. Coming here was more a career move than a stock move. I get much more excited about the stream of executives from all the big computer companies coming through our door all day long."

But Andreas also admitted that a recent house purchase that strapped him with heavy mortgage payments was made "betting a little bit" on a successful IPO.

"Will I celebrate tonight? No, not particularly. I have my son staying over and since I'm leaving for Christmas, today is our Christmas together. So this news today is like a nice little Christmas present. I'm taking him to dinner. And I'm giving him a nice eighteen-speed bike. You know, he's already called me on the phone and asked me how rich I was now? I'm going to have to temper that. I told him I was rich enough to send him to Stanford if he got good grades."

Another young man on the run at MIPS spent his morning in the manufacturing group focused almost exclusively on his job. This was Ben de la Rosa, 31, for whom the motto "In Memory of Your Youth" had been enscribed on the rock in the building's center divider. De la Rosa was generally considered the hardest-working man in the manufacturing building, if not the company.

An air force brat and the oldest of four children, Ben was born in the Philippines and spent part of his childhood in Okinawa and Japan. His father, who was Filipino, finally retired as a staff sergeant after twenty years' service, moved the family to California, and currently worked at the San Jose Post Office. Ben's mother worked at Signetics, a semi-conductor company just two blocks from MIPS.

Ben had actually lived in San Jose since 1970, his family deciding to give him a measure of stability while his father finished out tours in Thailand, Taiwan, and southern California. Ben's brother joined his father at the post office, one of his sisters worked for the San Jose police department, and the other sister became a housewife.

"I was interested in electronics, but I just never went into it. So, when the [map-making] company I worked for folded, I decided now was the time to change careers. I graduated from a vocational electronics school, a small one, while taking courses in college at the same time. So I ended up with an A.A. in industrial technology, with a concentration in computers and electronics.

"Well, it turns out my brother-in-law was working here at MIPS when the place was just a start-up, thirty or forty people. I couldn't get into any jobs at the time I graduated because Silicon Valley was kind of in a lull, and so when my brother-in-law asked if I'd like to make some money moving furniture at MIPS, I said sure. He told me it would at least be a way to get into a company to see what it was like.

"So I did it. Then I started helping out with other things. They didn't have a materials department—they had a materials manager, but he needed help in receiving. And so I sort of created my own job, helping out the engineering group with their parts and components and setting up a few things around the company.

"Now it's been three years. I started off in the stock room and learned all that, and then kind of took over shipping also. Then when my present manager came on [Judy Sims], she asked me exactly what I wanted to do. I was on a course of going into just materials, but she offered me some other opportunities where I could go into planning. I'm doing that now. My exact title is senior production control expediter.

"It's been a real challenge. There are times when it feels overwhelming.

"I really feel lucky. I kind of got in through the back door, but I feel I've earned it now. I've worked. We've done like six days a week, twelve hours a day for five days and then six hours on Saturday. But I've seen some of those production floor people come in seven days a week before."

And the IPO? "I've thought about it. It seems like that's what you build up for when you join a start-up. You hope for that. But this being my first Silicon Valley company, I haven't been really caught up in it. I'd heard talk about it because of other people that were here, that's why they moved from their other companies. Because of the founder's stock."

For Ben de la Rosa, Going Public Day could not have come at a better time. His wife, a personnel secretary at Ford Aerospace in San Jose, has just learned she is pregnant. Because of that, Ben admits to not yet having gone over the stock numbers with her: "I'm trying to keep her as calm as possible.

"I have run the numbers in my head. I called my mother. She's excited for us. It will help out with the baby. And my wife wants a new house. I'm the practical one; my wife wants to go out and do something with it. But I want to hold on, keep some of it.

"It means a lot to me that I was part of the beginning of this company, that I had a hand in it." Does he plan to leave MIPS? "That's a tough question for me because I'm surrounded by people who've been around; they stay for a little while, then they move on. For me, it's like I've grown up with this company, so it's pretty tough for me even to think about going off.'' One who did leave was Ben's brother-in-law, though he shrewdly used his option before departing.

"But the company has changed. There's a lot of new faces and the personality of the company is different. I do miss the small start-up company feeling and if I do move on that would be something I would look for in another company. I don't see going to a large company. I would probably go to another start-up. There's just that adrenaline rush you get trying to build a company. . . .''

Then Ben de la Rosa heads back to work. There's still a long day ahead.

Because Tom Riordan's tenure at MIPS is nearly as long as the company's history, he is one of the few immediate beneficiaries of the IPO. That is fitting, because for many people at the firm Tom Riordan *is* MIPS.

His company resume lists him as the "principal logic designer of R2/3000 processors, principal microarchitect of R2/3010 floating-point coprocessor, manager of M2000 computer system development, and director of CMOS systems—1985–present.'' In other words, without Tom Riordan there would be no MIPS. And all of that by age 33.

Tom was born in Florida. His mother was a nurse, and, like a surprising number of other MIPS employees, his father was a postal worker. Young Tom earned a B.S. in electrical engineering, a B.A. (pre-law), and an M.S. in electrical engineering from Florida Technological University in 1979. He had so little money that he lived in a trailer pulled by a beat-up 1972 Ford Grand Torino.

On the recommendation of a professor, Riordan applied for an engineering job at a number of tech companies and accepted an offer from the most famous of the batch, Intel. So, hitching up the trailer behind the Torino, he drove west to Silicon Valley, blowing a head gasket in Louisiana, but eventually arriving.

He stayed at Intel in Santa Clara for eighteen months, the car limping to work every day on two or three cylinders, until the division in which he worked was moved to Phoenix. Not knowing what to do, he called his old professor, who told him to go, but not to put down roots. So, Tom pulled the now-tired trailer down to Arizona and stayed there for another eighteen months. "It wasn't so bad. To be honest, I only slept in the thing. The rest of the time I was either at work or doing something else—sort of the way I am now.''

Riordan quit Intel in 1983, and, finding a job back in the valley at a start-up called Weitek, again dragged the poor trailer west. The job lasted only two years, but that was longer than the trailer, which Riordan abandoned in 1983 after having lived in it six years. From then on Riordan lived in a series of rented rooms in executive homes, guest cottages behind local mansions, and, finally, his own apartment.

While he was at Weitek, a headhunter gave Riordan a pitch about joining a brand new company called MIPS. Riordan knew of the company, because Weitek had dealings with it. He wasn't impressed: ''It was the way they were going to use this Stanford design, this university processor. At Weitek we sort of laughed and said, 'Those guys don't have a chance of making this processor a product in the real world.' It just didn't have any of the things—memory management, cache control—that it needed to be practical.

''Then three or four months later, the headhunter guy called and said, 'Oh, they scrapped all that and they're going to build their own processor.' In fact, that was why he was calling me. Now they were looking for designers.'' In the end, Riordan would design that MIPS processor. ''It was a fun, hard job.''

But then the hard times came. Riordan found himself having to lay off one of his people—a task he couldn't bring himself to do. An employee in personnel did the nasty job. ''I still owe the guy for doing that for me.''

At the worst moments Riordan even contemplated starting his own MIPS-like company, but realized that would have required starting over, ''and pouring all this very good work down the drain. . . . So our position was: 'Let's hang in there, finish the job, and in six months we'll either be here or we won't. So why leave now?' ''

Four years later Tom Riordan was still at MIPS. And on this morning, for his loyalty, he became one of Silicon Valley's big winners.

And the money, what did he plan to do with it? ''I have no idea. I haven't really thought of it. I'm not that kind of a person. I'm an engineer at heart. I live to create. I get bored. I may buy a house. I actually have a house in Phoenix, by the way, that I use strictly for tax purposes. I never lived in it. It was strictly an investment.''

Still, after five years of all-night work sessions and seven-day work weeks, the new wealth may buy a long-overdue private life. ''The reason the money means anything to me at all is because I can get married and have kids, right? And I know I can put them through college; I know that I can take care of them. And I can still be an engineer and create things without working strictly to put food in their mouths.''

Not that a wife and kids are in the offing. ''If I got married in the present time, I'd be divorced in a year because she'd never see me. It wouldn't work out. Currently I'm married to MIPS.''

As a true engineer, Riordan would search for a more precise explanation: ''You see, what I'm trying to say is that I'm not here to make money so that I can do something else. I'm here because this is what I want to do with my time. The big things in my life I've done in the last five years and am doing right now—the design of this processor set. Most of my dreams have come true.''

For most other MIPS employees, the seriousness of the morning merely masked an increasingly impossible struggle to make the day seem like any other. ''There are six hundred stories in the Naked MIPS Computer,'' as Joe DiNucci would say in his best television voice.

Here are some of them, their dreams as diverse as their lives.

Kent Price, 50, was senior quality engineer in the manufacturing group. Born in Springfield, Missouri, to a family of six children, he was raised on a dairy farm and remembers ''lots of cold mornings out milking cows.'' In 1963 the family moved to Modesto, California, because his mother wanted to be closer to her family and his father's asthma demanded he get to a warmer, drier climate. ''Besides, in the late 1950s and 1960s farming was not a very profitable venture. It was tough times. We wondered where the next meal was coming from.''

Kent's father became a postman. In time Kent's two older brothers went to work for Modesto city schools, one as an electrician and the other as a high school custodian, Kent's sister became a beautician, and his two younger brothers both became brick masons.

But Kent was headed in a different direction. He earned his A.A. in electronics at Modesto Junior College. Before his low draft number came up, he joined the navy and found himself, in 1970, stationed at Moffett Field in Mountain View, at the heart of Silicon Valley, in the ground maintenance crew for P3 Orion submarine surveillance planes. While there, he met his future wife at an engagement party of mutual friends.

''I considered re-enlisting, but my wife gave me a choice: her or the navy. I made the right decision. I stayed in Sunnyvale and got a job at Four-Phase Systems [a computer maker].''

He stayed at Four-Phase, located in Cupertino near Tandem and Apple, for nine years. "They were about where MIPS is at now."

But when Motorola bought the increasingly troubled company in 1983, Kent Price decided to leave. He joined Victor Technologies in the nearby Santa Cruz Mountains in the town of Scott's Valley. It was three months of a miserable commute. "A week after I joined them they started talking about reductions and cutbacks. Then it was one layoff a month, more than fifteen hundred people out of two thousand. I got it in the third round."

From there, Price went to the equally doomed Elxsi, where Jake Vigil was president. Three layoffs again, and Price's department was down to just him. Then he got a call from MIPS. Would he like a job? Yes, Price said. The next day there was another layoff at Elxsi.

He arrived at MIPS on March 31, 1986—meaning that he would be fully vested on his stock in just three months from Going Public Day. Price thought that, after two disasters, he'd found a company with a chance to survive. Then came the MIPS layoffs in January 1987. "I thought, 'Not again.' I had to lay off two acquaintances from my Elxsi days. My wife and I talked about moving back to Modesto or Missouri. To heck with this valley. We don't need it. But in the end we decided to stick with it. . . .

"In the long run [with the stock money] I'd like to do something on my own. Not necessarily electronics, but maybe something like woodworking or antiques. We have a small business now on the side, a family tree plaque we sell at Christmas craft shows.

"Maybe in five or ten years, before the kids get too old—they're 7, 6, and 2½—we'll move up to the Sierra foothills, like Auburn, and open a shop."

Wendy Paige's office has a sign that says, "Law Offices, Sweeney & Doberman." It was given to her by the sales department for her tenaciousness in negotiating contracts.

In her year and a half at MIPS, Paige has been on the move, traveling around the world cutting deals with the company's semiconductor partners and systems customers. She likes the work and the pressure, but it was not the career she'd planned. A graduate of the University of Massachusetts, she was the first female in her Scots-English family to go to college. The degree was in education, and she followed it with a master's in reading at the University of Hartford and then nine years of teaching in the Windsor, Connecticut, public school system.

"It was tough. Awful. I had kids come at me with knives and throwing chairs—and I was in a *good* school system."

She quit for a number of reasons, the biggest of which was the realization "that the superintendent of schools was paying two guys hired after me more money than he was paying me. . . .

"So I went to the University of Connecticut as a 30-year-old first-year law student. It was a rough gig. I got divorced as a result of it. I got served my divorce papers the night of moot court. But I still won the moot court competition."

At 33 Paige found a job at United Technologies. "In Hartford. It was fabulous digs, twenty-sixth floor, floor-to-ceiling windows by your desk, helicopter rides, it was really something."

She stayed for six years, working with UTC's Norden division. "I did a lot of international work: Israel, Europe, Far East, Europe. Good training for here. . . . But I also came to realize there's a difference between a defense contractor and a commercial company. Doing a government contract is like buying a used car and having to bring along your checkbook and your tax returns with you. It's a creepy business.

"What really made me walk was that my significant other accepted the position as the president of a company out here and said, 'I want you to come with me.' And I said, 'Time to change. California here I come.'

"So we came out here and bought a huge house in the Los Gatos hills—one of those 6,500 square foot things that looks down on the valley. . . . We went to Carmel every weekend and I spent most of my time at the health club or Nieman-Marcus. Just hanging and relaxing. Eventually I realized I liked shopping, but not full time."

She joined MIPS on May 4, 1988, hired by Joe Sweeney initially as general counsel for the Synthesis group.

"Sweeney said to me, 'Well, when do you want to start?' I said, 'How about Monday?' And he said, 'How about now? We could go right back to the office and you can get working.'

"The first thing Miller said to me was, 'The most valuable thing we have here is time.' He was right. With the IPO looming, nothing could slip. And with all these technology deals the company has been very law department intensive. It got rolling in January and just hasn't stopped.

"The interesting thing is that our technology and our organization is so new that we have to educate our customers about it. So here I am, back teaching again.

"I remember the first check we got from Siemens. I'm opening the mail and here's this regular envelope from Munich, Germany. I open it up and there's a check for $2.25 million! I was speechless.''

And the IPO? ''Well, the numbers for me aren't that big. Big enough for fun, but I already have a lot of fun. It's not going to impact my lifestyle. I tend to spend money on my family. I probably won't sell it. I'm sort of in this for the long haul.''

Tom Rohrs wears a Notre Dame watch to commemorate the fact that this Long Island boy graduated from the school in 1973 with a degree in mechanical engineering. He also holds a Harvard M.B.A. ''I like to go with winners,'' he says.

That includes Hewlett-Packard, where he spent eleven years, first in Waltham, Massachusetts, becoming general manager of that division, then in Cupertino, California, as the operations manager on the Spectrum computer project. ''They took pretty good care of me. It wasn't a skinny deal.''

But within months he was at MIPS. ''HP said, 'You're kidding,' when I told them. And I said, 'No, and I exercised my options yesterday.' . . .

''I can remember back at HP; the Waltham division was acquired through the acquisition in 1960 of the Sandborn Company and there were a lot of people in the sheetmetal shop holding a lot of Sandborn stock, which wasn't publicly traded. They used to play poker with it over coffee breaks. But by the time 1980 or 1981 rolled around, when they traded their paper Sandborn stock for HP stock, there were a few millionaires out there punching sheetmetal. And they just kept on punching sheetmetal because that's what they liked to do. It didn't make all that much difference who had a million dollars in the bank and who didn't.

''So I would suspect that there'll be some people here who may be smiling more broadly than others on the IPO day, but I guess I just don't think it's going to be that big a deal for all that many people.''

Jeffrey Payne proudly announces, ''I've been at MIPS since June 1986. I have the longest tenure of anyone in marketing.''

But what makes him even more unusual is that Payne is one of the valley's few second-generation entrepreneurs. ''My father has always been involved in start-up companies. He started two or three with various people and nurtured them and grew them and sold. The latest was called Challenge Manufacturing up in Emeryville. He sold that off and is retired now.

''I grew up in Saratoga [California], and except for three years of graduate school, I've always lived in this area. Graduated Saratoga High in 1974, then went to Stanford for a degree in math, computer sciences, and statistics. . . .

". . . MIPS was very different then from the way it is now. We were eighty-some people. Two people in marketing, one of whom was supposedly the vice-president. He left about a month after he arrived and was replaced by someone else. The company was very chip-focused. It was in a real start-up mode, where engineers would stay overnight and sleep on cots in their offices.

"Of that original group, probably only two dozen are left with the firm."

Dreams? "Sure, a house. I'm married. Have kids. I live in Willow Glen [a district in San Jose]. Possibly I'll move back to Saratoga. But nothing wacky. I'm not that kind of person. Nothing extravagant, maybe a nice vacation—assuming it's without the kids. . . .

"In five years I see myself in some marketing or sales management role, probably in a company about this size or smaller."

Barbara Campisi is another valley native. Small and pretty, she is an executive administrator, reporting to DiNucci, Jerman, and Boesenberg, with whom she came over from Apple. "It's been a big adjustment. This is what you call a small company. At Apple I had two assistants. And it's just been a whirlwind ever since I got here. It's hard to believe it's already been six months. It's been an absolute blur.

"I was born and raised in San Jose, went to college at San Jose City College, then went into dental assisting for ten years. I decided I didn't like that anymore and thought, why not try Apple? My sister had been working for the CFO there for several years.

"I joined Apple in 1985, when all the excitement about the Macintosh was going on. I got there the week it was introduced, and that was pretty exciting stuff. That was the division I worked for, helping people like Steve Jobs with presentations.

"After that I went over to the planning group in finance. And then Chuck came on board from Data General in Paris and I thought I'd try out this executive assistant stuff and see how I liked it. I did and I enjoy Chuck very much, which is the reason why I'm here.

"The real adjustment for me here is the technology. Being an administrator, it's always nice to understand what the products are. And for me it's really difficult; the stuff here is so technical compared to, say, a Macintosh. . . .

"I just made it in on the founder's stock. But being an administrator I didn't end up with a lot of shares. In a couple of years, when I'm vested some, my husband and I plan to do a little remodeling of our house. It's a little two bedroom, one bath place in Willow Glen which we love dearly and don't want to leave. Maybe we'll expand it some. The basic yuppie dream."

Barbara "Babs" Louie always wanted to be a musical actress. That's why she left community theater in San Jose, her hometown, and took off for New York City for a year. She went on casting calls and slept in the hallway of a tiny flat a block and a half from Carnegie Hall and lived on Chinese food—and in the end, came home.

That set off a decade of searching. She went to San Jose State, but didn't finish. She worked in summer stock in San Jose and Michigan and had a variety of temp jobs as a secretary and receptionist. She spent five years at a construction company and a year and a half more at Bechtel, as a secretary to the chief financial officer. That was followed by five years at an accounting firm. She joined MIPS in August 1987. She is now a legal and financial administrator.

But she is much more than that. Babs Louie has become MIPS's chief of morale. "Skip Stritter started and he kind of roped me into the first office Christmas party. The party turned out well. We have one every year now."

Soon Louie was called on to organize other events. "We created a yearly softball game, a golf tournament, a company picnic. Originally we were all in one building and then we expanded into this building and the engineers stayed in that building. And the old furniture stayed over there and the execs, marketing, and sales got all the brand new furniture. So soon we were calling this the Pit and that became the Palace. We built on that and started a rivalry, a fun rivalry, so we have softball tournaments and volleyball tournaments and tug-of-wars and everything. The Pit plays the Palace and we give the winner a trophy. . . .

"With the IPO, being in legal it's been rough. Most of it comes down to us. My dream, if the stock turns out to be strong enough and grows well, is to trade in my little condo for a real house. Then I can have a real big dog."

CHAPTER 21

Noon—Lunch Money

NOON WAS the first sanctioned moment when the people of MIPS could pause in their responsibilities and savor the meaning of the day. Most talked noisily as they left the buildings and scattered to restaurants throughout Silicon Valley.

One group—Chuck Boesenberg and all those reporting directly to him, Bev Jerman, John Hime, technical products group head Chet Silvestri, Joe DiNucci, Barbara Campisi, and several others—gathered on the other side of Sunnyvale, in the shadow of Hewlett-Packard's computer group complex, at the California Cafe. This restaurant, a cluster of converted railroad cars plunked incongruously in the middle of suburbia, and the Sports City Cafe, a mile away near Apple in Cupertino, were favorites of the MIPS crew.

The lunch, ostensibly a Christmas gathering, had been planned well in advance. Jerman: "There was a lot of joking and laughing and having a good time—and just a little bit about the day itself. Hu had brought this big cake that had 'Merry Christmas' on it. It didn't say anything about the IPO on it—of course, we couldn't be sure when. Anyway, we all had some.

"Then we got an idea. We'd spotted a table in another part of the restaurant where Cindy [Buttita, one of the company's three women officers] and two other MIPS people were sitting. So we decided to have some of the cake delivered to them. That was the initial idea. Then Jim Bellmire and Chet Silvestri get up, cut three pieces of cake, put them on plates, and drape napkins over their arms like waiters. Then we all got the idea, all nine of us, that we would go en masse over to their table and sing Happy Birthday to Cindy—even though it wasn't her birthday. So we all walk over there and we all sing and the whole restaurant claps.

"After that, back at our table, Boesenberg got up and called his broker. By then we were all looking at our watches because around one o'clock Chuck started asking us what time the market closed. Somebody said one-thirty our time, so by twenty after one he was asking, 'Where's the phone?' Then he called and came back and said the stock was at $19.

"One of the people there said he had called his broker at Merrill-Lynch and that she had told him that four Silicon Valley presidents had called that day to buy MIPS stock. And he quoted her as telling them that it wasn't going to trade any higher than 17 and it wasn't a good buy. But the CEOs were insistent and bought anyway. . . .

"You know, as I was leaving for lunch, Miller made an interesting comment to me. He said, 'Do you realize this is the last IPO of 1989, of this decade. And we're the youngest new company of 1990, the new decade?' We've got to capitalize on that somehow."

Back at MIPS, many of the desks in the management offices bore a two-page hand-written Xerox entitled "New Year's Resolutions at MIPS." Jerman's entry read: "Bev Jerman resolves to be quiet for all of 1990. She said, 'We have been quiet for two months now, and everything is fine. This proves that a lot of publicity is really not necessary.' "

In another part of Silicon Valley, venture capitalist Bill Davidow was having lunch with his old boss, Andrew Grove. Twenty years before, Grove, Bob Noyce, and Gordon Moore had founded the quintessential semiconductor start-up, Intel, now a multibillion dollar firm. Grove in recent years had been a strong critic of entrepreneurship, especially when "vulture" capitalists looted and weakened established companies in search of talented managers.

Now Andy was sitting across the table from just such a venture capitalist, discussing one of the most successful valley start-ups in years. And Grove was pleased, both for his old friend and because MIPS was an honest-to-God new U.S. computer corporation in the battle against Japan.

Davidow was pleased, too, but hardly about the riches he had made for himself. A fortune to a Ben de la Rosa or even a Dave Ludvigson was comparatively small potatoes to Davidow. The money from the MIPS deal would have little impact on his life. He already had the big house in Atherton, the architectural landmark home in Hawaii, and the helicopter ski trips in the Canadian Rockies. Davidow had already made several fortunes, with Intel, where he had been a senior vice-president marketing the company's microprocessors; with Tandem, where he was co-holder of the company's founding patent; and with Businessland, in which he had been an early investor.

For Davidow the MIPS IPO was important because it was a validation of his ideas, of his strategies, and of his venture capital acumen. As he saw it, the IPO was "the third trophy on my wall." He'd arrived too late for the Intel IPO, but he had had a hand in the going public of Tandem and Businessland. Now there was MIPS: "I can't say that MIPS wouldn't have happened without me. But I think it's happening better because I was involved and it's happening better because I helped Miller with some of the strategic issues and I've helped them with some of the marketing issues and he's had a sounding board."

Davidow knew that the success of the MIPS IPO would improve the image of Mohr-Davidow Ventures as well, making it more attractive to investors when the time came to create a new venture fund. It would also draw out potential entrepreneurs. "I'm interested in creating successes and not really in making money so much. That's because if you focus on creating a success and creating value for the customer, you're going to make money. As David Packard said, 'Profit is the reward for making a contribution.' "

But there was a personal element as well. For all his success, Davidow had long been a supporting player, albeit a major one, in the Silicon Valley story. In recent years, thanks to the successful investments and the authorship of two best-selling business books (*Marketing High Technology* and, with Bro Uttal, *Total Customer Service*), he had begun to move into the limelight. The MIPS IPO was the final step in Davidow's ascent into Silicon Valley stardom.

Not that the experience wasn't bittersweet. Only three years from being a line executive, Davidow still admitted to occasionally feeling odd about his role in dealing with MIPS. "I don't feel like I'm on the outside looking in, but there's definitely a difference between putting in a minority of your time on something and putting in all your time. I think that if you're asking whether 49ers fans enjoy winning the Super Bowl, well sure they do. And if you're asking did Joe Montana get more satisfaction out of it, I think he probably did. But also more pain."

Like Heidrich and Myers, Davidow had been kept up to date about the troubles with the SEC. He was up and dressed when Miller called with the good news. "I guess it was anticlimatic. If you're in a marathon and if at the end of the race you beat the guy by a yard, and you're scared as hell right up to the time you break that tape, I think that there's a different feeling of elation than if you're leading the guy by five minutes and you've got it in the bag.

"So, yeah, I was concerned about the stuff with the SEC, but I have so much confidence in what those [MIPS] guys are doing and such a belief in this company that whether they went public that day or a year from now, I didn't see it as a make or break issue. These guys were doing a fundamentally good job and they were creating value—and that is the most important thing. The world will compensate them for that. So I'm glad they got public, and I'm certainly glad for the return to our investors, but it wasn't 'Oh my god, we've made it under the wire.' "

If Davidow did have a concern, it was with the future, and the subtle interplay between the newly public corporation and its investors. "I didn't want this thing so hyped that the stock would shoot up to 95 and then go back down to 5. I was greatly concerned about investors' entering into this thing with unrealistic expectations. A [wildly fluctuating] stock can destroy the fabric of a company by disillusioning both employees and investors. What I wanted to see in the next few days and weeks was a nice, smooth climb in value. That's what makes people feel pretty good."

An even greater worry for Davidow was the internal changes that Going Public Day could bring upon the company. "There has to be something that holds a company together beyond making a lot of money; otherwise the company will begin to deteriorate as everyone begins to say, 'Now that I'm rich, I can do whatever I want to do.' You take an engineer who's making $80,000 to $100,000 a year and give him a million dollars and he's liable to say, 'Well now I can make $100,000 a year on interest without working. I don't have to put up with this shit.'

"The glue is that your people better love what they're doing, better be committed to the mission, better believe in winning. Because after the IPO a company moves to a phase where it can't create economic incentives for its people the way it once did. A new type of employee comes on the scene, one who is less entrepreneurial and more power-oriented. People who get their kicks having two thousand people know that they're the boss. People who enjoy a position of authority. The company has to learn to deal with this new type of manager."

Finally, there are the demands of a new constituency, the shareholders (including employees), that must be addressed. Too often these shareholders judge a company not by its long-term strategies, but by short-term results, as reflected in that day's stock price.

"That's one of the things I was talking about over lunch with Andy; about how the price of the stock begins to affect the behavior of the whole company. We were talking about why America is having the problems it's having competing with Japan. And Andy said that a lot of it had to do with the fact that executives like him had to answer to the public markets; that business decisions were often influenced by their impact on stock prices."

The day of the MIPS IPO was business as usual for Bill Davidow. A morning meeting with a potential investment, a young firm the size MIPS had been when he'd first encountered it. Lunch with Grove. The afternoon with one of his more troubled firms—a neat counterbalance to the good news of the day. Then he talked with his money manager, attended an Intel reunion at a restaurant in Cupertino, came home to a small dinner, and then waited with his wife for the return of their eldest daughter from college.

All in all, a fairly typical day.

Up the Peninsula in Menlo Park, in the venture capital enclave atop Sand Hill, two other directors of MIPS were accepting congratulations from their industry. Grant Heidrich and Gib Myers of Mayfield Fund had been with MIPS from the beginning, when it was just three scientists with a new idea about computer processing. The original business plan, which Heidrich kept in his files, was just a graph about computer performance scrawled on a single sheet of paper.

Heidrich and Myers had taken that team and that idea and built a company from it. They had given the team an office at Mayfield, had found them experienced managers, and, at predetermined milestones in the growth of the company, had given them hundreds of thousands of dollars. Later, they helped create the syndicate that would raise a total of $??? million to invest in MIPS.

In an industry where only one out of ten investments ever goes public, the success of creating a public corporation with $100 million in sales would have been enough to earn industry kudos for Grant and Gib. But the MIPS IPO was even more than that, and the venture capital industry knew it. It had added considerable luster to Mayfield Fund; it had affirmed the fund's philosophy of seed-round investments at a time when the industry trend was toward big-money later rounds; and, most of all, it had confirmed the wisdom and courage of Heidrich and Myers to stick with a company that many investors had believed dead. The industry knew it had taken guts to protect the interests of the secondary investors by stepping in and replacing MIPS's president, skill to recruit a top industry name from the East to take on a dying firm, and nerve to revalue the company downward and go out and raise new investors.

The venture industry was thankful, too, for what Mayfield had done; at a time when institutions were questioning the worth of putting their money behind high-tech venture capital, Mayfield had resolved some of their doubts with this spectacular MIPS offering. In an industry as incestuous and interdependent as venture capital, good news for one firm was good news for all.

Heidrich, young, blond, and rangy, and Myers, older, dark, and small, had been privy to every event and every decision in the history of MIPS. They had suffered as much through the weeks of battles with the SEC as any of the MIPS IPO team. And they were among the first to be called with the news.

Heidrich: "I got the call at 6:30 in the morning. The word was that the opening price was $17.50 and the opening trade at $20 and something. I immediately called Gib.

Myers: "I was on Christmas vacation. My mother had come into town from Illinois the night before. Grant said it had gotten off. I was ecstatic. But I have to admit I wasn't very surprised. The day before was the dramatic one, when everything was on and off. So I guess I had a high confidence it'd get off."

Heidrich: "I tell you those guys over there, Latta and Sonsini and the rest, did a helluva job. The dramatic time was the afternoon before, with the Quattrone article. Bob called me up and said, 'The deal's off. Ninety-nine percent chance. I don't know what we can do now.' He said, 'I'm so pissed off.'

"Luckily, I knew we could wait. The good news was that we were not a hostage to the date. We weren't out of cash. Some companies get to that window and they've got to go."

Myers: "We could've gone at the end of January, I guess. But it would have taken the edge off. It would have cost two points, three points—a huge amount of money."

Heidrich: "Anyway, we did it. I told my wife—she was deep into this deal—and then I went for a run. A euphoric run. Then I came into the office and told everybody. There was hardly anybody in here to tell, so I told all the secretaries. After all, they'd been living through this saga, too."

Myers: "I told my wife. Then I went down and told my mom. I explained to her what was happening. In the past she's often bought stock and hasn't always been successful. She hadn't bought any stock in MIPS."

Heidrich: "My mom had. I called her back in Illinois and told her. Then I called my brother, because he and his family were out here visiting us the day Skip Stritter and I had to fly back East for a second meeting with Bob Miller. I had to just sort of dump them here and take off. He's the director of the Brooks Museum in Memphis and a pretty sophisticated guy with business, so it's been fun for him because he's heard about this thing as it cycled through its various incarnations.

"Let's see. After I got to the office, I had a case of champagne and two dozen loony balloons sent down to MIPS and went off to a meeting with [Silicon Valley public relations guru] Regis MacKenna. I was working with a new company and I wanted to talk with him about how you position a whole new technology in a product market area. After lunch I got my hair cut. Hula [the barber] was one of the few people I talked to all that day who didn't know or care about the MIPS IPO."

The mood of the day also led both men to reminisce about the company and what they'd been through, each filling in the blanks in the other's memory. Together the memories went like this:

"Everybody loses sleep over it. Many sleepless nights years ago, early on. 'What's going to happen?'

"We knew it was so great and yet it was falling apart and that was the really difficult bad period.

"I remember going to these famous things called 'Mash Bashes,' named after John Mashey [MIPS vice president for systems technology]. After the layoff I went to one of these things after John kept saying, 'You really got to come down. These people really want to talk to you.' So I did and God, all these people were grabbing me by the lapel and saying, 'Why are you laying people off?' 'Why are we cutting back?' Just these really challenging comments and questions. It was tough. . . .

"I remember how it all started. It was when we first went in to interview Jim Clark about Silicon Graphics. We were down there and

John Massouris was wandering around and Clark grabbed me and pointed at the Moose and said, 'That is a brilliant guy and he's got some neat ideas. Follow up on them.' . . .

"I remember, back at the worst of the tough times, when Hennessy, Massouris, and Stritter all came over to my house at 9:30 at night and we sat in the library for three hours. They said, 'Look, the board's got to do something. It's even worse than you think. We need to have a discussion, try to figure things out, get rolling.' They wanted to get rid of the president, Vaemond Crane.

"You see, it takes a tremendous amount of effort to really understand what is going on in a company. Five managers can have five totally different perceptions about what's going on. Take that one step removed, and you've got the predicament of being a director. You've got to make a decision, but if you make the wrong one everybody walks out. Or, if you make a decision prematurely to ask a CEO to leave and you don't have underlying support from management, then the whole company can be gone in a matter of days.

"You hear the story that the board always waits too long to make a decision like that, which is true—but you have to wait too long because you can't just take a chance on that kind of decision. There's too much at stake. So in fact what's happened is that by the time you make the decision, you've done a lot of homework and others in the company have come to you and you've been able to solicit from them who they will support. Luckily, I've never had a situation where management was supporting the wrong person. It always comes together, but it takes a long time and it's so delicate because you don't want to show a lack of support for the CEO prematurely, because all of a sudden you're undermining him and that tips the table.

"But I tell you, swinging the ax like that is tough. He's your guy after all. I can still see that boardroom and all of us sitting around it, giving Crane the news."

The memory of the MIPS coup d'etat remained painful and Grant and Gib soon left it for other anecdotes. Like the day a month before when one of the board members was flying in from Japan for the MIPS annual meeting. "He's at San Francisco Airport and he's late; he's only got twenty minutes until the annual meeting and he's rushing through customs. He flips his passport down and it's got his MIPS card in there. And the customs guy says, 'MIPS. Isn't that the company that's going public? So tell me, why are you so much better than Intel?' The customs guy!"

That reminded Heidrich of another story. He pointed at three Balinese wooden puppets that decorate his office. He explained how he visited the sculptor, whose father was a brahmin, in the same compound where the family had lived for eight hundred years. During their conversation Heidrich found himself talking about MIPS. "But the sculptor just couldn't understand the idea of a giant computer being reduced to a single square of silicon. So I gave him one of the MIPS chips encased in lucite. And I realized that for him it was equivalent to magic. Which, when you think about it, I guess it is."

A few days later, when the confusion had passed, Heidrich, now a high-tech brahmin himself, sat down and typed a stream-of-consciousness note on his feelings about the day. It said in part: "Sense of relief, euphoria, great pride in the people and the company. In spite of perceptions of VC and technology, we defied gravity. The Mayfield process works. Great personal accomplishment to have helped. Played a sparking role in founding and development of company. Almost a paternal feeling.

"I do not like the obvious, easy stuff. I like things that change the world. How people do things. How they think about the world, themselves.

"Feeling this is a start, an enrichment of an opportunity, a tremendous vote of confidence. An affirmation. Done so much in so little time. Taken the bull by the horns and run with it. It does reaffirm; yes, dreams do exist. They do come true if you believe in them and work at them. Just like what I've been reading to my 3 year old. Dreams, dreams, dreams. . . ."

But on this day there were more immediate, earthly concerns—new start-ups to help, new investments to be made. And so, during the day Grant Heidrich walked down the hall to an office where, like the three MIPS scientists four years before, five postdoctoral molecular biologists were trying to get their new company off the ground.

"They'd seen all of us buzzing around and they'd obviously gotten infected by the excitement. And I said, 'I want to tell you about the heritage you are inheriting here. You've got a tall mountain to jump over. Not long ago the guys from MIPS were sitting there just like you. And this is what can happen.' They believed it. And I believed it, too. MIPS is a reminder that it can happen."

CHAPTER 22

Afternoon—The Dam Breaks

BY THE MIDDLE of the afternoon any effort to make this like any other day at MIPS was gone. Employees gathered to chatter, cheer, and laugh everywhere in the company. By three o'clock the workday was over. John Hime, who'd been receiving visitors all day to check the stock price, broke out a bottle of Glenfiddich and announced the party had begun.

Nearby, a young business development engineer named Rob Jensen accidently and poetically captured the essence of the MIPS IPO. Fresh out of school (a photograph of the Santa Clara University engineering building hung in his cubicle), Jensen had found himself at MIPS in October facing a seemingly impossible job: assembling and testing all the equipment in the MIPS booth for a major trade show (Unix Expo) less than forty-eight hours after the earthquake. Short of people and time, he'd somehow pulled it off. In recognition of his superhuman effort, at a company-wide meeting in November, Jensen had been awarded a pressure cooker.

Now, on the afternoon of Going Public Day, he faced a new, if not so daunting challenge: how to keep a bottle of champagne cold. The ice he had, but what to put it in? He remembered his award. And thus, with the perfect symbol—a champagne bottle in a pressure cooker—MIPS began to celebrate.

Soon a group of headquarters people gathered around this totem. In the center was an animated Chuck Boesenberg, the third member of the road show troika. Eleven months before, when he'd left Apple, Boesenberg had been quoted in several trade publications as saying that he'd "always worked for big companies—IBM, Data General, Apple—and now I'm going after my Silicon Valley dream." His mention in a *Fortune* article about workaholic baby boomers had earned him the nickname around MIPS of "Boom Boom Boesenberg."

Raised in the northwest suburbs of Chicago, Boesenberg had attended a small engineering school, Rose-Hulman Institute of Technology, "because I wanted to play quarterback and my parents would only let me play football if I majored in engineering. And I had to find a school that was small enough for me to play but still had an engineering curriculum. I went on an army scholarship.

"In the end I only played two years, and the second year I switched to defensive halfback.

"After graduating I had a four-year army commitment, got commissioned as a second lieutenant, and spent the next three and a half years in Frankfurt managing an IBM 360/40 data center. This was 1971 to 1974. Ended up a captain.

"I got out and went to work for IBM in Chicago, Los Angeles, and Atlanta. Sales and marketing positions. Then I went to work for Data General, where Bob Miller was and I was the area director for the Southeast. Then I managed Europe, the Middle East, and Africa for DG. . . .

"After that I came out here to work for Apple. I was recruited through a search person named John Holeman, and, after I gave him Miller's name as a possible candidate, Holeman recruited Miller to MIPS.

"Because of all of these career moves, my family lived in five cities in six years. So I had a military career where I didn't move anywhere and a corporate career where all I've done is move. So I came to Silicon Valley with the intention of never moving again. I built a house in Saratoga and put in a vineyard that won't produce anything for four years and that's just fine with me. Because I'm not going anywhere. Nancy and I have two kids, an eighth grader and a sixth grader, 14 and 11, and I made a commitment that I'd move anywhere for my career until my oldest reached junior high and then I was going to stay put. I beat it by a year.

"What brought me [to MIPS] was that I wanted to do something where the company was in a more formative stage and ten years from now I could look back and say there's part of me in that company. When I ran Europe for Data General I managed two thousand people. When I managed sales and marketing at Apple, I had three thousand people. In those kinds of jobs you become an administrator—and I wanted to roll up my sleeves and get back into it. I also wanted my Silicon Valley dream of a company going public. I had great confidence in Bob Miller and that was very, very important to me.

"It was Bob who recruited me. After I moved out here, every three or four months our families would have dinner together and over the last year Bob started talking to me about joining MIPS. And he got more and more serious the last year.

"Finally one Sunday afternoon Nancy and I went to Bob's and Barbara's house for dinner and tennis and Bob and I took a walk. As we walked by my car, we stopped and started talking the deal. We came to an agreement on the terms and conditions of my coming to MIPS by writing on the trunk of the car in the dust. . . ."

"It's so different. Today I was running around making the slide that's going to go into a slide presentation. At Apple I'd have had a twenty-person staff I'd give the idea to and they'd go out and make ten alternative slides for me to pick from. . . .

"I don't think going public will change my life. I've been fortunate. We have our place in Tahoe for skiing and our home in Saratoga. But it will give me the opportunity to give my children whatever college they want."

Had Chuck Boesenberg now fulfilled his Silicon Valley dream? "No, going public is only the first step. The real value is to have this thing work, to look back four or five years from now and see that MIPS has reached its potential. That's the true Silicon Valley dream. I'll really celebrate when MIPS is a billion-dollar company and its RISC architecture is totally established."

But by three o'clock even Boom Boom Boesenberg couldn't help but talk to an attentive group of about twenty employees about the experiences of the road show. He told again about the car accident in Paris and recalled his reaction to the sight of Miller's car being hit: "Oh my God! They just killed our president!" His audience, with champagne and Scotch in hand, laughed noisily. Standing slumped in his office doorway, even Ludvigson managed a smile.

Employee: "Did you hear? The moon is in Capricorn right now. I can't remember exactly what that means, but one of the things the moon is supposed to symbolize is money. So there's this really neat astrological thing, like the stars are all lined up for this to happen today, right?"

*   *   *

As a rule employees don't talk about the magnitude of their stock options. And one person who may appear overwhelmed by his sudden wealth may actually have seen less money than another employee who acts disappointed.

Beyond the listings in the prospectus of executive stock compensation, little is publicly known on Going Public Day about the biggest beneficiaries of the event, such as the founders who may still hold a sizable fraction (several percentage points, that is) of the firm's outstanding stock.

The consensus around MIPS was that the biggest winner on Going Public Day was Skip Stritter—perhaps $10 million, some guessed. After all, he was a founder, and unlike Massouris he was still with the firm, and unlike Hennessy he held not only a board seat but also a line position. If anyone at MIPS had made a Big Myth Silicon Valley Score, it had to be Stritter. And no one seemed to begrudge him a dime of his new fortune.

Stritter, 42, sat in the Sports City Cafe. It was early in the evening and the place was only beginning to fill up with people from Apple and Tandem. Some of the owners, members of the San Francisco 49ers, were there, drawing considerable attention. No one noticed the tall, lanky, red-headed man in jeans sitting at a corner table, who was, in his own way, a superstar.

Stritter sipped his beer. "We always said, a little bit tongue in cheek, a little bit serious, that having no business plan was an advantage. If you have a business plan 12 inches thick with spreadsheets, all the VCs do is cut it apart and say 'this number doesn't look right.' So instead, we just went over the technology, the use of people, and what we thought we could do and they bought it."

Stritter was born near Boston. His mother had been a chemist, stopped working when her children were born, then later went back to teaching.

"There's an interesting coincidence in all this. Two and a half years ago, almost to the day, Grant Heidrich and I flew back to Boston to interview Bob Miller for the presidency of the company. As we're driving out from Logan Airport things start getting more and more familiar. It turned out Bob lived right across the street from my old high school! We said, 'We better check this guy out.'

"Ultimately, two things clinched the deal: Number one was that Bob had really researched MIPS; he knew all about us and had a good idea of what it needed and what he wanted to do. Number two was that Barbara cooked a good meal and we were hungry.

"Getting back to school. This was '65 to '68. Dartmouth in those days was a pioneer in computing. Timesharing was being invented. That wasn't why I went there—I went because I loved to ski. But I ended up playing a lot in the basement of the computer center—trying out Sam Adams Beer and its competitors—and found myself getting interested in computing.

"This was the beginning of the Vietnam stuff and there were some protests, like when General Hershey, head of the Selective Service, came up to give a speech. Everything was okay for me because graduate students got deferments and I was going to go to graduate school. Then I remember coming home from skiing one day and a couple of my buddies were in my room holding a newspaper that said graduate deferments had been aced.

"So, after I got my degree, I immediately went to work at Bell Labs on some supposedly 'important' work. And Bell Labs had this great program where they send you to get your master's degree."

That's how Skipper got his master's from Stanford, as well as a deferment. A year later, in 1970, Bell Labs sponsored him to go back and work on his Ph.D. Stritter arrived at Stanford just in time for a sit-in protest that shut down the engineering labs. "That was the day I arrived for the qualifying exam. The next day they canceled school for the rest of the quarter.

"I finally got my Ph.D. in 1976. It took six years. During ski season I got out of Palo Alto every weekend. Why would I want to graduate? I was even the ski coach one year when we went to the nationals. It was great. I still have ties there; Stanford is very important to MIPS. In fact, just yesterday I was over there with the assistant dean of engineering. We have some programs that we do with them."

Was this a counterbalance to the MIPS support for Texas A&M? "Absolutely. All those free computers to those Aggies. I was a professor at the University of Texas for a while, so you can imagine how I feel about giving computers to Aggies.

"One thing we did when we started MIPS was to donate a small number of company shares to Stanford as a thank you. A lot of the technology that this company is based on was originally developed at Stanford.

"Anyway, getting back, after I got my Ph.D., I went to Austin,

Texas, to work for Motorola. I ended up working on the 68000 micro-processor for the next three years.''

The 68000, one of the first 16-bit microprocessors (it is used, for example, in the Apple Macintosh), was one of the most influential computer chips ever designed. To this day, Stritter's name is most commonly linked with that device. When *Upside* magazine polled its executive and venture capitalist readership for the all-star executive team of Silicon Valley, Stritter was selected as the valley's top research and development person.

Stritter only says, ''The 68000 worked out very nicely and it was very satisfying. Motorola understood that it didn't understand. That was important, because that led them to say, 'We're semiconductor guys but now we're starting to build computer stuff.' So they went looking for computer people—and somehow, that meant me.''

By 1979 Stritter was ready to come back from Texas. ''I missed Silicon Valley, the feeling, the excitement of knowing what's going on, being involved and tapped in. I didn't have that there. My colleagues from Stanford were all here, too. I wanted to know what all the neat start-ups were, what the new technologies were, and be part of them.

''I mean, here in the valley, you can just sit in a bar like this and overhear everything important that's going on in technology in the world.

''So I came back to California with no job. I consulted for a while to keep things going while I was looking for a job. One of the people I talked to was over at Apple working on a secret project that would become the Lisa. It was a nice design and it used an AMD 2900 mi-croprocessor. Well, we got to talking and I was able to convince him to take a closer look at the 68000. And it turned out in the end that's what the Lisa was built with. The Lisa self-destructed, but by then the Macintosh was based on the 68000, too, so I was a little bit instrumental in all that.''

The pay was $4,000 for four days. Unfortunately, no royalties.

That wasn't Stritter's first instrumental act. Back when he was still with Motorola, Forrest Baskin, Stritter's old advisor at Stanford, called. He was desperately searching for Motorola 64K DRAM memory chips to use on a new computer board he was designing, the Sun Stanford University Network Computer. Stritter agreed to help. ''I probably shouldn't tell this, but the statute of limitations is up by now. I went down to the test floor at Motorola and there were these big fifty-gallon drums full of reject chips ready to be destroyed. So I filled up my briefcase with a bunch of them, sneaked out past the guards, and shipped them to Forrest. He and his people culled through them and found enough that worked right.'' The SSUNC would be the beginning of Sun Computer.

Finally, Stritter took a job at Nestar, a computer networking company, and stayed three and a half years.

''By the fall of 1983 I was getting itchy. It was time to move on. In December I left Nestar and began hanging around Stanford, renewing my acquaintances with, among others, John Hennessy. We got to talking about ideas, what companies were starting, what should be happening here.''

Hennessy, with a visiting scholar from IBM, John Massouris, was working on a MIPS chip. Stritter joined in.

Soon thereafter, a call came from Gordon Bell, a computer legend, who had just shocked the industry by leaving DEC and joining a young company called Encore that wanted to be an umbrella for entrepreneurial teams. Bell knew of Hennessy's group and invited them back to Boston to make a presentation.

''It didn't click for us at Encore. But what did click was the idea of starting a company around this technology. So, inadvertently, Gordon Bell started MIPS.

''This was January 1984. Pretty soon John, John, and I were meeting for breakfast once a week at the Cookbook restaurant on the El Camino Real near the school. . . .

''Pretty soon we were meeting every day. We'd meet about 8:00 A.M. and we'd get done at noon. We had the same table every day. They knew us. We didn't even have to order anymore. Moose would have waffles with fresh strawberries and John would have a certain kind of omelette and I would have my English muffin and sausage patties and grapefruit juice. The same thing every day.

''And that was the start of MIPS.

''By the spring we were talking both technology and business plan, although frankly we were pretty naive about business issues. We were technology people. But we felt that the combination of Hennessy from academia, Moose from industrial research, and me from making commercial products was a compelling combination.''

The team then went out in search of money, using any connection and acquaintance they knew.

"We went to a lot of places. I had met Grant Heidrich when I was at Nestar. So that's how I knew Mayfield. . . .

"We talked not only to Mayfield, but several other investors, many of whom are now MIPS investors. But they weren't into seed round investments. And we had several offers. We also had some arguments. In one case we got seduced by a sweet-sounding offer, but the way it was presented wasn't palatable. They said, 'Here's an offer. We'd like your answer in two days, and we'd like you not to talk with anybody else in the meantime.' Well, we were already having conversation and we did talk to someone else, though not about this offer, and [they] found about it and they got mad at us. But that was okay, because we realized we didn't want to work with them.

"In the end, it was with Mayfield we felt the most comfortable. And it's worked out perfectly. They've been wonderful supporters. They said, 'There's an office you can use.' We were reluctant, but by then we'd already agreed on a deal: $1.5 million, a good first round in those days.

"And we got started. On August 28, 1984, we were sitting in a lawyer's office because we decided that things were getting serious enough that we ought to incorporate. And so we grilled out this thing and bought our founders' stock and submitted the documents to the California corporations office. And the lawyer says, 'Okay, what are your titles?' And we'd never even thought about that. Hennessy was still involved as a professor at Stanford and didn't feel he could be an officer, so he became chief scientist. And Moose and I flipped a coin, literally. Moose lost, so he became president and I was chief financial officer. Ludvigson cringes when he hears that.

"We incorporated that day. Our first employee was Larry Weber and our first headquarters was an office and a Xerox machine at Mayfield Fund."

Five years later Hennessy is still at Stanford, Moose is running his own firm, but Stritter remains. "Oh yeah. This company is important to me. This is a big thing for me.

"One of the things back at the Cookbook restaurant we did right was to recognize that we weren't going to be management. We could help in technology or any place else we were needed, but we were not businessmen. We had seen the stories of big egos that invent something wonderful and then think they can be CEO—and they can't, and it crashes the company. None of us aspired to run the company . . . and that's why we've got this marvelous management team in place.

"It's all more than we ever dared dream about. We would talk about building a company, a place where great people could work and like it. To surround ourselves with good people. And that's all worked out really nicely.

"All of a sudden one day we looked up and the company had one hundred employees and it hit us that these people were coming to work here and depended on this company for a living. I always figured I could get a job anywhere. But these people believed in MIPS, they depended upon it. It was real. And that was a strange realization. And a satisfying one, too."

Big events lead to big thoughts.

Bob Miller sat in his office and pondered what had occurred—the sudden wealth that had landed upon his employees, the lives that had changed forever.

"It's the kind of thing that sends chills up my spine. The idea that you can make twenty millionaires from nothing. To me it's California Gold Rush stuff. It's so damn exciting.

"My son is studying international finance with a major in Japanese. I sent him a copy of that book by Morita and Ishigawa [*The Japan That Can Say No*], and he said, 'Oh, this is terrible. These guys are awful.'

"And I said, 'Brian, tell me something. How much of it was true? On a factual basis, how much was true? Forgetting the emotional stuff, isn't it true that American executives on an individual basis get more compensation than Japanese executives? Isn't it true that the Japanese invest in manufacturing, plant, and equipment at a higher rate than the U.S.?'

"I used to get into these terrible battles with de Castro [at Data General] about his goddamned slave labor plants in Bangkok. I'd say, 'Not only are you wrong from a humanitarian standpoint, but it's not productive either. It's not building anything. Manufacturing is a technology.' The Japanese understood that a long time ago.

"The fact is that if you piss away that technology, you're in trouble. People try to accuse me, because I take the subcontract approach in many cases to manufacturing, of being antimanufacturing. But it's just the opposite: I'm going to go where I can get it best, not cheapest. That's what a Sony would do. Their divisions can sell to anybody, but they can also buy from anybody, not just from their other divisions. Their only duty is to provide the best product. My model of Sony is forty tigers in the jungle, and if once in a while one of the tigers runs into the other, it's still two tigers going at each other. It's forty tigers in a jungle and not a helluva lot of control tacked on them.

"That's what I'm trying to do here. I may be CEO, but if you're the general manager I look to you to run the business. . . ."

But what about the complaint that the MIPS model requires a Bob Miller at its center? "I can't change that right now. But in ten years my goal is for that not to be the case. We will progress to ever-greater business autonomy, in the systems group, the software group, and the workstation group. The trick is to never let any of them grow into huge bureaucracies. Never let tigers turn into zebras. I call it the 'ass-to-teeth' ratio. Animals in the jungle that have more ass to teeth don't live too long. The idea is you always keep more teeth than ass."

His thoughts shifted to his old employer IBM, which he believed made a critical mistake by not selling its captive technologies—the guts of its computers, such as chips, monitors, and software—to anyone willing to buy them, including competitors. "That's what made me a heretic at IBM. I fought hard when I was in IBM to force the semiconductor guys to go out and compete in the open market. I will tell you today that that one decision could have changed the whole course of the industry and of IBM. It might have shut the Japanese out."

But what about the argument that IBM was so worried about antitrust that it was forced to leave its decisions to lawyers? "You can let every decision in your life be made by a lawyer because they are only too happy to tell you what you should do with your life. Let's say 10 percent of IBM's revenue is spent to screw around with the Justice Department. Okay, so that's the cost of doing business and add it onto the price of the semiconductors you're selling. And tell the lawyers to fuck off. That's what the Japanese would do."

Comparing Japanese executives with American executives, to the detriment of the Americans: "Did you read where Morita and his wife sat down for dinner with individual employees of every shift of every Sony plant in America? How many U.S. executives would do that? But that's what the worker wants. He wants that recognition and the individual attention. And that's what unions try to give him when management turns its back, or treats him like a useless piece of junk. . . .

"We're the ones with the natural resources. We're the ones that own everything. But if we're stupid and we misuse that, we can't blame the Japanese. We have to blame our own stupidity. If I'm a strident voice for anything, it's 'let's get the friggin' wake-up call in this country and stop talking out our weaknesses and start leveraging our strengths.' If you've got homeless people or a ghetto with 80 percent unemployment and the only choice is to deal or use drugs, then go solve those fucking problems. Give me a third of the Pentagon's budget and I'll go solve them—and I'll create ten new industries for U.S. companies in the process. . . .

"I'd love to be the ambassador to Japan. I think that Japan and the U.S. finding a way to be mutually productive and achieving a better understanding of each other is vitally important to the success of this country in the next century. . . ."

On the question of whether, until then, U.S. companies can really compete with Japanese firms, with their protected home markets and friendly deals with bankers: "Oh yes. There's one thing I'm most proud of about MIPS, the one that fits with being the 'model for companies in the twenty-first century.' If you go back to when Tom Watson founded IBM, you could only be white, Protestant, and male. Now look at MIPS. I don't think we've missed a nationality. I don't think we've missed one. I'm sure we have, without knowing it, every form of minority group that the government would ever talk about. And it all happened naturally. It didn't happen because some guy was trying to drive a set of numbers, like we had at IBM. That'll make you crazy. No, it happened here because it just came together that way. That's part of being MIPS. And, in the long run, that's the part that the Moritas and those other Japanese executives are going to miss. It's our competitive edge.''

CHAPTER 23

End of the Day

BY SIX O'CLOCK it was dark outside, but the branches of Red Bob's tree stood out in the light from the office windows.

Inside, a second bottle had been chilled in Rob Jensen's pressure cooker and emptied, and now it rested in the wastebasket with its predecessor. The groups of people were smaller now, quieter, and the lobby began to fill with goodbyes. More and more offices and cubicles sat empty, their phones intermittently ringing four times before the callers were shuttled off to the phone mail recorder.

A few of the employees were leaving now for an early Christmas vacation, but even most of them would return tomorrow for the hurriedly announced company Christmas-IPO party. The company had, in the past, held Christmas parties at one hotel or another, complete with a live band. Employees anticipated that this year the event, celebrating Going Public Day as well, would be the ultimate blow-out, as flamboyant and memorable as the much-publicized Apple and AMD parties. Some engineers were overheard speculating, only half jokingly, that the live band this year might be the Grateful Dead.

But the on-again off-again nature of the negotiations with the SEC ruined whatever plans had been made. A week earlier the deposit on the hotel reservations was given up, and now Babs and crew were reduced to holding the big celebration, the most important one in the company's history, among the microwave ovens and vending machines of the MIPS cafeteria. The only hope was that the excitement of the occasion, a half-day off work, and several cases of champagne would redeem the pedestrian surroundings. In addition, there was a surprise hiding in one of the storage rooms: cases of the lucite cubes containing miniature copies of the MIPS prospectus. These cubes were usually awarded only to top management, the underwriters, and the lawyers on an offering, but MIPS had decided to give one to every employee.

By half past six the headquarters building and both of the other MIPS facilities were nearly empty, the employees heading off to local watering holes to celebrate or home to share the big news. The top management had agreed to gather at Birk's, an elegant wood and brass steakhouse in Santa Clara at the base of a sleek office tower. "The family can wait," said one as he headed out the door.

From the parking lot one could see that the departure of the executives had left one wing of offices darkened . . . except for one still brightly lit window. There, as every day, one could see Jake Vigil sitting sternly at his desk, typing and pondering at his computer terminal. Not even Going Public Day could divert him from work that needed to be done.

A Jaguar sedan roared up. The window rolled down. It was Joe DiNucci: "I'm taking my family out to celebrate. My 18-year-old called me to congratulate me. He's at UCLA, very mercenary. He understands. He said, 'So Joe, what's on the agenda for tonight?' I said, 'Michael, we've got to talk vesting and all that,' but he didn't want to hear about that."

At eight o'clock the crowd at Birk's was feeling good. About twenty MIPS executives and managers had taken over one end of the crowded bar and were shouting to one another over the din. Jobe was there, as were Jerman, Hime, and Kyriakou. DiNucci stopped in. Even Ludvigson was there, having found enough second wind for a drink before the long drive home.

Jobe was talking in his Texas drawl. "Bob Miller called and left a message on my answering machine while I was out jogging and so I came back, saw my answering machine was going, popped the button, and listened to Bob saying, 'Hey, we're out! We went effective this morning.' And I thought, holy shit, this is great! I was so concerned about whether we really would trade today or not and if we didn't, that we might not make it until next year.

"Then the next thing I thought was I better git my butt to the office. I got to make sure we make the quarter. I've still got that 'Make the quarter, make the quarter, make the quarter' attitude going. So to be honest, I haven't celebrated much today. I've been spread out working, calling people, trying to get the orders in, being sure we're in good shape.

"The numbers are good and the quarter's going to be fine. I don't feel too vulnerable. To tell you the truth, I don't feel much different at all. My net worth is the highest it's ever been, but it sort of feels like monopoly money. It's not like I can take it and spend it. We've still got to build this company. We've got to make this company last for a long time.

"So tonight I'm just having a couple of pops with some friends who helped make this thing happen. And make sure I'm either in good enough shape to drive home or I'm calling Alpha Cab to take me home.

"Hey, you know what makes me feel good? This company is now so well financed that I can compare balance sheets with anybody. I mean, our company is now valued 50 percent higher than Data General!''

That remark brought cheers.

The talk then turned to cars. Hime, it seemed, already had his order in for the new Mercedes SL coupe, though it wouldn't be delivered for ten months yet. DiNucci and Jobe swapped stories about how fast they'd drive their Ferraris, including a race with a Testarossa down the usually quiet and residential Foothill Expressway, and a 150-mile-an-hour run on Highway 50 in Nevada.

Then Jobe found out that one of the ladies present was single and wondered aloud if she'd ever gone to dinner with a multimillionaire. The group laughed.

Andreas, drink in hand and tie loosened, stood looking on in amazement. "It's not the money," he said over and over, "it's not the money, though the money's nice. It's the excitement. It's being right here at the nerve ending. It's like Bill Gates at Microsoft, Steve Jobs at Apple. It's the excitement of being right there when the big deals are happening."

Back at MIPS, Jorge Quesada and Enedina Navarro began their shifts. Jorge, 21, wore a new canvas bomber jacket over a MIPS shirt and Reeboks. Enedina, 26, wore a Camel cigarette T-shirt. For them, janitors with Specialty Building Services, this day was like any other—except that there was more garbage than usual to clean up—and tomorrow was expected to be even worse.

The notion of Going Public Day had no meaning for either of them. Quesada was born in Uruapan, a small village in the state of Michoacan, Mexico. His father was an agricultural laborer. He has two brothers and a sister. He says (through a translator), "I came to California in 1985.

I came alone. I have worked as a field worker and on an assembly line. That seasonal work was hard and a friend told me that there was good work here.'' He worked in the plastics industry, making picture frames, and in electronics assembly at Pyramid Computer. After that he became a janitor, because the money was good. He's worked at MIPS now for eighteen months.

Jorge lives in the barrio on the East Side of San Jose. Two of his friends are also janitors; the other still works at Pyramid. In his spare time he likes to detail his V-8 Buick Skylark, drive around, and go dancing at the Copacabana.

''I expected something better than what I had at home. I had nothing. Here I have something.''

He stays in touch with his family and says they worry about him. That makes him a little homesick. Someday he hopes to go back on visits.

In the meantime Jorge Quesada dreams. He wants ''to learn English to get a better job, and then go back to school to study electronics.'' He would also like to marry a girl from his village and bring her up north.

Jorge says he'd like to work at a company like this, because everybody here is ''courteous.'' Still, he admits, they seem to work awfully hard at MIPS. Sometimes he will see them still at their desks at four or five in the morning.

Enedina came from San Pedro Jesistan, a little town on Lake Chapala in the state of Jalisco, Mexico. Her parents were farmers. She is the eldest of seven brothers and five sisters. She came with a brother to the United States just a year ago. He's a janitor, too, in one of the other MIPS buildings.

The two came to join three other brothers, who were working as farm laborers in Watsonville. Enedina spent three months picking blackberries. It was terrible.

She and the four brothers finally moved to San Jose. They share a place downtown and come and go throughout the day and night to various janitorial and laborer jobs. Enedina has little spare time, as her brothers expect her to do all the cooking, washing, and ironing. And then there is English class. Sometimes she finds time to go dancing, but never to the movies. Sometimes she watches movies at home, but in English only to help her learn. Her favorite movie is *Gone with the Wind*, but her favorite stars are Julio Iglesias and Ruben Blades. She doesn't have a boyfriend. ''My brothers chase away,'' she says in halting English, then laughs.

Enedina has a dream too. She would like one day to be a hair stylist, perhaps even open her own shop.

Ysidro Ramos, 31, is Enedina's and Jorge's boss. He is operations manager for Specialty Building Services. He has a splint on his arm from a bone graft and a goatee; he is wearing a MIPS shirt, jogging pants, and tennis shoes.

"I was born in a small town in the state of Jalisco called El Irullo. My father is a construction worker. My mother is an assembler at an electronics company here in the valley. They are separated. My father's living in Guadalajara and I'm thinking of bringing him up to live with me and my wife and my son.

"I came to the States in 1975. I wanted to go to school, but I couldn't because there were so many of us and I had to help. I picked cucumbers and sprayed insecticides. I have four brothers and three sisters. One is in LA; he's going to UCLA and wants to become a lawyer. Three others are still in high school or junior high. One sister decided to go her own way, has two kids, and works at Apple Computer. Another sister works as an assembler at Diasonics with my mom. Another brother kind of got away from the family because he changed religions. We're Catholic and he became something like Mormon. My mom and three of the kids live on the East Side. I live in South San Jose. I'm married and have a boy 20 months old.

"My wife works. She's an accounting technician for the county of Santa Clara. She wants to get her CPA. She works during the day and I work at night."

Ramos is a man on the move. He earned his high school degree at age 22 and then went on to junior college. He dropped out, to his regret, because his English still wasn't good enough to keep up. So he had to put his lifelong dream of becoming a policeman or fireman on hold.

It is still on hold, thanks to a chain of unexpected events. He was taking the occasional junior college course to prove to himself he was ready, and when he was just about to sign up full time, "my wife got pregnant." He took care of the infant while his wife worked. When he was finally ready to take the fireman's academy exam, he discovered he needed a bone graft in his arm to repair an old fracture. Again the dream was put on hold.

In the meantime, though, Ramos built a comfortable life. He worked as a janitor for one of the larger local janitorial firms. Then he got a job at an electronics company. "They were going to pay for me to go to school to learn electronics, but unfortunately they went bankrupt."

But the salesman from the janitorial firm called soon after and asked if Ramos would like to join him in starting their own firm. Ramos agreed and in the process became an entrepreneur. Now his business card reads Operations Manager. He knows what going public means. "Sure, it's what America is all about. It's the only place you can really accomplish what you set for yourself." That's why he put on nine people tonight instead of the usual four: "I didn't want them to go home too late."

MIPS's Going Public Day has affected Ramos personally as well. His partner wants him to take a piece of the company, hold equity. But Ramos has resisted. He still has his dreams of being a policeman or a fireman.

But what he's seen today has made him think. "Who knows?" he muses, "There are big janitorial companies out there that started out with nothing and made it big by getting contracts with the right companies. Maybe we could do the same thing and grow with this company."

Gib Myers took his wife and mother to dinner at Masa's on the wharf in San Francisco. "We were sitting there and I didn't even notice that at another table were John Doerr of [venture capital firm] Kleiner Perkins and a bunch of guys from Lotus.

"We ordered cocktails and the waiter comes back with a very elegant bottle of champagne. It had a note on it that said, 'Congratulations on the MIPS IPO. You did a great job.'

"It was a particularly nice gesture because Doerr was very involved with Sun. Back when we were out raising money for MIPS, we had a hard time with Kleiner Perkins, and Doerr was a lot of it, because he really believed in Sun and was promoting Sun and didn't really see our side of the story. Now it had all worked out fine. So the champagne was a really nice thing on his part."

That night Connie Nga Dang sat down and wrote a letter to her husband in Vietnam. Her letters were usually filled with updates on the lives of their children, but tonight Connie would tell her husband about the extraordinary thing that had happened to her that day.

Bob Miller also wrote a letter that night. But his was to his baby daughter, asleep at the other end of the house. This would be one of the most important days of her life, though she would not know that for years.

Sitting at his desk, nearly twenty hours after he'd awakened, looking out through the darkened trees in his back yard, and surrounded by his father's old train set and momentos of a thirty-year business career, Miller wrote a letter to the future.

He recounted, for the young woman his daughter would one day be, the events of this singular day. Miller knew that when she read this yellowing letter, he and Barbara would be gray, that he would be not at the apex but at the end of his career, that this shining day would have receded into the distant past.

Signing the letter, Bob Miller brought the MIPS Going Public Day to a quiet end.

Index

281